THE
FIRST YEAR
OF LIFE

A Guide For Parenting

THE
FIRST YEAR
OF LIFE
A GUIDE FOR PARENTING

By
Nina R. Lief

Edited by
Mary Ellen Fahs

Sadlier

Los Angeles   New York   Chicago

Photo Credits

Cover photos: Erika Stone from Peter Arnold, Inc.
Elizabeth Braun: Page viii (FAHS)
Barbi Lindsay: Facing page 1 (bottom), pages 24, 48 (both), 68 (top), 116, 140, 162, 184 (both), 206 (both), 228 (all)
Mark Mittelman: Facing page 1 (top)
New York Medical College: pages 68 (bottom), 88 (all), 252 (both)
N.Y. News: Page viii (LIEF)

Art Director: Ron Wickham
Design Coordinator: Barbara A. Grodsky
Cover Designer: Gail Schneider

International Standard Book Number: 0-8215-9895-3

Library of Congress Catalog Card Number: 81-53003

For Victor Filler Lief,
whose early encouragement,
perceptive criticism, and loving support
made this effort possible.

CONTENTS

INTRODUCTION ix

CHAPTER ONE   AGE: **4** to **8** weeks 1

CHAPTER TWO   AGE: **8** to **12** weeks 25

CHAPTER THREE   AGE: **12** to **16** weeks 49

CHAPTER FOUR   AGE: **16** to **20** weeks 69

CHAPTER FIVE   AGE: **20** to **24** weeks 89

CHAPTER SIX   AGE: **24** to **28** weeks 117

CHAPTER SEVEN   AGE: **28** to **32** weeks 141

CHAPTER EIGHT   AGE: **32** to **36** weeks 163

CHAPTER NINE   AGE: **36** to **40** weeks 185

CHAPTER TEN   AGE: **40** to **44** weeks 207

CHAPTER ELEVEN   AGE: **44** to **48** weeks 229

CHAPTER TWELVE   AGE: **48** to **52** weeks 253

BIBLIOGRAPHY 275

INDEX 283

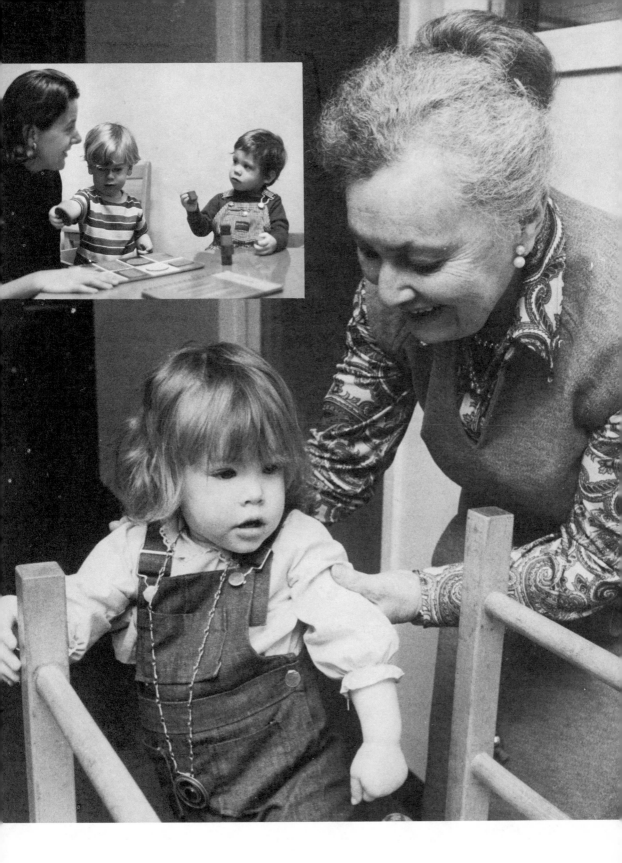

Dr. Nina R. Lief (**full page**) and Mary Ellen Fahs (**inset**) with children at
the Early Childhood Development Center.

INTRODUCTION

Much research has been done on the crucial importance of a child's earliest years, but little of the knowledge and understanding derived from this research reaches the parents, who have primary responsibility for the child's care and development. To provide parents with this information as well as with support and encouragement in their roles as parents, New York Medical College and the New York Junior League established the Early Childhood Development Center in 1974.

At the Center, small groups of parents (usually from eight to ten adults) and their babies meet with a trained group leader in weekly discussion sessions. The curriculum for the discussions is based on the best current information regarding a child's emotional, social, and cognitive development, as well as on the real-life concerns of parents, as expressed in their questions. The links between appropriate childrearing methods and developmental theory are continually demonstrated, thereby enabling parents to see how childrearing techniques directly influence the infant's cognitive, social, and emotional development.

The major aims of the Center's program is to assist parents guide their children toward healthy personality development and to help mothers and fathers derive enjoyment and satisfaction from their roles as parents. While other programs have emphasized the physical and cognitive aspects of a child's development, the Center is more concerned with helping the parent understand the emotional and social side of that development and the importance of parent-child interaction in this process.

The curriculum used at the Early Childhood Development Center has been published in a hardcover manual, **The First Year of Life: A Curriculum for Parenting Education,** New York: Keyway Books, Inc. (a division of William H. Sadlier, Inc.), 1979, designed for those professionals and lay persons who wish to set up similar programs. Parents' questions and professional comment on child development and childrearing have been adapted from the curriculum manual in this paperback volume.

This book is divided into twelve chapters covering the first twelve months of life. Each chapter begins with a brief description of the child's level of physical, intellectual, emotional, and social development at that interval. The monthly developmental highlights are followed by the discussion—as it took place with parents at The Early Childhood Development Center—of a series of topics relating to child development and childrearing issues as well as parents' feelings.

Throughout the text, different typefaces have been used in a consistent way to facilitate the presentation of the material. Regular roman type indicates professional comment on child development and childrearing. Boldface type indicates comments and questions of parents.

Every effort has been made to avoid sexist use of pronouns in referring to the gender of the babies who form the subject of this book. This explains why the pronoun referring to the baby is sometimes masculine and sometimes feminine, and why the gender of the pronoun appears to change arbitrarily from section to section.

Similarly, throughout the text the parent is more often referred to as the mother, rather than the father. This is not due to any sexist orientation but simply to the fact that the great majority of the parents who provide the major amount of care during the first year of a baby's life are generally mothers. It is our belief that parenting is a shared male-female responsibility, and the word **father** can be substituted for the word **mother** in most cases.

Further, a growing number of mothers of children under a year of age are working outside the home. Because the child's needs regarding nutrition, attention, and discipline are similar whether his or her parents work, topics throughout the book will discuss the variety of ways that parents in differing circumstances may meet their children's needs. The purpose of this book is to foster the healthiest possible growth and development of the child and to make parenting less stressful and more enjoyable.

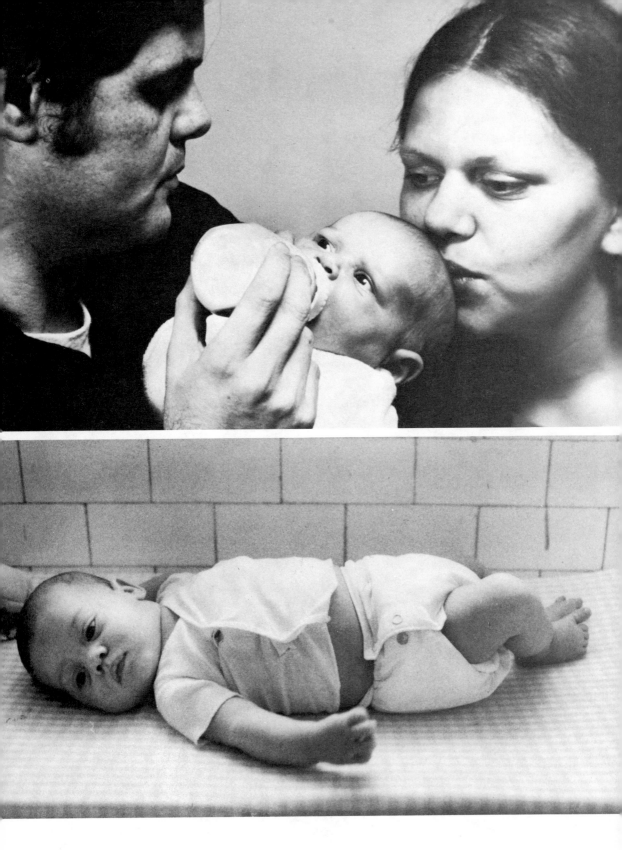

(**Top**) Parents with one-month-old infant;
(**bottom**) Characteristic tonic-neck (asymmetrical) position
of one-month-old infant.

Chapter One

Age: 4 to 8 weeks _____

For most parents, the newborn infant seems to be doing very little; but a closer look reveals that the baby is engaged in small but exciting activities. In the earliest weeks of life, the baby holds himself with hands fisted, one above his head and the other outstretched. His legs are pulled up under him, so that his posture is asymmetrical. The baby is sensitive to touch all over and is aware of how he is being held.

Intellectual development and learning begin with eye contact and visual tracking. This ability can be encouraged by dangling a red ring on a string about eight inches in front of the baby to see if she will look at it briefly. In the coming weeks, the baby will begin to follow the ring with her eyes. (A red ring is one of the most useful toys a baby can have. The red color attracts the baby's attention more than the usual pastel shades of nursery toys.) When a rattle is placed in the baby's palm, she may grasp it reflexively before dropping it. If the grasp is maintained, this is an indication of more advanced motor development. If one makes a sudden noise, like ringing a bell, near the baby's head, the baby generally reacts by either a diminution of activity, a startle of the whole body, a change of expression, or by crying.

At this age, a baby's face is impassive, and a seemingly vacant, indirect stare at surroundings is normal. This stare becomes focused with maturation and stimulation. Looking at the parent's face, staring at surroundings, and listening to sounds are all early signs of socialization.

MOTHERS' FEELINGS ABOUT HAVING A CHILD

Most mothers have special feelings about having a child, and these feelings differ from mother to mother. Some mothers want children very much. Some feel that their children arrived at the wrong time; they wanted them earlier or later in life. Some never had experience with babies; others are very confident because they have had experience with younger members of their own families. Some may have wanted a girl and others a boy.

How did you feel about having a baby? Did you feel ready?

> "We were just so delighted when she came. We had wanted a baby for such a long time. We feel she is more important than anything else in our lives, and she makes us happier than any of the other experiences we have ever had. But, still, I always wonder if I'm doing the right thing."

> "I certainly wanted the baby, but I feel I'm a little too old and have had no experience with children. When my husband left me the first morning and I realized I was alone with the baby and he was my responsibility, I just panicked. I guess that's why I'm here."

This feeling of being responsible for another human being who is small, helpless, and utterly dependent on the parents is often frightening, especially if a person has never had any experience with newborns. One has endless questions. This is one of the reasons for this program.

> "Well, I am a trained nurse used to infants, but this one is mine, and it's a different feeling. I need help too. I feel I know about the physical part, but I want to learn about the baby's feelings and how I should treat him."

That is a very good point of view. We will become more concerned with emotional development as the physical problems of child care become less pressing.

Did most of you immediately feel a sense of love for the baby or has this feeling been developing gradually?

> "My baby is a month old and, much as I wanted him, he still seems like a stranger to me. I can't believe he's mine . . . maybe because he just cries and sleeps a lot, and doesn't seem to respond as though I meant something to him. He leaves me with kind of a 'blah' feeling."

This is a very apt description of how many mothers and fathers feel about a new baby. Not all parents have an immediate feeling of love and affection, and they find the baby unresponsive. Few new parents know what to expect of a newborn baby. I know from asking this question many times that frequently a parent's mental picture of a newborn baby is actually that of a four- or five-month-old infant smiling in an endearing way from the cover of the **Ladies' Home Journal**. This is surely the picture of a baby anyone would fall in love with at first sight. But don't worry. Your baby will appear this way when he is older, and your feelings for each other will develop in time.

"I am so glad you said that because I was having some of the same feelings, and I thought that there was something wrong with me—maybe I wasn't cut out to be a mother, or maybe my baby wasn't all right. I just didn't dare say it to anybody."

It is good that you are finally able to express these feelings. You know now that others have had the same experience, and that there is nothing wrong with you or the baby. The feeling of having the baby belong to you, and you to him, is a process that takes time to develop. One of the topics that we will be discussing throughout this program is how parents can move through this process with understanding and enjoyment.

MOTHER'S NEED FOR HELP—FATHER'S ROLE

Having a new baby and trying to keep house just as you did before the baby came is a very difficult job and one for which mothers often need some help. Are you finding this hard? How are you managing?"

"My big problem is how to get the shopping done. I don't have a carriage yet, so it's a little hard. I've resorted to calling the stores on the phone, but that always turns out to be more expensive."

In some families the father can help with the shopping and pick up needed items on his way home. Often a friend or relative is willing to lend a hand. However, there are some families without relatives or friends in their neighborhoods, and these people do have to rely on the telephone until they get organized.

"My problem is that I haven't adjusted to being awakened at night to feed the baby. I never get any sleep during the day when the baby is asleep because I try to get my housework done. What I wouldn't give for a full night's sleep!"

This kind of fatigue is very common among new mothers. Some mothers feel it more than others. It is quite an adjustment, but there are ways of coping. One good solution is to have a nap during the day when the baby is asleep. That way you will be able to enjoy the baby more and accomplish more. Another solution is to have father take over for a while, so that you can have a rest. The father will feel more needed and will get to know his baby better as well.

"Those are good ideas, and I have used them, but still I can't get the laundry done, the house cleaned, and the meals cooked because the baby takes so much time. Sometimes it's only two hours between feedings, and each one takes time. So, some days I never get anything done, and my husband just can't understand why things don't run just the way they used to."

No one should expect a household to be run exactly as it was before the baby came. There must be some changes and accommodations to the baby's needs. The housework is less important than the mother's and baby's health. To make matters even more difficult, the baby's schedule is very variable at first, before a pattern is established.

THE BABY'S NEUROLOGICAL DEVELOPMENT AND RHYTHM OF ACTIVITIES

"When do babies begin to see and hear?"

The development of the baby's central nervous system begins with the head. The mouth is the first organ for sensation and exploration. Hearing is fairly well developed at birth; even a premature baby in an incubator responds to a soothing voice. A baby's vision is blurred at first, but soon he can see the parent's face and distinct patterns. His attention can be drawn momentarily to brightly colored objects within a range of about eight inches.

"When will my baby be able to lift her head up?"

As babies respond to sound and sight, the first movement of the head is from side to side. At about four weeks they begin to lift their heads. Then gradually they begin to use their hands, slowly becoming competent with them. Next they master the arts of sitting, crawling, standing, and finally walking. Thus, development proceeds from the head down to the arms and hands and finally to the legs and feet by about one year of age.

Parents seem to like to encourage their children to walk, but most children will develop this motor ability unaided. Development of visual attention and speech, however, need parental encouragement. Parents can stimulate visual attention with mobiles and other visually attractive toys. They can encourage the abilities of listening and speech by talking to their children.

"At what age will these developments occur?"

Development generally follows this neurological sequence from the head down to the legs and feet. Parents will be reassured to know that each child has his own maturational timetable and develops various abilities during different weeks and months of life. Some children walk earlier; others talk earlier. Each child is a unique individual. We should not compare children to see who is ahead of whom. Instead, we should watch their development and note the unique and marvelous differences among them.

Each child also has her own genetic endowment, her own inherited characteristics, her own rhythm of activity. This cannot be changed, but parents can assist the infant to achieve her or his potential, so that there will be the maximum possible growth and a happy interaction between child and parents—and fulfillment for all.

Most of us have had a pattern and rhythm to our lives. Each of us has a biological clock; we don't each get hungry at the same times or need the same amount of sleep. Much as we knew things would be different after the baby came, few of us could foresee just how it would affect us. This is partly because we were not aware that each baby has his or her own biological clock and rhythm, which may or may not coincide with our notions of what this clock or rhythm should be. Yet parents have to adapt to their baby's rhythm because the baby, with her immature nervous system, cannot adapt to her parents' time schedule. At first, the baby takes up a great deal of time. As the baby gets older, however, patterns are established according to the baby's particular biological clock. You will come to understand your baby's needs better; child care will take less time and be more enjoyable.

Sleeping, Waking for Feeding

Child-care books tell us that infants sleep most of the time and only wake for feedings. While this may hold true for some babies, many do not follow this pattern. They seem to sleep for shorter intervals and need to be changed or fed more frequently. Also, some babies have certain periods when they take long naps, while at other times they take short naps. Gradually, the parents will be able to adjust their housekeeping and resting to coincide with their baby's napping patterns.

I wonder how you have adapted to your baby's rhythm and kept up with his needs.

> "He has changed our lives completely. We can't count on his sleeping when we want to eat. In fact, dinner time, when my husband comes home, is the most difficult time to get the baby to sleep."

It is very difficult in the beginning to meet your baby's needs in such a way that you can continue your own routines. The problem of management is difficult, and some compromises have to be made. Each family must select for itself which personal and social activities are important, and which can be given lower priority.

> "I'm having a different concern: it's not that my baby won't sleep or wakes too soon, but that she sleeps past her feeding times, sometimes for five or six hours. Then I get worried and go in to look at her to see if she is breathing. I don't know if I should wake her or let her sleep."

All parents get anxious when babies sleep too long. All of us have heard stories that make us worry. It is natural and right to go in and check on the baby at intervals, whether she is sleeping overtime or not. You have to get to know your baby. From the start some babies begin to wake and sleep at predictable intervals, so parents can plan their days accordingly. Others remain unpredictable for months. We no longer believe in fixing "time-clock" schedules for babies—waking them to be fed or forcing them to wait if they are hungry. There is a good body of experience now which indicates that the baby who is fed on her own time schedule, according to her own needs, will eventually have fewer feedings and get into a schedule more easily than the baby who is fed according to a fixed schedule set by the clock. We have also found that if the baby is awakened for a feeding when she is not hungry, she may not take the feeding well, thus frustrating the parents as well as the baby. There are even some babies who wake so hungry that they take the feeding too fast and become gassy and uncomfortable.

Parents have to get to know which system works best for their baby. You have to experiment and use your own judgment. This takes a little time and patience, but it can be achieved. Some parents manage to do this in the first weeks; for others it may take as long as three months. As the baby's pattern is established, parents are able to reestablish a pattern of their own, and life takes on a more satisfactory tempo.

Burping—The Anatomy of the Stomach

Parents also have to learn when the baby is crying for a feeding and when the cry means there is a burp that must come up. Indeed, the whole technique of how to burp your infant has to be learned by trial and error.

Just lifting some babies to a sitting position on the parent's lap and rubbing the baby's back gently brings up the burp. Other babies need to be held high on the parent's shoulder, which acts as a support for the baby's abdomen. Still other babies do better being patted as they lie across the mother's lap. Some babies burp quickly; some take a long time. Some have to be burped during a feeding; others only afterward.

In any case, burping is an important part of the feeding procedure and if done patiently and consistently, can help prevent crying after feedings and difficulty in sleeping—situations that are frustrating to baby and parent alike.

Babies often spit up with a burp. Some do a great deal of this, and sometimes most of the feeding is lost. When a lot of spitting occurs, the baby may need a little more food before settling down, or may wake earlier for the next feeding. Mothers soon get to know which is the better method for burping their baby.

Are any of you having difficulty with the baby's burping and spitting up?

"My baby takes forever to burp. I have tried holding him over my shoulder and patting his back. I have also tried sitting him up, but nothing helps much."

The important thing is not to try to hurry the burp. Take plenty of time. The parent's tenseness and desire to hurry communicate themselves to the baby and keep the baby from relaxing to bring up the air. Perhaps you are not giving your baby enough time.

"I have the same experience. Waiting for a burp may take fifteen minutes. Then the bottle has to be warmed again, and the entire feeding and changing routine takes most of the morning or afternoon. There is no time to get anything done between feedings!"

Most parents are not prepared for the amount of time it takes to perform the ordinary tasks of feeding, burping, and changing a baby. It comes as a shock. Sometimes parents think there is something wrong with the baby, but there is nothing wrong. This period in the baby's life will not last forever. It may be shortened by taking it easy and not feeling rushed by the need to get housework done. At first, some things may have to be postponed until the baby and mother develop a pattern for burping, and until the mother becomes more adept at baby care. It all comes with practice.

Knowing a little about the anatomy of the stomach may help you to deal better with burping. The stomach looks like a bottle with the neck at the top; it contains an air bubble. If the baby is lying down when she is fed, the bubble will be at the bottom of the stomach under the food the baby has eaten, and will need time to work its way to the top for emission of the burp. Sometimes this air bubble pushes some of the food ahead of it, and spitting up occurs. If the baby is held at the proper angle—almost sitting in the mother's arms during feeding—the bubble will come toward the top of the food, and the emission will be easier. Sometimes, even with these precautions, some of the air is trapped, and the burp needs to be expelled at a later time. It's a good idea to hold the baby after a feeding for a long enough time to allow a final burp to occur. Sometimes this final burp only occurs when the baby is on her stomach in the crib. Each mother gets to know very soon how to cope with burping her baby.

"I was always told that putting a baby on her stomach was dangerous, that she might choke if she burped and spat up a little food."

Actually, it is safer for the baby to be on her stomach because the force of gravity will cause the milk to flow right out of the baby's mouth. If she is on her back, there is more chance to aspirate the milk that comes up. Most healthy babies can lift their heads away from the wet spot by themselves unless they have actually vomited the whole feeding. In any event, it is a good practice to look in on the baby occasionally after she is put to bed to be sure that all is well.

There are other reasons for crying. Some babies cry when they are wet or have had a bowel movement and are uncomfortable.

Many mothers are annoyed at the number of necessary diaper changes. This varies from day to day and does not last forever. Mothers soon learn to tell the cry that signals a diaper change from other kinds of cries.

Breast-fed babies usually have more frequent bowel movements

Frequency of Wetting and Bowel Movements

7

and looser stools with more variation in color than do bottle-fed babies. Some babies have only one or two bowel movements a day. Some babies do not have movements every day and are comfortable without them. If they are uncomfortable without them, seek medical advice. If the movements become too frequent, or if the stools become loose, or large and foamy, also seek medical advice.

Do any of you have concerns about the many changes of diapers?

"For one thing, it's got to be quite a problem having enough diapers on hand so as not to run short. I don't mind the crying when he is wet. I just didn't have any idea a baby could use so many diapers in a week. I just wonder what mothers did when they had to wash them by hand."

It does come as a surprise to find out how frequently a baby wets, but this frequency is perfectly normal. After all, a baby's total intake at first is purely liquid, the bladder capacity is small, and sphincter control has not yet developed. This is just another item about babies which may not have been emphasized sufficiently in your prenatal classes.

"I don't use synthetic diapers because my baby got a rash, and my pediatrician advised using regular diapers. I do them in the washing machine at home. There are about fifteen to eighteen a day. It's not difficult to do, and the rash has cleared up."

It's good that you have found a solution to your problem and can now cope so comfortably. Your experience shows again that each baby is different and may need special ways of handling.

"Does a baby have to be changed every time she is wet? Should you wake a baby to change her?"

It is best to change a baby as frequently as she wets, especially if the wet diaper annoys her. It is not necessary to wake a baby from a daytime nap to change her, unless the baby has a sensitive skin or the doctor has advised you to do so. Sometimes it is a good practice to change a baby before you go to bed at night, so that she won't spend such a long time in a wet diaper and run the risk of developing an annoying diaper rash. There are many creams now that are used to protect against this kind of discomfort. Again, each mother has to find out for herself what system works best for her baby.

"There is one other question that bothers me, and that is how many bowel movements are normal for a baby. Also, does the color matter? I've heard so much about diarrhea and how dangerous it is. My baby has a soft greenish movement after almost every feeding. Sometimes it's curdy, so I worry even though my doctor tells me not to."

Breast-fed babies usually have more frequent bowel movements, and these are often green and "curdy," as you say. This is perfectly normal. If that is the usual occurrence with your baby, there is no need to worry. However, if there is a change to more frequency and a watery consistency, then you should consult your doctor.

Formula-fed babies usually have less frequent bowel movements, and these are apt to be smoother and more yellow in color. The color simply indicates how rapidly the stool has moved through the digestive tract. Green stool shows most rapid movement; yellow slower. Darker brown may indicate constipation. Most formula-fed babies have one or two movements a day. However, there are some babies that may skip a day without a movement and are perfectly comfortable. If the baby seems uncomfortable, then the doctor should be consulted for a change in formula or another remedy. Each baby is different, and, here again, parents have to learn what is normal and usual for their baby.

Ideas of the age at which to introduce semisolid foods (such as cereal, fruits, strained meat or vegetables) vary with pediatricians. There may also be a difference in which food they suggest first and the order of introduction. These differences are really not important. What is important is that the feeding experience should be a pleasant one for both baby and mother.

Feeding Semisolids from a Spoon

We have found that most babies accept a cereal feeding when it is introduced at the second morning of feeding, either before the bottle or after the first pause in the bottle feeding. At that time, offer the baby a little loose cereal off the tip of a spoon. Let her sip it as though she were drinking it. After rolling it around in her mouth, the baby may swallow it. If she likes it, try another sip. If not, continue with the bottle or breast feeding, and try again in the same way the next morning.

Do not expect to feed half a jar of semisolid food to your baby the first time. If you have such expectations, you are likely to be disappointed. Infants rarely respond immediately to change. You should not expect your baby to get a major part of her nourishment from the spoon at this stage in her life. You should only try to make taking food from a spoon a new and happy experience. It is a learning process. When your baby has learned to eat semisolids, and this may take several weeks, you can then make spoon feeding a larger part of the meal. In no instance is forcing worthwhile because it can set up the beginning of an eating problem which may later carry over into oppositional behavior in other areas.

Babies usually have an innate sense of their own capacity and what foods agree with them. Babies with allergies usually prefer foods that agree with them or make them feel the most comfortable. At the onset of an illness as yet unrecognized by the parents, babies often refuse to eat. Parents should respect and think about their baby's eating preferences.

"My pediatrician is opposed to starting semisolid feeding too early, but all my friends with babies of the same age as mine have already begun to do it, and that bothers me."

Your pediatrician may be very wise in his advice because he knows that most of the nourishment a baby receives at this age is still from milk, and he may feel your baby is not ready for spoon feeding. Early spoon feeding is the vogue at present, but it is not necessarily best for all babies.

"My baby spits the cereal out. Should I keep trying?"

It sounds as though your baby is not ready or does not like the food you introduced. Give up spoon feeding for now, and try again later. If it still doesn't work, ask your pediatrician about another food, but do not force your baby to eat from a spoon. There is no rush.

One procedure some parents follow in trying to spoon-feed their babies is to insert the full spoon into the baby's mouth, so that no food spills on the outside of the mouth. The mother gets every drop in, but the baby may find this shoveling technique a most unpleasant sensation. Indeed, the baby may respond by clamping her mouth shut when the next spoonful is offered. This response indicates that the mother has set up a resistance to spoon feeding. Often, the mother compounds this error by attempting to force the food in if the baby resists.

Another habit some mothers develop is to wipe the baby's mouth after every spoonful to avoid messiness. Babies usually find this annoying, and it may make them uninterested or irritable at feeding time.

"That's just how I've seen mothers feed their babies, and I thought that was the correct way!"

It is not a question of whether this technique is "correct" or not, but a question of whether the technique allows both mother and baby to derive pleasure from the eating experience. Clearly, in most cases, it does not. Some babies may accept the shoveling type of feeding, and the mothers are satisfied because the food gets down. However, later eating problems may be related to this early form of feeding.

Stimulation: Overstimulation and Soothing

Playing is a pleasant way of stimulating the baby. It can produce pleasure for both baby and parent. Indeed, it is such fun that sometimes the parent overdoes it. Usually when the baby tires, he will no longer pay attention, and the parent gets the signal that it's time to stop. However, we have all been bombarded lately with newspaper and magazine articles about the deleterious effects of understimulation and the resulting slowing down of development. While this is a correct observation, it may make some parents a little overzealous and cause them to overlook their baby's fatigue signals. It is important to be able to gauge how much stimulation a baby can tolerate.

Overstimulated babies "tune out" visual stimuli and will not respond to adults who are too overwhelming in their approach. They can be upset by overstimulation and become restless and fussy. Also, a lot of activity sometimes makes them cry and fret before going to sleep.

Sometimes when we interpret the baby's need as stimulation, he really needs soothing. Each baby needs to be soothed in his own way. Some simply require holding; some a little gentle rocking or patting; some singing or soft talking; some only a change of position; some feeding. Parents soon learn to recognize how best to soothe their baby.

What experiences have you had in playing with your babies?

> "Well, the baby would respond to play for only a short time some days, and that upset me. Now he seems to respond more, but the other day we were getting on fine when all of a sudden he began to cry. I thought he had a cramp or a burp. Now I'm beginning to think I just wore him out."

Until you have had enough time to get to know your baby's responses to play, you may misinterpret the fussiness of overstimulation. Sometimes parents become annoyed when they don't understand the situation. If they are showing the baby off to friends and he becomes fussy, it may cause embarrassment.

> "That happened to us last Sunday when my husband's parents came to visit. We showed them how the baby holds the rattle once or twice. Then Grandpa tried, and that was okay. But when Grandma tried, the baby just dropped the rattle and began to cry. Grandma thought he didn't like her, and that upset her. Maybe he was tired from overstimulation. I'll tell her; she will be so glad to hear it. Now we'll look out for that."

In addition to avoiding overstimulation, it is also important not to expect too much of babies. They don't like being 'shown off' any more than adults do.

> "What about the danger of having a baby near a color television because of radiation?"

That is a valid concern. It is important to keep the baby at least four to five feet from the set. In addition, television may be overstimulating. As a result, it may not be a good baby-sitter, although we have come to use it as such. A recent university experiment has found that babies respond to visual stimuli earlier than first thought. If overdone, however, this stimulation produces fussiness.

DEVELOPMENT OF BASIC TRUST

Patterning and Sequencing in Relation to Basic Trust

We have discussed the need to understand a baby's rhythm or biological clock. We will now turn to the need to establish a schedule for the baby. We do not mean a precise hourly schedule, such as feedings at six, ten, or two o'clock, but a sequence of activities in a regular order. This kind of sequenced schedule not only makes life easier for the parents but also has a definitely beneficial effect on the baby. It helps organize the baby's understanding of the life he is to lead. When the activities on the schedule are done in the same sequence each day, the baby will acquire a sense of knowing and remembering what comes next.

For example, at the first waking in the morning, the mother may change the baby, feed and burp him, and then put him down in his favorite sleeping position for another nap. At the next waking, she may bathe and then feed him. It is good if these activities continue in this order each day.

When the daily activities are repeated with this kind of regularity, the baby can begin to remember the events of his day and can then begin to anticipate these events. This gives him a sense of security and trust in the world around him and the people in it. This sense of trust is a very important cornerstone in personality development. It gives the baby a feeling that he will be cared for in a predictable way and that he can rely on his parents for this care. If basic trust is not established early, the baby may become an anxious, insecure, suspicious person. Parents, therefore, play a vital role in their baby's personality development beginning at an early age. An orderly life pattern also contributes to the development of memory and logical thought. We will discuss the intellectual aspects of this topic later.

Have you begun to get the baby's day to follow some regular sequence?

"My pediatrician gave me a schedule to follow. It gives the feeding time for the formula. I've been trying to follow it, but it just doesn't come out right. Doing things one after the other without watching the clock will make it easier for me. I won't be feeling that there is something wrong with my way of taking care of the baby. Not being able to keep up with the clock made me so uneasy. Maybe that made the baby uneasy too."

Trying to live by the clock on the wall rather than by responding to the baby's biological clock often leads to an unsatisfactory relationship between mother and baby. One becomes tempted to force the baby to eat when he is not hungry and then not respond when he is.

"I began trying to do things 'on time' but found it made me tense and always off schedule. Now I go along with the baby, and we are all happier. Is that what is called 'feeding on demand'?"

Yes, you could call it that. I would prefer to think of it, however, as responding to the baby according to his needs. It will be easier for you in the long run because when the baby's biological clock takes over, a definite pattern, which you will recognize, will be established. It may interest all of you to know that studies have shown that babies fed this way often require fewer feedings and are more comfortable than babies kept to a strict timetable. At first the baby's schedule will be unpredictable, but when the mother becomes familiar with the baby's needs, the baby soon settles into a fairly predictable rhythm. He will become comfortable as his needs are met; and the groundwork for basic trust is being established.

"I guess I was lucky. My baby seemed to respond to the schedule started in the hospital, and she continued it at home. She just eats and sleeps at the same times—eight, twelve, four, eight, twelve, and three or four in the morning. It just happens that is good for us because my husband gets home at seven p.m. and can give her the eight p.m. bottle while I fix dinner."

You are lucky that your needs and the baby's coincide so well. This is the arrangement most parents expect, and they are, therefore, disappointed when it doesn't occur quickly. If, however, the parents are properly 'cued in' to the baby's needs, a schedule that suits both parents and child usually does come about in time.

There is another way in which the parents give the baby a sense of trust—a feeling that someone will help him when he needs it—and that is by responding when the baby cries as quickly as possible. This is an important subject, over which there has always been controversy. Many people think attending to a baby's cry "spoils" the baby.

Crying, Spoiling, and Picking Up in Relation to Basic Trust

How do each of you feel about this? I am sure you have all been concerned about your baby's crying and whether to respond promptly or not. Perhaps you've been advised about what to do by someone in the family, a neighbor, or friends. What do you do when your baby cries?

"It seems too me that everything you have been saying is what my mother and other relatives think is catering to the baby. They say if I pick him up every time he cries, he will always cry, and that I will become a slave to him. They think he has to learn early that crying doesn't pay."

And what do you feel about that?

"My instincts tell me to pick him up, and that's what I do when we are alone. I get along fine, but when my mother comes over, well, then I get very tense and don't know what to do."

This is a very common situation. There is such a misconception about 'spoiling' children and what to do about crying. A great deal of study has gone into clarifying this important subject.

In the past, recognized scientists and many lay people advocated picking up babies when they stopped crying to teach them that crying didn't pay off in getting attention. To be sure, a baby will eventually give up and stop crying, but we think this may have deleterious effects on character development. It may produce either a child who has no hope or trust in his surroundings and becomes passive and submissive, or one who stores up much frustration and anger and becomes very demanding.

Crying is the only language babies have. They are saying something is needed, perhaps only a change in position or a soothing word. Perhaps they need a change in diaper or another burp, and they should get a response from the caretaker—be it mother, father, or baby-sitter.

Research has been done about the relationship between crying and mother's response, notably by Dr. Ainsworth at Johns Hopkins University. She has shown that babies who are picked up when they cry are those who eventually cry least, while those whose cries have not been heeded become the "cry babies." What really "spoils" a child is inconsistency in handling. Responding to a baby's cries part of the time and ignoring them the rest of the time is confusing to the baby. He may become irritable—and you feel you have a "spoiled" child. What has really happened is that your child has become insecure because of inconsistent handling.

You will find that as you 'tune in' to your baby's needs and give the appropriate responses, the baby will become less anxious, more comfortable, and more easily satisfied. Your relationship will become mutually satisfying and set the basis for attachment and affection.

"How can you get this over to parents and relatives who criticize you?"

I would say very sweetly and politely that this is your baby. You know they brought up their children the way they thought was best. More is known about babies and their emotional development now, so you would like to use this information and do what you feel is best for your baby. If you make a mistake, it's your problem—you are the one who is with him most of the time. Child psychologists believe it is best to pick up the baby and find out what he wants. Because he is so young, crying is his only language. When you explain your behavior that way, there may be a better acceptance of your way of doing things. You have to be your baby's advocate to protect his immature nervous system from unnecessary stress.

How many here have arrangements for regular pediatric care for their babies? Are you able to call for assistance whenever you feel you need it? We ask this because we have found that many mothers are afraid the doctor will think their questions foolish. We feel that the doctor should be available to answer any questions about diet and health that are of concern to you: what to do for a cold, loose or hard stools, vomiting, fever, rashes, and the baby's reaction to new foods, etc. The job of the doctor is to answer those questions, and a mother must not be intimidated. Pediatricians are there for you, not vice versa.

Relations with the Family Physician or Pediatrician

However, there are large areas related to behavior and development about which these specialists may not be prepared to answer questions. For example, the doctor may not be prepared to discuss with you just how much, or in what way, to stimulate your baby's play, or what to do to stimulate speech. He may not be prepared to help with the development of the baby's personality. His major concern is the baby's physical health, and he should certainly be consulted about that. We will try to answer questions relating to the baby's emotional, intellectual, and social development.

> "It is good to know there is someone to ask the questions that the doctor doesn't have time or experience to answer. I find the doctor is often too busy to answer even the questions he should answer."

Often doctors are very busy with sick children. However, most pediatricians do have a telephone time for answering questions. Naturally, they would prefer not to be called during busy office hours unless the call is really urgent.

> "That's true, but often what I think is urgent, the doctor dismisses as of no importance."

To a new mother many things which are not very urgent may seem so. As you develop experience, however, you will be able to recognize what is really important. Perhaps we can help you do this.

STIMULATION: WAYS TO SPEND TIME WITH THE BABY

Now that the babies are getting older, staying awake longer, and becoming more curious about their surroundings, you, as parents, can utilize this time for appropriate stimulation. One of the most important forms of stimulation is talking to the baby. Babies respond to voices around them, particularly the mother's voice. Many people think babies can't understand, that language stimulation should come later. Do any of you feel this way?

Language

> "I do feel that way, but sometimes I just can't help talking to the baby, and then if others are around, I feel a little silly. I know she can't understand what I say, but she turns and

looks at me very hard when I talk to her and sometimes seems to have a little glimmer in her eye."

It is true babies do not understand what you are saying, but they can tell intuitively from your tone and the expression on your face if you are pleased and happy or angry and upset. They respond best to musical, rhythmically modulated speech. The human voice can be very soothing to babies. Even a premature infant in an incubator can be soothed by hearing the comforting voice of a nurse. Responding to the human voice seems to be one of the infant's very early abilities and should be encouraged. All babies who are healthy and not confined will learn to walk according to their own timetables. While they make sounds spontaneously, babies do not learn to speak a language without being spoken to; they must have speech models.

Some parents talk to their babies as they care for them or as they move about the baby's room cleaning and arranging things. The baby listens to the mother and, when she pauses, tries to respond by making some gurgling sounds. It is important to repeat these sounds back to the baby; the baby soon gets the idea that the sounds she makes evoke a response. This is communication and the beginning of conversation, another link in establishing trust and attachment.

Very often talking to the baby evokes a smile rather than a vocal response. Smiling is also communication. The first smile is a great moment for all parents. How many of you have experienced this already?

"At what age do babies begin to smile? I thought my baby smiled at me, but my mother said it was only gas."

Babies begin to smile responsively at varying ages. The responsive smile is generally preceded by a glimmer in the eye. It is sometimes possible to evoke a smile at about eight weeks, but a spontaneous social smile comes at about four months. The more a baby is spoken to and the more she sees her parents' smiling faces, the earlier she is apt to respond.

"My baby just looks at me very seriously when I talk to her. I haven't been able to make her smile, but she seems to be intently watching my mouth move. She looks as though she wants to say something."

Babies usually make some responsive gesture. They may give a little grunt or coo, purse their lips, move their tongues a little, or just look at you intently. All of these responses should be viewed as communication. Some parents poke the baby's face to stimulate a response. But in this case, the baby is responding more to touch than to speech. Babies get tactile stimulation from being held, dressed, burped, and comforted. Parents must make a conscious effort to give early speech stimulation.

Another form of stimulation for this age is visual. Dangle a bright toy about eight to ten inches from the baby's eye level. (A red ring is one of the best toys for this purpose.) When the toy is in the baby's line of vision, move it back and forth saying some special phrase like, "See, see" or "Look, look." Approve and smile as the baby follows the toy with her eyes. At first the baby's visual range will be very limited, but at about three months she will be able to follow an object through 180 degrees.

Babies can also be stimulated to grasp the dumbbell-shaped rattle when it is placed in one of their hands. They may reflexively grasp the rattle without as yet recognizing that they are holding it. They may wave it up and down. This stimulation should be offered daily at playtime. Both parents should participate in it. They can get a good deal of pleasure noticing how the time the rattle is held in each hand slowly increases, which hand is stronger, how much the baby waves the rattle, and how happy the baby is with the parents' attention.

How have you been trying to play with your baby?

> "I talk to the baby and hug him, but I haven't tried playing with the ring or rattle. I thought he was too young. My husband talks to him too and chucks him on the chin or cheek to try to get a response, but there isn't much reaction yet. He just stares into space. Sometimes he seems to watch me but for only a couple of seconds."

The responses you can expect now are visual tracking and grasping. As the baby's nervous system gradually matures, you will see more and more response. This development is fun to watch.

> "I'm glad to hear that. My husband and I try once in a while, but the baby doesn't often respond. So my husband has decided he has a dumb child. I guess we don't know what to expect."

There is nothing wrong with your baby. It does help, however, to know what to expect; that is the purpose of our discussions. If you continue to play with the ring and the rattle and to stimulate with speech and smiling, you will see the baby's responses develop. Each baby has a different timetable. Some babies respond earlier than others to visual or vocal stimulation. Don't worry about what other babies are doing. It's fun to keep tabs on your **own** baby—she's the only one that counts for you.

Parents can also give babies physical stimulation or exercise. Here are a few exercises you might want to try: (a) While the baby is lying flat on her back, grasp the baby's hands and gently extend the baby's arms towards you until they are straight and you feel a little tension. This will stimulate the baby to flex her neck and lift her head

Visual and Tactile Stimulation: Games and Toys

Motor Stimulation; Large Muscle Stimulation

slightly off the surface. This exercise is a good way not only to strengthen the baby's neck by practice in flexing the neck muscles but also to strengthen the abdominal muscles which contract as the baby lifts her head. Our only caution is that the parent should not pull the baby's arms so that the baby's shoulders are lifted up, leaving the baby's head on the surface. The whole point of the exercise is to get the baby to lift **her own** head up. If the baby does not respond by flexing her neck muscles and lifting her head, the parent should discontinue the exercise and try it again in a few days. (b) Place the baby on her stomach and see how well she can lift her head. Call to her from above her eye level, so she will try to look up. Then call to her from below eye level, so she tries to look below the level of the surface she is lying on. By the time babies are four months old they can do this well. The exercise can be developed into the game of 'Peekaboo' which both parents and child will enjoy—and which will also help strengthen the feelings of attachment. (c) Draw the opposite knees and elbows of the baby together a few times. Each knee can be flexed toward the abdomen, and each arm and elbow toward the chest and back out.

None of these exercises is essential because babies squirm, kick, and move about if given the freedom to do so. However, they are a way of playing with the baby, a way of interacting and having fun with the baby. This is important for both parents and child.

How many of you have tried any games or exercise with your babies?

> "I have seen you do the one where you extend the baby's hands toward you and the baby begins to pull his head up. My mother says a baby's head always has to be supported, and I could damage his neck if I do this exercise. I didn't dare try it."

In general, people are worried about injuring a baby's neck. The baby's neck and head are attached by very strong muscles, and the head won't fall off. You will notice, however, that we don't jerk or pull the baby's head up. We simply put a little tension on the extended arms, and this stimulates the baby to lift her head herself. With practice and growth, the baby is able to lift her head higher and higher. By five or six months babies can pull themselves to a sitting posture if someone gives them support by holding their hands. It is fun to see this ability develop. If you do this exercise the way we have described it, no harm will come to your baby. (See photograph facing page 89).

> "We do push his legs on his abdomen and have found that he is able to expel his bowel movement more easily. He is happier and more comfortable."

I am glad you discovered that. All of the little exercises we have been discussing help to build up the muscle tone, so that the baby can take care of normal physiological functions more easily. In addition, these exercises are fun for you and the baby.

Being taken out of doors in the carriage is stimulating because of the change of air temperature, the motion, the new sights and sounds. The baby is often soothed to sleep by the motion or by the fatigue produced by the stimulation. The seemingly simple activity of dressing for the outdoors can be both stimulating and fatiguing for mother and child.

Going Outdoors: Stimulation from Dressing, Outdoor Air, a Change of Scenery

Have you been taking the baby out regularly?

> "I can't seem to manage it every day. By the time I get the baby all bundled up, my clothes on, the diaper changes and bottle together, and the carriage out, it's almost time to come back."

It does take organization. The first few times are hard, especially if it is cold, and there is so much to get ready. But once you get a routine set, you will find it easier. It will be helpful for the baby to be in a different environment, and taking the baby for a stroll will permit you to get out of the house.

> "I go out as often as the weather permits. The fresh air helps the baby sleep. I get my marketing done and meet people. Everyone says, 'What a cute baby,' and whether they really mean it or not, that makes me feel great."

Mothers often enjoy dressing children up, and babies get a feeling that others are pleased with their appearance. At first, preparing for a stroll with the baby seems like a lot of trouble, but as you become adept at infant care, it will become less difficult.

> "On the whole, I think I'm doing pretty well. Certain days are bad. The baby cries a lot, and I don't catch on quickly to what's bothering her. When I do finally figure it out, I feel good."

As you get to know your baby better, you'll "catch on" faster. Your ability to respond quickly and appropriately will lessen the amount of crying. Most young babies cry a good deal more than one unfamiliar with infants would expect. Babies cry to make adults understand what they need. The important thing is not to think that there is something seriously wrong with you or the baby if the baby cries. You'll soon be able to tell whether the baby's cry means hunger, wetness, gas, fatigue, or simply the need for entertainment or loving.

It is important to realize that the loudness of a young baby's cry is not always proportionate to her need. At this stage babies cry just as loud for a small discomfort as for a big pain. Because of the immaturity of their nervous systems, they do not have the capacity to modulate the cry in proportion to the need. Their reactions are all or nothing. The intensity of the cry may not, therefore, mean anything. It is important, however, to calm the baby to see what specific attention is needed.

CARETAKING AND ATTACHMENT

Some of you who have not planned to devote all of your time to your babies may be beginning to wonder about the appropriate time to resume your jobs. You have given the babies a good start with your undivided attention, and the babies are getting more settled in their routines. Some of you may be wondering if your baby will be just as well off with another caretaker, such as a maid, neighbor, grandmother, or other relative. Others of you may be deciding that you are enjoying child rearing and that the quality of caretaking is more important than you realized. You are probably also aware that the question of who should take primary care of the baby is widely discussed among professionals and parents alike. Each of you will have to decide what is best for your baby and your family according to your own circumstances. We will all share our thinking on this subject so that you will understand all aspects of it.

Some believe that a baby should get used to being taken care of by several people. However, there is now a large body of research and experience which points up the baby's need to form an **early** one-to-one attachment to the mother, the father, or other caretaker, so that later in life the baby will be able to form attachments and relate well to other people. In order to form this attachment, a baby needs to see the same face as she feeds, to feel the same arms hold her, so that she gets a sense of familiarity with that particular hold, face, voice, and smile. This familiarity establishes the baby's sense of security and attachment. If the relationship is primarily with the mother, a baby can also get used to the father at certain feeding times, or diaper changes, or playing times. However, one person should remain the primary caretaker at first.

We talked earlier about the surprise mothers felt when they didn't have a sense of closeness to their babies when they were first born. Are you now beginning to feel that sense of attachment more than you thought you were going to at the beginning? Do the babies seem less like strangers now?

"Oh, yes. It's an entirely different feeling. I'm really getting to know the baby and love him—not just deriving pride and fun out of dressing him up like a doll, the way it was before. Now I think he is getting to know me. His eyes follow me around the room, and he kicks and smiles when I come in. It's different."

That's a very important awareness that you just described, and it's what makes child rearing fun.

"When you first talked of feeling attached to the baby, I just didn't think that would happen to me. I didn't think I liked babies. But now I can't wait for my baby to wake. I miss him when he is asleep, and tiptoe in to look at him. I'm not the same me."

So you are really having a whole new enriching experience which you didn't know you could have. You can't get that out of a book. It has to be experienced to be understood.

"We've had a hard time with our baby. He has had a digestion problem and cries a lot, so I have to hold him. At first I resented the baby because I didn't want him in the first place. I wanted to go to graduate school, but the pregnancy was too far along for an abortion, and I had to give up school. But now when I get him comforted, it gives me a sense of being needed and close to him, and I like that. What happens when babies are taken care of by different people?"

The sense of attachment that we are discussing is lacking in the development of many children in their own homes when care is divided and inconsistent. In children's institutions where there are three eight-hour shifts, care is even more inconsistent. Often attendants cannot be assigned the same babies to care for each day. It is difficult to replicate the consistency of parental care. Institutionalized babies grow up trying to make attachments to anyone and everyone; they have difficulty in making permanent attachments later on.

We consider early binding attachments important because of their relationship to later attachments to spouse and children. Good early attachments also prepare the child for coping in learning and school situations. The child's early relationships are important for future healthy personality development. Though much of early caretaking is time-consuming and tedious, the attachment that develops at the same time is vitally important. Parents can gain satisfaction from caretaking when they understand what they are doing and why it is important. We are not trained to be parents, but it is an achievement as important as, if not more important than, any other career. When we know how to do a job well, we enjoy it more. The same holds true for parenting.

"You talk more about attachment to the mother. Isn't the father just as important?"

The child's attachment to the father is, of course, important. We talk more about the attachment to the mother because in our society it is still, usually, the mother who takes primary care of the baby in the first years. The father is home only at night and on weekends, so that his contact with the baby is not as consistent. However, with planning it can be made consistent. The father can always take over a specific feeding or bathing or playtime, so that the attachment to him can be developing simultaneously with that to the mother. There are some families in which the mother is the one who goes to work, and the father is the primary caretaker. In such cases, the primary attachment is to the father, and the mother arranges specific contacts with the baby. In other families, both parents have to work and the baby may be left with a grandmother or other caretaker, who becomes the primary caretaker.

We will talk further about how to manage if both parents must or want to work. There are stages in the baby's life when it is more appropriate for the mother to resume work. Most people have thought that the ideal time for this is when the baby is six months old. Actually, this may be the most difficult time for the baby because by the age of six months she has begun to form binding attachment to the mother. Also, at about five to seven months comes an awareness of the difference between mother and others. This is, therefore, a difficult time to leave the baby with a new caretaker. If a mother must return to full-time work in the baby's first year, it is better, in our opinion, to do it when the baby is about three months old. In this way, the baby begins to form an attachment to the other caretaker. The mother will then need to set up her own particular routines with the baby, so that attachment forms with her as well, much in the same way it does with the father.

Each of you will have to decide what is best for your family. We are here to help you in any way that we can. We would be happy to talk individually with any of you about your plans.

The important issue to understand is that a child needs the consistency of the same caretaker—mother, father, or other person—so that a binding relationship, which is the foundation of healthy personality development, can be established.

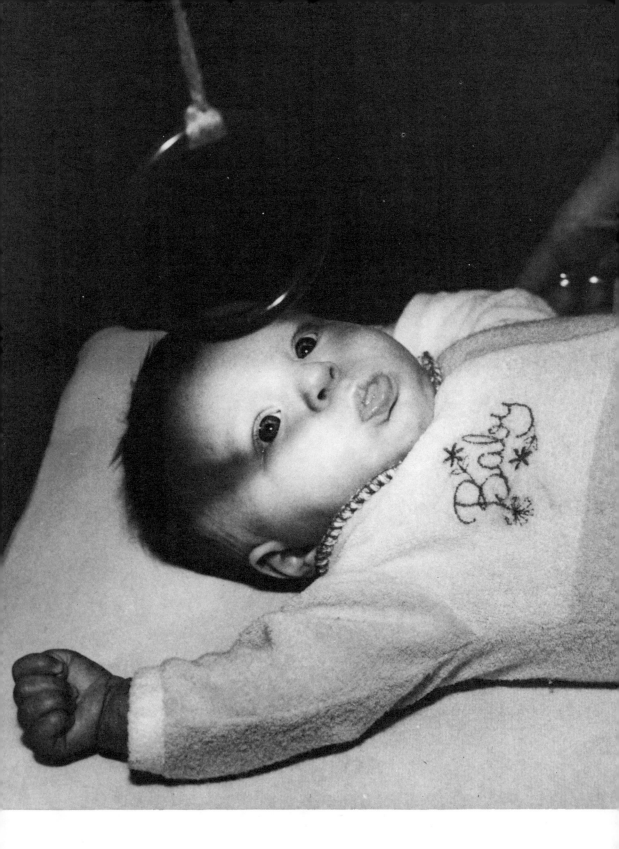

Two-month-old infant visually tracking
a red ring dangling from a string.

Chapter Two

Age: 8 to 12 weeks

By eight weeks, the baby can control her head much better. She can lift her chin farther off the surface on which she is lying on her stomach and may even look around. During the exercise described on page 18, in which tension is placed on the baby's extended arms as she lies on her back, the baby will be able to lift her head further off the surface as well.

The baby is much more attentive to the red ring dangled about eight inches above his head. He may even be able to follow it briefly. The baby can hold the rattle or red ring much longer in each hand. The strength of the baby's grip with each hand may be tested by gently pulling the toy away. This may give some early indication of handedness, which will be of interest to parents.

Now when the baby hears a loud noise near her, she may not react with her entire body, as at four weeks, but there should be a change in facial expression. The baby is more alert and expressive, and may have begun to smile. The baby looks much more directly and definitely at the parent and at others.

The baby may begin making sounds in response to the parent's smiling and talking. The baby's lip and tongue movements are his first attempts to reply. The baby's facial expression now changes in response to contact with adults and surroundings. The baby is gaining the ability to visually track the parents as they come and go around him. By now, some babies have progressed to only one night feeding. (Any feedings after the early evening feeding and before the first morning feeding are considered night feedings.)

_____PARENTS' FEELINGS AND EXPECTATIONS

Parents are usually NOT prepared for what the baby is going to be like. Most people's image of a baby is that of a four- or five-month old, perhaps one who looks like the babies on magazine covers—healthy complexion, smiling, and responsive.

What were your expectations?

"I never went near a baby until I had my own, and it was quite a shock to see how little he was. He seemed so frail, and I was afraid to touch him. I guess I visualized the older 'cover' baby you just described."

"My baby brother was born when I was twelve, and I had a lot to do with taking care of him, so I thought I was experienced. But it really isn't the same with my own baby. I guess my brother was older before I took care of him, and my mother was always around."

Being totally responsible for your own baby is a different experience, and your responses depend on previous ideas and experiences. Is it different for those who have their second baby?

"Well, I am not as scared as the first time, but I didn't have a good experience with my first. I had no idea what to expect and made mistakes. That's why I'm here."

What you have just described is a very common experience. Even mothers who have studied child development in school or taken prenatal classes are shocked to find how unstable the infant's body processes are and how minimal his initial responses. Your babies are living in totally new environments, and their systems need time to adjust and stabilize. This process takes varying lengths of time, depending on the baby's maturational rate and general health. Early responses, though seemingly minimal to many parents, are achievements for a new baby. It is an achievement when the baby opens his eyes to glance at the parent who is cooing at him. Grasping a parent's finger when it is inserted in his hand, sucking his bottle well, and getting up a burp are all achievements for an infant.

At the same time, learning to comfort the baby so he stops crying is an achievement for parents. Most new parents feel their baby cries too much. The seemingly unending needs of some small babies often upset new parents and make them feel like prisoners. Caring for a tiny being whom you don't always understand can be very frustrating. It is very normal to feel this frustration and important to talk about it honestly. If this sense of frustration becomes too great, parents may lose control and become abusive. Most of us have angry impulses when we are frustrated, and we all need to find ways of releasing the tension and anger without hurting others.

The important thing to remember at this period is that both parents will soon learn to understand their baby's needs. You will learn how to comfort the infant by going through a series of trial-and-error maneuvers—feeding, changing, burping, rocking, and talking. Soon you will learn which is the right step to take, and the baby will settle down. Parents can then feel some relief and satisfaction at the baby's and their own accomplishments.

Your babies are now about two months old. Are you beginning to understand their needs better? Are you becoming less worried?

"I think I'm getting better at burping the baby, and she is less fussy. The feedings are taking just as long, maybe longer, because I'm allowing more time for burping and getting settled, but her sleep time is getting longer, too."

That sounds like a great deal of progress. What else are you noticing?

"I think the baby is a little more responsive. I think she is at last beginning to smile."

Many of you expected the baby to smile, return your hug, and seem pleased to be your baby right away. You were prepared to give so much, and the baby seemed unresponsive. Now you are beginning to have different feelings.

Are you beginning to feel that the baby is more of a person, not just a "chore"?

"I can't say yet child care is not a chore, but I'm beginning to understand the kind of response a baby can make, so I'm getting more satisfaction."

"It seems to me that the baby always had a personality, but he wasn't reachable. Now he is beginning to follow me with his eyes and to smile. I've learned to talk to him and can see his mouth move as though he were trying to answer. I'm getting a real feeling for him, and the fun of having a baby is beginning to come true for me."

Feelings About Baby Talk

"The baby still takes too much time, but some of the routines are becoming more automatic and less burdensome. I'm beginning to take time to talk to the baby too. I was wondering about 'baby talk' and if that was all right?"

We have been encouraging you to talk to your babies, responding to their sounds, repeating them, and letting the babies respond to you. Some of you may consider this "baby talk," but it is actually appropriate speech stimulation. We encourage you to make cooing and other pleasing sounds to the baby which the baby may imitate. The baby feels the warmth and pleasure which you convey, and responds. This vocal interaction results in speech stimulation, communication, and strengthening of the ties of attachment. When we offer a bottle to a baby and say "baa' tle" with the proper inflection, that distinguishes the sounds for the baby and is still good English. If a mother says 'lé che,' that is still good Spanish, but it is easier for the baby to distinguish the sounds. There is nothing fatally wrong if a mother says "baa' tle," provided she says "bottle" later on when the baby's development is more advanced.

Do you have other ideas about this?

> "I have always said before I had a baby that I would never use baby talk, but now I realize that what turned me off was the 'itsy-bitsy-baby' way some parents spoke to older children who could already talk."

Your point is a good one. There is a difference between infantilizing an older child and responding appropriately to an infant. The former retards the child's speech; the latter enhances the establishment of communication and attachment. The parent's response has to be appropriate for the child's age and level of development.

Fathers' Feelings About Parenthood

Fathers have an important role in providing stimulation for the infants. Often they need encouragement, however, because they feel that babies are fragile and they are afraid of hurting them. Sometimes they are concerned about disturbing the babies.

The mothers have been telling us in the past weeks about the changes that their babies have made in their feelings and their lives. Fathers, too, must be having new experiences and feelings, and we would like to discuss that with you.

Is the experience what you expected or different?

> "We went to Lamaze classes, and I was very involved in the whole delivery process. But I didn't know, and I don't think anyone ever discussed, how much time and effort babies take. It all appears so easy—they just eat, sleep, and have to be changed. Well, you can forget that right away. Even if they are on a schedule from the start, just one feeding from start to finish can take an hour and a half sometimes."

> "Our baby really hasn't been more trouble than we thought, but I would have liked to come to these sessions sooner because I feel so involved and want to be sure my wife and I understand things the same way."

> "I don't think it's a father's job to care for such a small baby. It's a job for mothers. When our son is older, say a year or so, then I think I'll be able to do more. I'm just not good around small babies."

We seem to have a variety of feelings—from wanting to be more involved or involved earlier to feeling out of place with a small baby. These are all natural responses. One feeling that seems to prevail is the lack of preparation for the time and energy it takes to care for an infant. Though you may have heard it, it doesn't fully sink in until you experience it personally. Fortunately, this is not a permanent situation. As the baby matures and the parents come to understand the baby's needs and how to satisfy those needs, the baby takes less time and her schedule becomes more routine. The parents and the baby get to know one another, and some of the ways the parents related to one another before the baby was born begin to return. Gradually some of the social activities that the parents used to enjoy—having friends over for dinner or going out—can be planned again.

> "When do the night feedings stop? That's the hardest part. My wife is knocked out at the end of the day, so she is asleep by nine. I stay up for the late night feeding at eleven or twelve. She gets up for the four or six o'clock feeding so I can sleep to seven to have some energy to go to work."

When night feedings stop varies with each infant. Usually it occurs when the baby is between three and six months old. It depends on each child's metabolism, weight, and biological clock. The early morning feedings will gradually come later as well. Mothers tend to try to get housework done to please their husbands, but it would be better for the mothers to nap while the baby does so they can make up for lost sleep.

> "The part of having a baby that bothers me most is the spitting up. How long will that last?"

Spitting up may last until the baby is about a year old, but she will do it less and less as time goes on. The reason a baby spits up is that she has a gas bubble underneath the food. The tummy is shaped like a bottle, and the gas bubble is at the bottom. When you hold the baby up, this bubble comes to the top and pushes out the food in front of it. The reason we adults are better able to keep food down, although our stomachs are also bottle-shaped, is because the nerve controlling the muscles is matured and can keep the muscle closed. But with the babies, these are not developed yet and the maturation time varies with each child.

We have been mentioning the difficulties with a new baby. What aspect of having a baby is fun?

> "My big kick comes from giving the baby a bath. That's our thing together. I seem to be less afraid of dropping the baby, so my wife is glad to have me give the baby her bath."

> "I have a good feeling when I feed the baby and hold him. He relaxes in my arms and takes his feeding well. And if he burps well, I feel I have it made."

> "So far, there doesn't seem to be much to crow about. He opens his eyes and stares once in a while. That's about all. He doesn't seem like anything to me. I just don't feel he is any-body yet."

> "I can't wait to get home from the office and look at her. Just seeing that she is alive and well and has made it through another day is fine with me. Then my wife tells me how well

she ate and burped, and how her bowel movements were. While we are talking, I chuck her under the chin, and I think she likes it. There is a kind of a smile. That's great!"

Different aspects of the baby's development affect each of you, very much as the mothers have been affected. Each parent responds to the baby differently, and each baby responds to her parents and her surroundings differently. There is a great deal of difference in parents and their babies. Each one of us is unique. We need to remember this about the baby, so that we don't try to fit the baby into a stereotype.

Fathers' Roles in Stimulation

It used to be considered that a quiet baby was a good baby. The thing to do was to leave a baby alone and let her sleep. Visitors might peek into the crib, but the baby couldn't be touched or upset. The object was peace and quiet at any price. Now, however, we have learned through observation and experimental studies that babies need stimulation. They need body contact, auditory and visual stimulation. But they need stimulation timed to their level of development, so that it is appropriate for the baby and rewarding for the parent. We use our knowledge about how the nervous system matures from the head down and from the center out in the way we stimulate the baby.

The infant is born able to hear, so we can stimulate her hearing response by ringing a bell farther away and then nearer her ear. The baby's earliest response will be the startled reaction of throwing the head back and arms out, or blinking the eyes, or even crying. We can also stimulate babies with a music-box type of toy placed in or above the crib.

The best stimulus is the parent's voice. However, the baby can sense at a very early age whether that voice is loving and approving or harsh and critical. Even a premature infant crying in an incubator can respond to a caretaker's voice and be soothed. So, even though a baby cannot understand what you are saying, the tone in which you talk to the baby is very important.

How have you fathers been trying to stimulate your babies?

"I know so little about babies. I am really afraid to touch him. If he is quiet, I don't want to upset him. If he is crying, forget it. He's my wife's then."

"I guess my contact is just to chuck her under the chin a little to see if I can get a response of some kind. There isn't much yet."

"Sometimes when I put my finger into his hand, he curls his fingers around my finger. I pull on it a little, and then he seems to look at me. But that's about it."

You all seem to be trying to get a response from the baby, so let's talk a little about what the baby can do and what you can do to experience more fun with the baby. When you talk to your babies, you will see them work their mouths trying to respond. They may even break into a smile when you do this. Although the baby doesn't understand what you say, she knows if you are pleased and responds to your tone and expression. This kind of exchange between parent and child is very important for early language stimulation.

Have you noticed this response?

"To tell the truth, I feel like an idiot talking to such a little baby, so I guess I don't do it enough and think the baby is unresponsive. But from now on I'll try. It doesn't have to be baby talk, does it?"

No, it doesn't have to be baby talk. Warmth and friendliness need to be conveyed. What you say doesn't matter, just how you say it.

"Well, I'm one of those 'idiots' that loves to talk to the baby, and it gives me a great thrill when he curls up his mouth and acts as if he wanted to answer back."

"I thought it was too early, so I never tried."

"I do talk to the baby, and I noticed the motions or grunts he made. But it never occurred to me that it was a kind of reply. That's really great!"

A baby's visual development also needs stimulation. Visual ability develops a little later than hearing. At first the baby has a random kind of gaze. She sees objects in front of her, but the outlines are hazy. When the baby is about a month old, if a brightly colored object (such as a red ring) is dangled at the right distance and angle, the baby may glance at it momentarily. In the next month, with stimulation and maturation of the nervous system, the baby begins to follow the ring a little way. By three months, she may follow it through 180 degrees. The baby also begins to follow the parents as they move about the room. The sequence of visual development is fun to observe and is enhanced by parental stimulation.

How many of you have been noticing this change in your babies?

"We haven't been able to get much response with the red ring. In watching you here, I think we were holding it too far away. It makes us anxious when she doesn't follow quickly, so we avoid doing it. We are anxious about her vision because both of us have such poor eyesight."

It is easy to understand your feelings and your protection against anxiety, but it is much better for the baby to have visual stimulation.

One study has shown that the babies near the nurses' station in a large infant ward, where there was much movement, had better visual responses and general development than did the babies at the far end of the ward, where there was less opportunity for stimulation.

> "When we first noticed that the baby followed us when we moved around the room, it was a great thrill. Now we use it as a game."

> "Won't the baby develop vision anyway, whether we stimulate her or not?"

Yes, she will, but you can enhance the development by stimulation. More important, the parent can use visual stimulation to develop an avenue of communication and interaction which is pleasing to both parent and child. This pleasant interaction is the beginning of a good relationship.

You may have also noticed that a very young baby keeps her fingers clinched in a tight fist most of the time. Later the baby's hands unclench, and her position becomes more symmetrical. This is an important sign of development.

The babies can now flail their arms around and kick, but they can't reach. However, they can hold a rattle in their hand if it is put there. At first they hold it momentarily, but as their grip strengthens, they hold it longer. At this stage, parents should be putting things into their baby's hands. This activity demonstrates the maturation of the central nervous system from the head to the hand.

Have you been playing in this way with your babies?

> "Actually, no, I couldn't say I was making a game of it because she drops the rattle right away. I thought it was too soon and I'd just be picking up the rattle over and over again."

Certainly, that is the situation now, but you can watch the development of the hand coordination by regularly stimulating the baby to grasp the toy. One day you will notice that the baby will hold it a longer time. Soon she will hold it by intention instead of reflex, and that will be quite a thrill.

> "How long does that take?"

For each baby it is different. Each baby has his or her own maturational timetable. One baby's grip will be slow in developing. Another baby will grasp the rattle very quickly and fling it about occasionally, even hitting herself with it. Each baby will reach that stage. It is fun to observe how babies arrive at it. The red ring is a good object to use, and so is a small dumbbell-shaped rattle, which the baby can grasp easily.

"How long should you play like that with a baby of this age?

The length of time varies with each baby. There should be at least one special time set aside in the day when visual, auditory, and tactile stimulation is engaged in. One can also do this at each changing before putting the baby back to sleep after feeding. Sometimes the baby will show signs of overstimulation. She will turn away, cease to pay attention, or get fussy. As parents get to know the baby better, they can tell what is enough. Sometimes there needs to be a quiet soothing period after stimulating play, so the baby can relax and go off to sleep. Sometimes the baby just goes off to sleep on her own. Parents soon get to know what their baby's style is.

Men and women often have different feelings about parenthood. In the last section, we discussed several aspects of child rearing from the fathers' point of view. We are interested in knowing how the fathers felt about the discussion at Fathers' Night and how the mothers feel about the fathers' attitudes.

Mothers' Reactions to Fathers' Feelings About Parenthood

"My husband was interested in hearing what we talk about and how things are discussed. I think just seeing the whole group together with the different babies was very interesting and important to him because he never sees any other babies."

I am glad you mentioned that he noticed the different types of babies. The interesting thing is that each baby is so different from the others. Most people, when they think of babies, think that all babies are the same. But babies aren't the same, and they're not the same from day to day.

"I think that my husband always thought that babies were easier to take care of than they are. He was able to see that it is a big job for all mothers and fathers, and that it isn't just the two of us that find it hard work."

"Well, my husband found out that babies can have their good days and bad days, and all parents get upset when there is a bad day. But I think he'll be able to take it in stride now that he understands."

Was there anything specific we could clear up for him? I remember he asked why people laugh when he tells them you come here.

"Well, he puts it this way, 'The baby is going to school,' and of course people laugh. But he didn't really explain it. He just said 'school.' The next day he really explained it fully to his mother."

"It's really the parents who 'get something' out of these discussions. It helps them enjoy their babies. That's how I see it. My husband liked seeing the other babies here. It made him feel good that his baby was louder and more aggressive than all the rest."

It seems that certain aspects of our meetings were made clearer to your husbands, and also that some of their feelings about their babies became clearer.

Some fathers appreciate their girl babies being gentle and girlish. Other fathers like it if their girl babies are aggressive. They all like it if their boys are aggressive. When you see a lot of babies together, you see that yours has a special personality and special characteristics that other babies don't have. You really can't compare babies.

"My husband liked seeing that other parents have a hard day if their babies have been very difficult. We just felt that other parents didn't feel the way we do sometimes. We thought it was just us."

Yes, it's very hard in the early months, and that's why it's really important to have somebody look after the baby for half an hour so you can both go out for a walk. It's important to know that you are being irritated, but that it's not the baby's fault; the baby is not doing it to try to "get your goat," which is one of the natural feelings that parents have.

You felt there was something wrong with you. Now you know that's not so. Everyone has the problem once in a while; some people can handle it more easily than others.

It may help you to know that at some of these difficult times some kind of change is taking place. It may be a response to a dietary change; it may be a change in growth; it may be that the baby's nervous system is developing to a new level that the baby is not quite ready for. So the baby is a little bit frustrated and shows it by crying. Crying is a baby's "language." You say it's frustrating because your baby can't talk but he is talking; when he's crying, he is saying something. Our job, as caretakers, is to try and "tune in" to what the baby is saying. That's what we are trying to learn.

PATTERNING AND SEQUENCING IN RELATION TO BASIC TRUST: A REVIEW

We have been discussing consistent stimulation, and this activity fits into another topic which is very important. We will talk now about patterning and sequencing. We do not mean a rigid time schedule, such as feedings at six, ten, and twelve o'clock, bath at five, and bed at six. That used to be considered the correct way to set up the daily pattern. We are not so rigid now. What we do consider important is that each procedure come in a regular sequence. If the first activities in the morning are changing, feeding, burping, and then sleeping, this sequence should be followed each day. If the next activity is a bath, then a feeding, and then going outdoors, this sequence should be followed regularly. Soon the baby begins to remember the sequence and comes to rely on it. This pattern helps to organize her life and, by consistent repetition, she develops a sense of trust in the parent and an awareness that her needs will be taken care of in a dependable way. This consistency is the beginning of basic trust.

This sense of trust in the parents is one of the essential elements in healthy character formation. Having a regular pattern also helps the mother to organize her day. She does not impose a schedule on the baby, but she responds to the baby's needs. She soon learns whether the baby is apt to take a longer nap in the afternoon or morning, and she can arrange to do her housework or rest during those periods.

Sometimes other relatives become impatient. They often urge that a regular time schedule be followed and that the baby be allowed to cry so that she learns to conform to her parents' time schedule. The impression is that the parent is spoiling the child by accommodating to the baby's pattern. They think the baby is spoiled if she is picked up and tended when she cries.

How have you been dealing with the patterning and sequencing of the baby's activities during the day?

"Establishing a pattern—is that one of the purposes of these discussions?"

Our overall purpose is to help the babies establish the kind of personality which will help them to reach their maximum potential with the endowment that they have, for each baby is differently endowed. Some children will be more interested in muscular activities, some more interested in visual things, some more interested in academic work. We hope to help them to reach their maximum development. We have learned from experience that there are certain important items that help them along that way. Patterning and sequencing is one of them.

It is important because it helps both parents and baby in organizing their lives and, in so doing, gives the baby a sense of knowing what to expect. This helps the baby develop a sense of trust in her caretaker.

Spoiling

"In our family we are having some discussion and disagreement. My wife picks the baby up when he cries. I don't see how she can ever get him to fit into any kind of schedule if she does that. If the baby is left to cry it out, he will know crying won't get him anywhere. My wife is just too softhearted."

"We began with the same idea, but as we experimented and got more experience, we found out that our baby cried for something. Now that we have sort of caught on, he cries less and less, and there is more peace around the house."

It seems to me that one of your major concerns is about "spoiling" the baby. Although the first weeks may be more difficult for the parents because the baby's timing may be unpredictable, studies have shown that as parents begin to tune in to their baby's timing, the baby is more contented, requires fewer feedings, and is easier to take care of. As to spoiling, it has been shown that the babies who are picked up when they cry become the babies who eventually cry least. The babies who have sometimes been picked up and sometimes left to cry, or those who have always been left to cry, are the ones who become clinging, whining children.

Always picking up the baby when she cries gives the baby the sense that her parents are reliable and available to help. Crying is the baby's first language and her only way of conveying her needs to the world around her. Crying may mean the baby needs to be turned over, or cuddled, to be fed or changed, or wants a little attention.

"I think our baby often cries just to get attention. Right now it seems she wants undivided attention."

That's right. As she gets older and can do things for herself, she will not need undivided attention. Now she needs it, and lots of people think that if you pick up the baby every time she cries, you are spoiling her.

"When she started to teethe, she began screaming so much that we couldn't understand what was wrong. The only thing we could imagine was teething. So we took her to the doctor, and he said to give her all the nursing she wants, and sure enough that's what it was."

That's right. You might have taken the attitude that she needed discipline. I am glad you didn't feel that way, but there are parents that do.

The behaviorist school of psychology believes that you should condition babies in that way; it used to be very popular years ago. The baby will finally stop crying, but that baby may become an unhappy, cranky person, not trusting anyone around her. Another baby might become inhibited, without the drive to achieve all that she could achieve. We have people in our clinics who have been brought up that way and are having problems that are not easy to solve. Because we have had those experiences and because it has been so hard to treat those patients, we recognize that the problems begin very early. We are trying in this program to prevent such personality problems.

"Are there no occasions when you should let a baby cry?"

Such occasions are rare. When you get to know your baby, you may find that if the baby is overtired, she sometimes needs to cry a little to settle down to sleep. That's her way of doing things. Once the parents know their baby well enough, they get to understand and respond to the baby's needs, and the baby cries less and less. 'Cuing in' to the baby enhances this process, as does the baby's growing trust in her parents.

"After a whole day with the baby, I get very tired and angry."

That's why it's very important sometimes for Papa to help when he comes home. It's very important for mothers to have some time away from the baby.

"Sometimes I yell at him, and then I feel terrible for the rest of the day. I feel I did something to his personality."

It may be difficult for the baby to understand why his usually pleasant mother suddenly lost her temper. We are all human and occasionally we all lose our tempers. Problems arise when our responses to the baby are unpredictable and inconsistent **most** of the time. If a mother feels she is having a bad day with the baby, she should call for help from a neighbor. Perhaps she should take the baby out in the carriage to change the scenery and mood. There are days when babies are hard to comfort. It may help you to know that babies behave rather badly on days just before there is a change in their development. As they are reaching a new stage, they have a feeling that things are not in equilibrium. The important thing to remember is that the baby is not going to behave like this forever. As you learn to cue in to the baby, there will be fewer days when you yell or feel like yelling. Parenting should be fun most of the time, and we are trying to help you get fun out of the experience.

"I understand that it's a good idea to come here. But I am amazed when I tell somebody about it at the office. They laugh. They think it's a big joke."

They think you don't need to train to be a parent?

"That's it exactly."

In years gone by, most people had large families. These relatives could hand on knowledge of child rearing from generation to generation. Now, we live in very small apartments—just father, mother, and the baby—and there are no extra hands to help you and no one to verify that what you are doing is right. So there's a need now for this kind of program, especially when the population of this country is very mobile and has lost many of its family ties.

Our purpose is to try to supply the missing support that young parents used to have. In addition, we are making available to parents the experience and new information gleaned from recent research on child development in the critical first three years of a child's life.

PLAYTIME

Regular Playtime with Parents

We have already mentioned how parents can stimulate their babies by playing with them. As the babies grow older and sleep less, they will need more playtime. There should be at least one time each day for play when there is a real face-to-face interchange of cooing and talking, a period for dangling a red ring with a smiling interchange, a time to watch the parent move around the room. For some babies play becomes the routine after certain feedings. Often this is the early afternoon feeding. In some families it is the evening feeding when Daddy comes home, so he can participate. After a playtime, there may need to be a simmering-down period when the baby is changed. Sometimes another sip of the bottle or breast is needed before the baby is put back to bed. Each family has to establish this playtime in a way that works best for it.

Playing Alone with Toys

Some of you are beginning to bring toys for your babies to hold. At present, the babies do not realize that the toys are in their hands, but it is good for them to have practice gripping the toy and flinging it. Some of you have reported that they are beginning to notice their cradle gyms. Some have even banged them accidentally with their hands or feet. Because they are beginning to coordinate more, this accidental contact will soon be purposeful.

Have you been noticing this?

> "Yes, that's the new thing, but it amuses him for only a few minutes. Then he gets tired and wants to be picked up. Then I get his musical mobile going, and that entertains him another few minutes. Perhaps he's alone for five minutes. Shouldn't it be longer? It hardly seems like any concentration at all."

Five minutes of concentration is a very long time for a baby of this age. A mother would like to have the baby amuse himself longer because she needs more time to get things done, but for the baby five minutes is a long time. Sometimes the baby's play can be prolonged if the parent plays a little, introduces another toy, or recognizes the baby's pleasure with a pleasant remark. The baby can then follow his own interests for another brief period of time.

Periodic communication with the baby gives him a sense of pleasure and enhances his trust in the parents, who are available in good times as well as bad. All of this helps create a good reciprocal relationship between infant and parent. It's one of the fun parts of parenting. Gradually the baby's concentration span increases, and he can play longer alone because he has experienced the frequent return of his mother or father to cheer him on.

How many of you have been trying to do this?

"I've been noticing how excited our baby gets when he hits his cradle gym. He likes to see it move when I hit it for him. It takes the monotony out of baby care now that there is more play. It's fun to watch."

"By talking, coming back to the crib and putting another toy in, or banging the cradle gym, I've managed to get the baby's room cleaned up or the laundry sorted. The day is going better. I don't mean such devices always work but he entertains himself more than he used to."

"My baby still likes to watch his mobile or communicate with a red doll I put in the crib. He hasn't discovered the cradle gym yet."

Each baby responds somewhat differently. Each baby's timetable for responding is different, and each response is different. That's what makes it so interesting getting to know your own baby. Each discovery is a milestone. The parents' overt recognition of each new activity enhances the baby's development.

Although the babies are only between eight and ten weeks old, one will occasionally get his fingers in his mouth and suck on them. When the baby's hand lands near his mouth, it is accidental, not purposeful, behavior. In the next month this hand-to-mouth activity will become more frequent and purposeful. Most parents have negative feelings about babies sucking their fingers, especially their thumbs.

Putting the Fingers in the Mouth

How do you feel about it?

"I don't want my baby to suck his thumb. I think it's a bad habit. So I put a pacifier in his mouth instead, but he spits it right out. Then I don't know what to do."

Most mothers don't recognize that the baby's ability to put his hand to his mouth is an achievement representing increasing coordination. The baby's hand is the first pacifier which he can control. He may put his hand to his mouth repeatedly when he first becomes aware he can do this wonderful thing. This annoys parents, but it is a natural development and shows progress. Babies usually acquire this skill between three and four months of age, but there is a great deal of variation from baby to baby.

When the baby can put his hand in his mouth purposefully, he can also hold a teething ring, the red ring that you have for play stimulation, or another firm toy. He will suck or chew on these toys as he does with his fingers. If the baby is teething, this activity will be comforting.

"Is the pacifier a bad thing to use? You hear so much pro and con about it now. What do you think?"

Pacifiers

We think the hand is a better object for teething than the pacifier. The pacifier has another function. It is good for babies who do not get enough sucking. Often bottle-fed babies take their feedings too fast and need more sucking. Breast-fed babies usually stay at the breast long enough so that they do not need extra sucking. When a pacifier is placed in a baby's mouth, it is not a stimulus for hand-to-mouth coordination, nor is it a good teething ring. There is another drawback: Pacifiers are often dropped on the floor or street, and keeping them reasonably clean becomes an extra chore.

"Then you are not absolutely against pacifiers?"

Pacifiers are useful for babies who need more sucking time. One often sees parents taking the baby's hand out of his mouth. This is very frustrating for the baby because this hand-to-mouth activity is a natural part of his motor and cognitive development. It is also one of the first ways a baby learns about his own body. A baby sucks his fingers less when he is able to hold other things and put them into his mouth. Parents can assist this process of exploration by putting appropriate things in the baby's hand.

Babies who need more sucking may need the pacifier. A pacifier should not, however, be used to stop the baby from crying every time she opens her mouth. She may be signalling that she is hungry or thirsty, or that she needs to be held or comforted. As parents get to know their baby, they learn what this finger sucking means and can respond appropriately. The more parents tune in to the baby's needs, the more secure the baby becomes. This helps establish a happy relationship between parents and child.

"What about those two- and three-year olds who walk around with a pacifier?"

One needs to know what the past history of that child is, what kind of need is being satisfied, and what sort of deprivation this child may have had earlier in order to answer this question. What these children are doing has some meaning which the parents may or may not understand. Many children seem to need a bottle or pacifier, or to suck their thumbs, in order to go to sleep. There is some reason why they need to do that.

"But isn't it more natural for a mother to pull the baby's hand out of his mouth than to let him suck his fingers?"

I think it is the most common adult response, but that doesn't mean it is correct. We must remember that this activity is comforting to the baby and provides a means for the baby to begin to understand that these fingers belong to him. This is the beginning of his realization of the extent of his body.

Constantly pulling the baby's thumb out of his mouth is very frustrating for the baby. It is an unnecessary kind of frustration. Frustration leads to anger, which babies express by being fussy. A conflict develops between parent and baby which is unproductive and can lead to an oppositional relationship. The development in a child's personality structure of a feeling that he has to battle his parents can begin early, often on this kind of seemingly innocent little issue.

"Do you think that you always have to give in to the baby?"

I would not call it "giving in to the baby." In my view, it is understanding the baby's needs and trying to satisfy them appropriately. If the baby sucks his thumb, I feel that this signifies something. The baby either needs an object to bite on or suck, or he needs other diversion. The parent must try to determine what the baby needs, and supply a teething object for teething needs and longer breast or bottle feedings for sucking needs. A pacifier should be used only as a last resort. If the baby needs diversion, the parent can offer a toy or talk or sing to him. Parents will learn what the right thing is as they come to understand their baby's needs. Instead of a conflict, a reciprocal relationship develops, which not only gives pleasure to both baby and parents but contributes to the baby's sense of basic trust. Parents also feel satisfaction from being able to "tune in" correctly to their baby.

One of the reasons you are here is to learn how to understand your babies' needs, so that some of these early conflicts may be prevented. We hope your babies will not need to have pacifiers when they are two and three years old because you will have understood their needs and satisfied them in other ways.

In general, we get too concerned about how long a baby has a bottle, or a pacifier, or is breast-fed. The tendency has been to wean babies too early and too abruptly—that is, when the mother, not when the baby, is ready. It may be appropriate for children to continue with at least one bottle until they are two or three years old.

Beginning of Conflict Between Parents and Baby

BABIES' INDIVIDUAL DIFFERENCES AND PREFERENCES

All of this reemphasizes that our job is to understand and "tune in" to the child's needs at each stage of development. In addition, each child has his own individual style. Some babies are frightened when they are given a bath and cry throughout the whole process. Others may not sleep well in their cribs but will sleep in their carriages.

Have you noticed any preferences that your babies have?

"I find the bath the most difficult thing to handle. I've tried everything—warmer or cooler water, sponges and wash cloths. I've tried a little plastic tub and the sink. I've tried having a toy that he likes in the tub. I've tried changing the time of day. I even had my mother give him a bath, because I thought it was my inexperience, but he still was terrified. So now I just give up, but I feel badly because I know a baby should be bathed daily. Now I just hold him and sponge him off, which he doesn't like either, but it has to be done. Then after the bath is over, he is very happy, and that puzzles me."

There are some babies who take a very long time to get used to their baths. Most parents are a little tense themselves when they begin to bathe a baby. This tension communicates itself to the baby. Some babies are sensitive to exposure. You can begin by first sponging off each part, covering that part, and then going on to the next so the baby does not feel exposed. Then when the baby seems used to that, you can try submerging one leg at a time in the tub, then finally more of the body till the baby is in the tub. As we've discussed before, the intensity of a baby's cry does not necessarily signify the amount of discomfort. Babies still cannot modulate their cries. For the babies who do not like baths, it helps to give the bath as quickly as possible. Sometimes a baby can be distracted by talking or singing in a soothing tone.

The important thing is to find the most suitable way for your baby and then repeat it in the same sequence each day. When a pattern is established, the baby begins to respond to the procedure and gains a sense of security and eventually pleasure. In some families, bath time is a fun time, and the whole family likes to participate. Fathers often enjoy bathing the baby and look forward to it.

"My baby is the kind that loves his bath and hates his crib. If I put him in his crib at night, he will cry and won't go to sleep. The minute I put him in his carriage in his room, he quiets down and goes off to sleep."

For some reason he may feel more secure in his carriage. Perhaps it is smaller than the crib and he feels less exposed. As you can see, each baby has his own individual likes and dislikes. It isn't always easy to tell why, but it is important for each parent to respond to the baby's individual needs. Each baby needs to be treated differently. We adults make a mistake in expecting all babies to be alike. We are not all alike, so how can they be?

"I understand that we are all different, but it seems to me that you are recommending that we cater to our child's every wish. There are some things that we all have to learn to do in life. Why not start young?"

What needs to be started young is the feeling that parents can be trusted to give comfort and security. The child who has this feeling of basic trust will be ready when he is older to cope with the difficulties and hardships of life. At this age, he needs attention. If he gets appropriate attention now, he won't crave it later when it is not appropriate. He will be able to cope later if he is helped now to feel secure.

By now, some of the babies have established a sleeping pattern that suits the parents' way of life and all is well. Some babies had what seemed to be a pattern, but some development like the onset of teething has disturbed this pattern.

Establishing a Pattern

Have any of you encountered this situation?

"That's just what I wanted to talk about. My baby was a good sleeper until a week ago, but now she wakes once or twice during the night. At first I didn't mind this, but now I'm getting tired of it."

Usually a baby who has had a good sleep pattern will return to that pattern when the discomfort is over. Most prospective and new parents worry a great deal whether a baby will sleep or not and whether they will be up all night.

How many of you anticipated this?

"That was the first thing my friends warned us about when they found out we were having a baby. But, so far, our baby has not kept us up much. Each time there has been a good reason, such as a cold, or a tooth, or a tummy ache when a new food disagreed with her."

Some parents are needlessly frightened ahead of time. Other parents never anticipated anything but a quiet, sleeping baby; it's a shock for them when the baby cries. New parents who are called upon to be up day and night really have difficulty coping and need help. All feelings of affection for the baby may be driven away by sheer fatigue. This situation is hard to deal with in our nuclear families where there are often no relatives nearby to help the new parents. Also, in a large, impersonal city we often have no friendly neighbors to lend a hand. A father who has been working all day comes home to find the household in an uproar—no dinner ready and a distraught mother with a crying baby. Some fathers can size up the situation and lend a hand. Some, in fact, like the role of rescuer and want to help. Others become angry and feel that their wives are giving too much attention to the infant and not enough to managing the house.

How are you managing?

"My husband was an only child and was very indulged, so he just couldn't cope with my not being available to have his dinner ready on time. Now he is getting to know and like the baby, so the situation is not so bad. But I still think deep down he resents the attention the baby gets."

That is quite a common situation and makes it hard for both parents. If you can talk about the problem, it is easier to deal with. It may help your husband to understand that you are also having to make a lot of adjustments.

> "My trouble is not that the baby wakes so much, but that I have difficulty getting back to sleep. I just can't do all the things I need to because I have to nap during the day. The situation's better now, but I was lucky because my husband understood and really helped a lot."

The majority of infants do eventually sleep at regular intervals, waking only for changing and feeding. A few do this from the start. Others get into a pattern if their parents follow a regular sequence for the day's activities in a patient and relaxed way. You may bathe the baby regularly either morning or evening. You may take her out after the second morning feeding or the first afternoon feeding. If you do all of these things in a regular sequence which suits both parents and baby, gradually the baby's life will get into a pattern. This pattern will give the baby a sense of security and trust in her parents because she gets a feeling for what comes next. This pattern also gives some organization to the parents' lives. Then, the mother can gradually get to do more of the neglected tasks.

Each of you has to find the best way of settling your baby for sleep. If she fusses a bit, you tolerate it; but if she cries, you try to discover the reason and comfort her. You may need to hold the baby for a while or rock her a little.

You know there was a reason for those antique cradles: babies need some rocking. In primitive societies, they are carried on the mother's back or hung in a swing fixed to a tree branch, where they are lulled to sleep by swaying in the breeze. It is only in our scientific, mechanized world that babies are supposed to go to sleep without some sort of soothing motion.

We can, however, develop familiar patterns of activities that lead up to sleep. For example, the parent can sit in a relaxed frame of mind, feeding the baby, patiently getting up the burps, and playing with the baby if she seems inclined. Then the baby may be changed again and put on her side or stomach to sleep. Most babies prefer a certain posture for sleeping, and just putting them in this position cues them in to the sleeping situation after the routine of feeding, burping, and playing.

Are you beginning a pattern of the sequence of events leading up to sleep?

> "Well, the sequence that seems to work best for us is to give the baby his evening bath, then a bottle, and put him in his crib on his stomach with his pet toy, a calico cat, in the corner where he can see it. He squirms around and moves his hands and feet. Then he settles his head in a comfortable position, sometimes with a little whimper, and goes to sleep."

That's the idea. You seem to have found a good pattern for your baby.

"Do you think bathing the baby is better at night than in the morning? Does it help the baby to get to sleep?"

For some babies bathing at night helps them get off to sleep more easily. Each mother has to decide what is the best way for her and her baby.

Father's Role in Establishing a Sleep Pattern

What we have been discussing is the usual manner of establishing a pattern, and this is intimately connected with establishing basic trust. The father should also become part of this process, so that the baby counts on him and he becomes a part of the process of developing basic trust. There should be a certain feeding, or perhaps the bath, which the father regularly takes over. He can also help with the bedtime routine.

Sometimes, particularly at night when he comes home and the mother and baby are overtired, a father may step in and soothe both by his reassuring presence. Often the father, who hasn't seen the baby all day, wants to play with the baby. When he has had enough, the father puts the baby down. But the baby has enjoyed the play and refuses to go to sleep or is too stimulated to settle down. In either case, it is necessary to have a quiet period with the baby giving her time to simmer down and relax. Then repeat your normal bedtime routine very quietly with no unnecessary stimulation. Babies often find it soothing when parents pat them a little, hum a lullaby, or turn on a music box or record. Sometimes babies may need an extra pat or an extra burp. If a regular bedtime routine is followed, the baby eventually cues in and gets into a sleeping pattern.

Colic and Its Relation to Parental Anxiety

If a baby cries a great deal, pulls her legs up on her abdomen, flails about, and won't sleep, she may be having colic. She may also sleep for a very short time and then wake up crying. If this is the situation, the baby's doctor should be called. The doctor is the one to decide whether the feedings need to be changed, whether there is an allergic reaction to some food, or whether some medication is needed. Fewer babies seem to suffer from colic than used to be the case, but there is always a small group of them who have a real problem.

There are also babies who appear colicky but are only a little uneasy because they sense the tenseness and anxiety of the parent. As parents become more certain of their roles and begin to cue in better to the baby, the so-called colic ceases.

Is this happening to some of you now?

"I'm glad to say my baby is responding better. I think it is because I feel more secure as I see him progress from day to

day. Knowing that this is something that we have to learn together, that it doesn't just happen to some and not to others, helps me keep trying. It's like practicing a sport. The more you do it, the better you get at it."

Other Upsets to Sleep Patterns

There are some babies who are very light sleepers, and families tiptoe around whispering when the baby is asleep. But this is rarely necessary. Usually a baby who is sleeping can sleep through the usual household noises like those made by the washing machine, cleaning, the radio, the television set, or conversation. The baby gets used to these household sounds. However, they do startle and often wake if there is a sudden loud noise—a car backfiring, a fire engine, a clap of thunder. Then the baby may become frightened and need comforting. Sometimes a single such episode breaks up a sleep pattern, and the pattern has to be patiently established again. This is upsetting to parents, but the interruption will not last long if handled appropriately.

Has this happened to any of you?

"Yes, we went to visit my mother, and there is a fire house next door. The engines woke the baby for several days while we were there. When we were about to leave, he began to sleep through the noise."

"We have a dog that barks when the doorbell rings, and that wakes up the baby. I'm hoping the baby will get used to it. I put a sign on the door asking people not to ring the bell because the baby is sleeping, but sometimes that doesn't help either. We may have to get rid of the dog."

That would be a sacrifice, I'm sure, but you may have to do just that if the baby doesn't eventually learn to ignore the dog's barking.

"How long should a baby sleep in a day? I've heard that they should sleep about twenty out of the twenty-four hours. Mine doesn't do that."

Many mothers ask that question. It may come as a shock that a minimum of fourteen hours out of the twenty-four is average for a good many babies.

Do Dreams Upset Babies?

Occasionally babies will also be upset by their dreams. Recent research on sleep has involved a device which registers rapid eye movements (REM). Rapid eye movements are interpreted as indicating dreaming and have been found in infants. What babies dream about is, of course, speculation. Because they often startle during sleep, it has been suggested that babies may be dreaming of falling or floating. As they grow older, they dream of events that have occurred during the day. Sometimes, if you watch sleeping babies, you will see them making sucking movements. It's conjectured that they are dreaming of nursing. The subject of babies' dreams requires much more exploration.

"I'd like to ask about traveling. We've been going away weekends to a farm. What is the baby aware of?"

Traveling with a Baby

She is certainly aware of the change. How was she during the trip?

"The first time she cried and didn't sleep at all. The second time I took the carriage toys that detach, and she slept on the trip, but when we were at the farm, she didn't sleep well."

Your baby was certainly aware of the change in surroundings. Sleep disturbances will be a common indication of this awareness. Babies feel comfortable with sameness—the same room, the same pictures, the same toy in the crib. This is the consistency that they need to develop a sense of security and trust. Babies do not respond well to constant shifts. If a family decides to go away on a long trip, say for the summer, the baby has time to adjust. It is hard for a baby to adjust to a new place each weekend. However, if you are going to your farm regularly, the baby will begin to feel at home there in time, especially if you bring along enough of her favorite things.

We're not advocating that parents should stay home every weekend, but you do have to realize that the baby may not adjust readily, and you should not be too disappointed if she doesn't. If you find your baby is a good traveler, you can take advantage of it.

Again, there are individual differences and each parent has to tune in to his or her child.

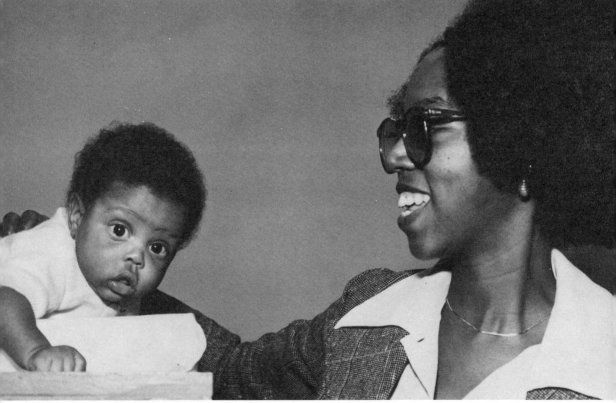

Three-month-old infant lifting head
from prone position with mother's encouragement.

Chapter Three

Age: 12 to 16 weeks

Parents will notice more developmental changes at this age. When the baby is lying on her back, she holds her head so that her face is more straight up, rather than to the side. Now the hands are not held as tightly clenched and are open more often. When supported in a standing position, the baby lifts one foot momentarily. When turned on her stomach, she braces herself on her forearms and holds up her head to look around, keeping her hips on the table.

Most babies can now follow the red ring through an arc of 180 degrees when it is dangled above their heads as they are lying on their backs. This is a skill that improves with practice and may be used as a play activity which enhances parent-child interaction.

The baby now holds the rattle or ring placed in his hand more firmly and may even glance at the toy. Glancing at the toy is a big step forward in development. If the parent holds up two objects, such as a cup and a small block (preferably a one-inch red cube), the baby may glance at each of them, showing that he can attend to two things of different sizes at the same time.

When a parent talks to the baby, the baby may observe the parent very intently and then smile, coo, or chuckle. Her vocal response may be accompanied by some physical activity such as waving the arms and legs.

The babies may also be looking at their hands now and pulling blankets or clothes over their faces. Parents can utilize the latter development in a beginning "peekaboo" game. (Some parents may worry that babies will smother if they cover their faces, but there is no need for worry because the babies will do this only momentarily and plenty of air can get through baby clothes and bedding. Thin plastic materials such as cleaning bags are, however, **exceedingly dangerous** and should be kept away from the baby.)

CENTRAL NERVOUS SYSTEM DEVELOPMENT: FROM HEAD TO HANDS ____

In one of our earlier sessions we mentioned that the central nervous system matures from the head down. We pointed out that the baby first hears and then sees. She learns to turn her head from side to side. Gradually she lifts her head by herself when she is face down, and with her parents' help when she is on her back. She is becoming more successful at these activities. She is lifting her head higher from both positions. Parents can now observe these achievements, and show the baby more emphatically how pleased they are.

Have any of you begun to experience this?

> "My baby is able to get her head up ever so much more. Each night, her father watches to see if she has made any progress. He gets a big kick out of it—as much as the baby does, I think."

This is a very good way to engage father and baby in an interaction. Most babies are ready to play the "I see" game—an early form of peekaboo. When the baby is on her stomach, the parent gets below eye level, encouraging the baby to look down, and then slowly gets up again calling to the baby so she will look up. The baby will not be too good at this at first but this is a good time to start the activity. It is good for both parents and baby. Aside from stimulating motor and sensory development, it has other results which are as important. The parents get a sense of pleasure and achievement from the baby's response. The baby gets a sense of recognition and approval, which she may show by smiling or activating her hands and feet in sort of swimming motion. Parental recognition of this achievement helps the baby establish a good self-image. Beginning to acquire a good self-image early is very important to personality development.

> "Do you mean that the baby understands so young that she is doing something great? When she gets excited like that, I just worry that she'll strain herself. Everybody has been telling me we get the baby too worked up."

Of course, one has to use judgment and not get the baby overtired. However, stimulating the baby and giving her the feeling that she is doing something that you like are very important. This is the beginning of her positive awareness of herself. It is a small but very important beginning.

As we discussed earlier, the ability of babies to get their hands to their mouths is an achievement. Some of the babies may be putting toys which have been placed in their hands into their mouths. At first, the baby will not look at the toy in her hand and will not be aware that it is there. As the development of the nervous system progresses from head to hand, however, she will begin to look at her hand and what it is holding. She will also begin to play with her fingers, hold up her hands, look at them, and clench her hands together. For some babies this begins in the third month and is fairly well established by the fourth. When the baby drops the toy, she obviously can't retrieve it. Picking up and handing back a lost toy is another game parents can play with babies.

Have you been having this experience?

> "My baby is just beginning to do that, but as soon as he loses the rattle, he cries. It's getting to be a great nuisance."

It is too bad that you see the situation that way. It sounds as though you were giving your baby the toy to silence him, so you can leave him alone. It is better, however, to sit with him and retrieve the toy with a positive comment like, "Here's your rattle" or "Here you are." When the parent becomes tired or bored, a different activity should be started. It may be easier for parents to make this activity a positive experience by thinking of it as a game. It is important to realize that this game enhances spatial exploration.

As the baby develops the use of her hands, she can bring things to her mouth to explore their taste and texture. She may hold them up and look at them momentarily, thus getting some idea of size and shape. Then she will probably put them back into her mouth.

Early Exploration and Play

If the baby is propped up in a sitting position for a few minutes several times a day, she can explore her surroundings better visually. It is important for the parent to make available small toys such as rattles, inch blocks, and small stuffed animals that the baby can hold and manipulate.

Many parents, as we may have mentioned before, are disturbed when babies put things in their mouths and often inhibit this form of exploration. If you inhibit oral exploration, however, you deprive the baby of one of the ways she learns about the world, a way which is appropriate for her age and level of development. Of course, not everything should go in the mouth. Appropriate objects should be clean—but not necessarily surgically sterile—and non-toxic. They should have no sharp edges or parts that can be pulled off and aspirated or swallowed. There are many objects that meet these safety qualifications, such as the red ring and the small blocks which we use in the testing, empty thread spools, small terry-cloth stuffed toys, and small wooden shapes.

We have noticed over the years that oral exploration is one of the more difficult areas of a baby's development for parents to cope with. It seems to arouse anxieties concerning cleanliness and safety.

How many of your babies have reached this stage, and how do you feel about oral exploration?

> "I'm afraid my reaction is the wrong one. I can't bear to have the baby put things into his mouth, salivate over them, and

then drop them. Usually they fall on the floor. Then I have to wash them."

If you sit by your baby when he is experimenting with a toy, you can often intercept it before it falls on the floor. You could also have a supply of several rattles or rings and wash them all at one time. When you realize the importance of this activity to the baby's development and observe the growth of the baby's coordination, then perhaps you will get some pleasure and satisfaction out of it.

"I don't mind picking up the toy and washing it over and over again, but the baby gets her clothes so wet with the saliva. That's what I mind."

That's why bibs were invented. If your baby does a lot of salivating and chewing on toys, a bib will help you keep her clothes dry and fresh. You don't have to use a fancy bib, either; a small hand towel or diaper tied around the baby's neck will do.

"Why is it so important to let them do this now? I hate to see my baby messy."

The importance lies in the fact that this early exploration is the precursor of the drive to explore and learn later on in school. If this early form of the drive to explore is inhibited by the parent's attitude, the baby may not try, or be afraid, to explore later.

"This is a point of view I never heard before. I'm sure my husband will be quite surprised. He is so fussy! He won't come near the baby if the baby is even a little messy."

Teething

Some of the hand-to-mouth activity which you are noticing may not be entirely exploration. Sometimes a baby inserts her hand into her mouth to chew because she is teething. For some infants teething begins very early. Some of you have noticed an increase in drooling. This is a sign of teething. The need to bite on something may be another sign. The usual time for a first tooth to erupt (usually the lower middle incisor) is at six months, but this is very variable. Teething is not always accompanied by great distress, but it can be. Some infants have very thick gums and the teeth have difficulty in penetrating. There may be swelling and inflammation of the gum that make sucking and eating painful.

"Do babies get sick and have a fever with teething? I told my doctor I thought my baby's fever was due to teething, and she said it couldn't be."

Doctors do not agree on this. Some think the inflammatory reaction may cause fever. Other doctors believe fever during teething is caused by an accompanying upper respiratory or other infection. Whatever the theory, the baby is apt to be irritable and need soothing, emotionally and also locally on her gums.

"What should one do to comfort the baby if holding and rocking him isn't enough and he won't take a bottle?"

In our experience, rubbing the gums with a little ice or using a commercial refrigerated teething ring often helps temporarily so that the baby may be fed. Each pediatrician has his own approach to meeting the baby's and the parents' needs. Some use medication; some do not. We advise you to consult your doctors about this.

Teething is often apt to upset the patterning and sequencing we have been discussing, particularly the sleeping-pattern. Often a sleeping baby will bite down on a sore gum. This causes pain and the baby awakens. Sometimes it is hard to get the baby back to sleep again. At other times, just opening the mouth to cry relieves the pressure on the gums, and the baby quickly goes back to sleep by herself. Many parents find this irregular sleep pattern one of the harder problems to cope with and fear it will become permanent. Usually it is transitory, and as soon as the bothersome tooth has erupted, the usual pattern of sleeping will be reestablished.

Are any of you encountering much difficulty yet?

"My baby is drooling a lot. Aside from its being a nuisance to change bibs, I have had no trouble. I was wondering if the drooling meant teething because there is no whiteness in her gums and I can't feel any bumps."

Very often there is little evidence except increased drooling for a long time. Sometimes the gums are very swollen for weeks or months before there is any sign of a tooth. Sometimes there is no evidence of anything different until a mother hears a click on the spoon in the baby's mouth. When she investigates, she feels the sharp edges of a new tooth. What an exciting moment that is! Each baby teethes differently, and there is often a family pattern.

"My baby has been having a very runny nose and drooling but no fever. My pediatrician says she may be teething."

"My baby seems to cry for no reason that I can find out. I was beginning to feel she was just bad-tempered at times. Maybe there is a reason after all. It never occurred to me that she could be starting to teethe so young."

Some parents misinterpret an infant's bona fide need for comforting as malevolence, especially if the incident happens at night. They think the baby just wants to get them out of bed. Actually, a baby has no way of expressing her need except to cry; that is her language. As we have said before, the sooner the parent tries to meet the need, the less the baby will cry. To be held and consoled when she needs it gives the baby a sense of trust that the parent is available and trying to help.

"My first baby was cranky and had loose green stools for two days. It happened each time a tooth was coming. It seemed as though it would never end, but it did. I hope this baby doesn't teethe the same way."

It may become quite different. In any case, you now know that this period is intermittent. It is bad for a day or two, and then the baby goes back to her normal routine.

Visual Exploration and Stimulation

Many of you are wondering about how much the baby sees. Until the last fifteen years not much was known about infants' visual acuity and it was assumed they couldn't see too much. It is now known that the baby's visual system, though immature, is functional at birth. From the earliest days, babies are able to orient towards visual stimulation and have the necessary muscular control to focus with both eyes. There is, however, an optimal focus distance for babies of about eight inches. It is interesting to realize that a nursing baby's face is approximately eight inches from the mother's face. Objects nearer or farther than eight inches appear blurred to the baby for the first few weeks but then there is rapid development of visual ability. By now, you will probably notice your babies' fixing on small, distinct patterns like those on the bumper of the crib or on mother's dress.

"At first, I was worried that my baby seemed to pay so little attention; his stare seemed so blank. In the last week or so, I have noticed that he really seems to look at me and see me."

Parents are often concerned about the baby's early blank stare; they expect more and often worry needlessly about the baby's visual ability. Babies look intently at the mother or other caretaker during feeding. This is the beginning of visual exploration at the optimal focus distance for the baby. Babies also may stare at patterns or objects in their cribs which happen to be at the appropriate distance. Soon they begin to follow or track the parent visually as he or she moves around the room.

It is believed that babies pay most attention to bright colors, particularly red. This is why we encourage you to dangle the red ring in front of them to stimulate visual response. It is also why we encourage you to get toys that are bright, with marked color contrasts, so they will be visually attractive to the babies. It is fun for parents to play with their baby in this way and it helps visual development.

Babies become attached to these bright toys and feel more secure if these objects are nearby in their usual places. For that reason, it is a good idea to bring a familiar toy or two with you when you come here. These toys will help the babies make the transition from a familiar to an unfamiliar place.

By three months, most of the babies will follow the ring through 180 degrees and begin to see across a room. Around four months, they begin to develop depth perception, and their vision becomes more like ours. They continue to need visual stimulation, and we'll talk more about that in the coming weeks.

"What if the baby is a little cross-eyed? Should that be corrected right away, or will it improve by itself?"

Very often an infant's eyes do not focus on an object well because there may be an imbalance in the immature musculature. The muscle pulling the eye in one direction may be stronger than the muscle pulling the eye in the opposite direction, and this gives the baby a squint or cross-eyed look. This muscle imbalance may be present in one or both eyes and may correct itself as the baby matures. Stimulating the baby to use his eyes to follow a moving object may help to exercise the lagging muscle. If this condition persists beyond the first year, however, the baby's eyes should be examined by an ophthalmologist.

"How can you tell if a baby is going to be right- or left-handed?"

Handedness

It's not easy at first. At this age, the hand on the side which the baby turns toward—the one which is held up clenched—may be the dominant hand. Also, the hand that holds the rattle more firmly and longer may become dominant. At this age, parents should begin observing these signs. If a parent is left-handed, that is sometimes a clue. When the babies are five or six months old and begin to reach for things, they show the hand of preference.

"When can you finally decide?"

Some children are definitely left- or right-handed, and that is obvious very early. With other children you may not know until they are five or six years old. They may have mixed dominance and even reverse letters in school until that time. It is a good idea to hand something to a child in a way that will allow the child to decide for himself which hand to accept it with—that is, offer an object to a spot between the child's hands rather than directly to one of them. Sometimes right-handed parents unconsciously hand things to the right hand of a child. Then we discover later in school that the child is left-handed and is using his right hand, left eye, and left foot exhibiting mixed dominance.

"Does handing things to a particular hand cause any harm? I hand things to the baby's left because he seems to hold them best in that hand. My mother says not to do that. She says that I am making the baby left-handed and I must train him to use his right hand. Is that right?"

I am sorry to say your mother does not seem to be correct. If the baby has a preference for using his left hand, it should not be discouraged. Recently we have found that it was not a good idea to force use of the right hand because the nervous system is designed so that we are dominant on one side. Some people are meant to be right-handed and some left-handed.

"It does harm then to change the handedness?"

Often it does. At least, it may hold up the development of reading and writing skills because the eye-hand coordination isn't as smooth as it might be. In the old days everyone had to use his right hand in school. If a child had a preference for the left hand, he was trained to use his right hand. It is now recognized that some reading problems are related to this change in handedness. This practice has been abandoned, but some grandparents may not be aware of the change. I think they will be less insistent if you explain the change in practice to them.

FEEDING SOLID FOODS

Mothers are usually concerned about the quantity and variety of food that the babies are consuming. There seems to be more and more of a trend toward starting solids early and increasing their variety and quantity quickly.

"Oh, I began trying to give the baby cereal from a spoon when he was a month old, but he didn't seem to like it, so I put it into the bottle and made the holes in the nipple larger."

Did your doctor feel the baby needed solid food?

"No, I just thought the baby would be more filled-up and sleep better, so I did it on my own. He is sleeping longer, but I don't know if that's because he's getting the solid food or just because he's getting older."

"I tried a new food, lamb and vegetables, but the baby was very cranky the whole weekend. I don't know if it was the food or not."

Perhaps the lamb didn't suit her. I don't know what your pediatrician tells you, but usually the advice is to begin with a small amount. One may not need to be so cautious with all babies, but it is certainly wise when there is a family history of allergies. There is no need to rush into a variety of foods. It's best to be sure that each new food agrees with the baby and that the baby likes it. If the baby doesn't like a certain food, there is no need to force it on the baby. There are many alternative foods of equal nutritional value. Maybe, when you try the rejected food several weeks later, it will be accepted. Taste for different flavors develops at different times, and often a baby with a well-established habit of eating from a spoon will eat whatever is given.

Actually, at this age most of the valuable nutrition still comes from milk. The ability to eat solids well does not develop until after about six months. What you are doing now is getting your babies used to the sensation of spoon feeding and swallowing solids. The variety and quantity is not important yet. There is more chance your baby will be a good eater if food is not forced or shovelled in. Feeding is another area where an early conflict between parent and baby may develop. Feeding time should be a pleasurable encounter. It can be made unnecessarily difficult if the parent is anxious to get the food in, no matter how the baby responds.

"It upsets me when the baby doesn't finish every morsel. I know it shouldn't, but it does."

The baby's life doesn't depend on spoon feeding at this stage. He is just learning to eat, and not eating doesn't mean he is naughty or doesn't love you. Often, feeding a baby is equated with love. Giving the baby food means you love him; accepting it means he loves you in return. Actually, you will show your love more by respecting his level of development and need. Then you do not become a controlling, but a patient and understanding, mother. Good care of a child used to be measured largely by weight. We feel differently now.

"That's just the way my mother still feels. For her a fat baby is a healthy baby."

Recent studies show that longevity is enhanced by being thin. Obesity causes multiple health problems and shortening of the life span. Present knowledge indicates that if the cells of the body become accustomed to an increased fat content in infancy, they carry on this need through life, and it is difficult to get over obesity. Therefore, it is best not to overfeed infants.

"How much is enough, then?"

The baby will accept what he needs unless there is some special nutritional problem which should be discussed with your doctor. Most babies' capacity for food is very much less than adults think. It varies with each baby. Some are well fed on a teaspoon or two; others require half a jar of food at a time. The amount also varies from feeding to feeding and from day to day.

We also have to remember that some babies, particularly those in families with a history of allergies, seem to have an innate sense that certain foods disagree with them and will refuse to eat them. It is, therefore, safer not to coax a baby to eat a food which he persistently refuses.

ATTACHMENT: ITS DEVELOPMENT AND RELATION TO BASIC TRUST

We have talked in previous sessions, especially in our first sessions, about the sense of disappointment new parents may feel because the newborn infant seems so unresponsive. The parents may have

Parents' Initial Fears About Babies' Unresponsiveness

spent months dreaming about the new baby—how they are going to cuddle her and how she is going to respond and return the loving they give. Instead, at the beginning, the infant only occasionally opens her eyes long enough to glance about, perhaps not even in the direction of the adoring parent who is talking, cooing, or even rocking the baby. Sometimes the baby just yawns and goes off to sleep, or she may cry and show discomfort, much to the parents' consternation. Initially, parents have to be satisfied if the baby takes her feeding, burps, and goes off to sleep.

Do you remember that period? Do you remember some of you said you regarded the baby as a stranger and, much as you had wanted the baby, you were surprised that you didn't have the feelings you expected? That the baby didn't respond as you expected?

> "I remember that quite well. I was feeling very upset at the time because the baby was so unresponsive—by my standards. I was even worried the baby might be retarded. Now I know better."

> "The thought that the baby might be mentally retarded or impaired in some other way bothered me all the time during my pregnancy. Now I watch every movement secretly because I still have that fear."

This is a very common worry, and the infant's limited responses keep parents in suspense for a long time. Having the babies here weekly and learning what normal or appropriate responses are for the babies' ages, should be of some help in allaying the anxiety.

> "Would you tell us if you were suspicious or found something wrong?"

We would talk with you when we saw evidence of any problem because we would want you to get the appropriate assistance as soon as possible. An advantage of doing Gesell evaluations frequently is that they help in early detection of deficits. Most important, as you watch these tests, you see how differently each baby responds and that the maturational timetable varies with each baby. There is a very wide range of reactions that are considered "normal." No two babies begin to smile, sit, stand, or talk at exactly the same age. However, the developmental sequence is usually the same: Babies look around first, then smile, then turn over, then sit, then stand. Children in the same family may be very different; even identical twins do not mature in the same areas at exactly the same age.

> "Well, that makes me more comfortable. I remember that my brother was a fast walker and a slow talker, but he is a lawyer now."

> "I wasn't afraid that the baby was retarded, but I thought there

must be something wrong with me because I just didn't feel close to the baby. I was disappointed."

Mutual
Attachments

By now there is beginning to be a change in the baby's responses. All of these weeks, you have been trying to set up routines of feeding, sleeping, going out regularly, stimulating with toys, talking, cuddling, and comforting the baby. You have been advised to try to arrange the events of the baby's day in a more predictable sequence, so that she will get to know what is coming next.

We emphasize this sequencing because it helps the baby begin to develop memory. Also, by this repetition she will begin to develop a sense of trust in her parents and a feeling that things will be done in a dependable sequence. As the baby begins to develop this sense of trust, she begins to form a primary attachment to the person who has been taking most care of her. By now, the parents are forming the attachment to the baby that they expected to feel the very first day.

On the baby's part, attachment is a feeling that develops over time, with the gradual maturing of the baby's central nervous system and the growing understanding that there is a reliable person always ready to try to respond to her needs—perhaps even anticipate some of them. For the parents, attachment develops as they find they can satisfy the baby's needs and that the baby is thriving and beginning to recognize them. They respond as the baby watches them move about the room, gives them a special smile, coos, gurgles, flails her arms, and kicks her feet when they approach. Some babies can even manage to reach up when held to explore the parent's face or pull the parent's hair.

Have any of you begun to notice this? Do you think your baby is beginning to know you?

"I'm not sure my baby really knows me better than she knows the housekeeper, but she certainly responds with her eyes and flaps her hands when I come into the room. If that's attachment, we are there!"

"My baby may not be as attached to me as I am to him. Now I can't go out even for a little while without missing him. Earlier I just couldn't wait to get out; now, I can't wait to get back!"

Attachment
to the Father

"I know my baby knows me. He kicks and smiles and gurgles as soon as I get near his crib. That makes everything worthwhile—the diaper changing, the lack of sleep, the messy house, the confinement. I was wondering if babies have the same feeling for the father, and how they can develop it when their fathers are away as much as my husband is?"

We talked earlier about the father's role in establishing patterning and in developing basic trust. The earliest strong attachment is usually to the mother because she spends the most time with the baby.

The father, who is away much of the day, often has less chance to relate to the baby. However, this does not mean that he cannot have a role or place in the baby's day. There can be a feeding, playing time, bath, or bedtime routine that the father handles each day. In this way, the baby and father develop an attachment for each other. Soon the baby begins to know when her father is coming home and what the sound of the key in the latch means. Often the baby shows a great deal of excitement and enjoyment at the sound and sight of Daddy. Sometimes, the mother may have feelings of jealousy about the baby's interest in Daddy or feel "left out" when the father is engrossed with the baby. It is good to remember that fathers may often have had the same "left-out" feeling when the mother concentrated all her attention on the baby.

In what way or ways are you arranging for Daddy to get to know his baby? How much is he talking to the baby and playing with her? Do you think the baby is beginning to recognize her father?

> "My husband said the baby doesn't know who he is, so he spent the whole evening talking to her."

It is very important that the fathers talk and play with their babies, even if it means the babies go to bed later. The babies need to know both parents.

> "If I didn't keep the baby up a little later, my husband wouldn't see him at all. I wait to give him a bath until my husband is there. He enjoys watching the baby bathed and has even done it a few times. He likes to give the baby the bedtime bottle. Then we both tuck him in. I think they are beginning to have a real feeling for each other."

> "My mother says my father never touched us when we were babies and he never really learned how to deal with us. I decided early that I would see to it that my husband got to know his child. As a matter of fact, we both decided that before the baby was born. So my husband gives the first morning bottle while I make breakfast."

> "My husband is home during the day, so the baby gets to see him a good deal. However, I don't think the baby can tell the difference between us yet. Is that all right?"

That may be so now, but the baby is forming an impression of both of you as you care for her and play with her. Soon you will begin to see evidence of this recognition and attachment.

> "My husband doesn't do any feeding or bathing, but he spends a lot of time talking and playing with the baby. Although our baby seems to respond to all the members of the family, I think the response to my husband and me is a little different; she just seems more animated."

The development of an attachment to the mother, father, or other caretaker, and then to more people, is associated with basic trust, and is one of the most important beginnings of personality development. If a parent gives the baby a chance to develop this basic trust, the baby will have one of the most important gifts she will ever get in her life. Those children who have not developed an early attachment and trust may not be able to form appropriate and close relationships with others later in life. Their relationships remain superficial. Sometimes they are apt to be suspicious when it is not appropriate to be so. Children in institutions where caretakers work in eight-hour shifts and change frequently often have such problems. Parents who work must be careful that baby-sitters are not constantly changed.

We think this trust and attachment relates later in life to the ability to be involved with the teacher in school and with a drive for learning. A sense of attachment is a precursor to cognitive development.

"Are you saying that it is best for the same person always to take care of the baby, so she can form this attachment? Do you mean that only the mother should be responsible for child care?"

The baby needs to have a constant, consistent caretaker. That person doesn't necessarily have to be the mother, although in our society it usually is the mother. In some families, the mother works and the father is at home, so he's the caretaker. Sometimes, it's the grandmother or an aunt. The caretaker, however, should be constant. The baby needs to establish a feeling of security and relationship with one person. She will be forming attachments to her father and other family members as well, though these attachments may be less intense at first.

"Then what about day care?"

One of the drawbacks of the day-care system is that the personnel, no matter how good, shifts. No employed person keeps the hours that are required for a baby's care. Also, it is very expensive to replicate the one-to-one relationship needed by infants. Most day-care as we know it is more appropriate as the children get older.

"So the mother is always trapped!"

Parents often do not realize how important they are to their child's healthy development or how much time child care takes. **Someone** must make the commitment to create a special bond or attachment with the infant. The mother has traditionally done this but increasingly in the future, families may decide that the role of primary caretaker will be taken by the father or another person. The baby needs consistent care in the early developmental period. Once basic trust is established, the baby can begin to relate to other members of the

Mother's Feeling of Being "Trapped"

family, to close friends, and then to neighbors. Finally, the baby becomes a secure, social person. This development takes time, but the baby has to have a chance to form the first close relationship with his parents or a substitute caretaker to be able to make other social relationships later in life.

Most of you have worked and been very free to come and go. Your lives are very changed now; a lot of adjustments are necessary. Our society needs to be more supportive of and more sensitive to the concerns of young parents. Then there would be less inclination to feel "trapped."

Some parents may already be experiencing some aspects of attachment, such as when the baby will not let you out of her sight, even to go to the bathroom. This may intensify your feeling of being "trapped" and be annoying. This is, however, a normal stage in the development of attachment and lasts until the baby has had sufficient maturation and experience to know you will return. At this stage of her development, the baby does not know that you still exist if she cannot see you. She does not have that comprehension; she knows only what she sees. Therefore, it is best for the baby to be able to see the parent in the same room or through a doorway. You can reassure her by getting into her line of vision, calling to her or, best yet, taking her with you. Primitive people recognized this need and kept their babies close to them in papoose boards or slings. Now some mothers are adopting this custom by wearing carriers, and it works. When you disappear from sight, the baby thinks it is forever, just as you think it is forever when she won't let you out of sight. It is a stage in good, healthy development. In fact, we are concerned if a baby doesn't care if her parents come or go because this may indicate that the baby is not forming an attachment.

Have you begun to have this experience yet? How have you been dealing with the experience, and how do you feel about it?

> "I noticed my baby cried when I walked out of the room. I thought I had spoiled her by being with her too much. But I just couldn't let her cry, so I'd pick her up and carry her with me. I thought I was doing the wrong thing, but now I see that she needs that kind of attention."

If the baby cries when you leave, it is a sign of her attachment, and that is good. It shows normal, healthy development and progress. At times it may, of course, be inconvenient. If you understand that the baby's crying is her way of saying, "Please don't leave me; I can't do without you," then you won't feel as angry or trapped. Some crying is inevitable; we can't be "superparents" all the time.

> "My mother says I must let the baby cry, or the baby will be 'spoiled' and always cry for me."

We hear the comment all the time that responding to a baby's cry will "spoil" him. What we are dealing with here is the old concept that good children should be "seen but not heard." This is a misconception. A quiet child may be depressed, understimulated, or even autistic.

This is such an important issue that extensive research has been done on it. Many of these studies show that the babies who were attended to when they cried came to cry less and were able to relinquish their mothers earlier, while those that were allowed to cry without attention remained "cry babies" and were more reluctant to separate from their mothers later. We are concerned with the development of healthy personalities. The child whose needs are responded to will trust the people around her and have confidence in herself; she will not be a spoiled child.

NEW SENSORY-MOTOR DEVELOPMENTS

Turning Over

At the same time that you have been noticing the development of the baby's attachment to you, the baby has been displaying new motor activity.

The effect of the baby's new motor development on parents is different for each family and often for each parent. Now that the babies are beginning to turn over, some parents are very pleased. They regard this skill as an achievement. Other parents are not so happy because it's no longer safe to leave the baby alone on a changing table or bed. The new skill puts a new pressure on parents to guard the baby's safety. Perhaps some mothers feel this makes life more difficult and causes them more anxiety. Though this is indeed true, the development of the new skill is also a milestone in the baby's life.

This motor achievement is one of which fathers are often more proud than mothers. Mothers, however, often observe the developmental change first. It is fun to display this new ability to the father. It gets him involved, and he can help in safety precautions.

How do you and your husbands feel about your babies' greater activity?

"All the time I saw the baby struggling to turn over, I felt like helping him. Now that he can do it by himself, I'm glad, but it makes me nervous. I always double-check to be sure I have pulled up the crib side and never leave him on our bed anymore."

"My husband is very proud of this new achievement. But right away he ordered carpeting for the baby's room, so a fall would be softened a little. We also put heavy, shaggy rugs beside the crib and by our bed, and a heavier pad in the playpen."

All of those are good precautions because a parent can't be as quick as the baby sometimes. From now on, the babies have to be watched more carefully. At first it is difficult to keep an eye on the baby all the time, but in time doing so gets to be second nature.

Use of the Hands; Eye-Hand Coordination

In addition to the large motor advance of turning over, babies are now beginning to play with their hands, perhaps clasping them or just staring at their fingers.

The babies are becoming much more observant and can now enjoy more play with a toy. Now, when a toy is placed in the baby's hand, he may look at it or look from the toy to his hand. He is gradually getting the notion that he is holding the toy in his hand, that he extends to the end of those fingers holding the toy. This, too, is a milestone in development; it is the beginning of eye-hand coordination, a skill which becomes very important later on in school.

Have you been noticing this in your babies?

> "My baby holds the rattle and bangs it, but I haven't seen her look at it yet."

Each baby does that on his own individual timetable. Some babies look at their hands before they look at objects. It's great fun to see their concentration when they finally do notice their own hands.

> "My baby began last week. My husband and I get such a kick out of watching her look at her fingers. She screws up her face and looks at them very seriously."

When the baby begins to look at his fingers, it is very good to put a toy in his hand. That way, he can begin to explore new objects as well.

Sitting Propped Up

Are you beginning to prop the babies up to sit for a short time?

> "I've found the greatest infant seat. It is part of a walker, and the seat goes on at different heights. It's all padded like a chaise lounge. The baby can't tip over, and you can regulate the angle of the back. We feed our baby in this seat. So she is propped up and we have our hands free. She is also free and has a certain amount of independence."

The seat is one way to prop the baby up. You can also use a pillow in the carriage or the corner of the living room sofa, carefully watched, of course. The baby needs to begin to see the world from this angle and learn that there is more to observe than what he views lying on his back.

Of course, the view from his back is more stimulating if he can see a mobile. If the mobile also plays music, the baby will be more interested. The baby will watch for a few minutes while the parent does something else. However, it is tempting if the baby is quiet to leave him flat on his back too long. Now is the time to think about a little propped sitting—for five minutes or so at a time.

Some of you may find that sitting up also helps your babies burp and get rid of gas bubbles. They often burp on their own while sitting. Some may cry, and you may interpret this as not wanting to sit, but it may mean the gas bubble is hurting, and a change of position is necessary to help release it.

STIMULATION THROUGH PLAY ACTIVITIES

Toys are very useful in stimulating eye-hand coordination. A red ring or a red dumbbell-shaped rattle is especially helpful. Red is more attractive to babies than are the pale pastel colors used on most toys.

Appropriate Toys for Eye-Hand Coordination

The baby's attention span may not be long. He may soon drop the toy. He may even look for it momentarily. Then mother or father can retrieve the toy, and continue the game for as long as baby seems interested in holding the toy, looking at it, putting it into his mouth, waving it in the air, or banging it against the crib or playpen.

Have you begun to play this way with your babies?

> "I thought the baby was too young because he didn't seem to pay much attention to the rattle."

Babies may not pay much attention at first, but if you keep stimulating them with the toy as they mature, they will pay more and more attention to it. It is fun to watch this happen.

> "My husband does this with the baby while I'm getting dinner ready. That's his thing with the baby."

That's good interaction between father and baby. Now that the babies are beginning to play with toys, it is important to have appropriate ones. The best toys for children are those which they can manipulate. For babies, in addition to the rattle and ring, small one-inch cube blocks, empty spools of thread, and small toys with projections that can be gripped (such as small rag doll) are best. It is always a temptation to buy a big teddy bear, an enormous fire engine, a large doll. These are more fun for the parents than the baby. The baby can look at these large things, but he can't really play with them. He needs small things which stimulate his eye-hand coordination, toys whose manipulation he can master.

The babies are now at an age when they can pay more attention to cradle gyms and mobiles of colorful, simple shapes. These should be arranged over the crib, so that the baby may hit or kick them accidentally. Later on, as his ability increases and his central nervous system matures, he will intentionally put them into motion. The babies are now beginning to have a longer concentration span and

Attention Span; Establishing a Regular Playtime

may be able to amuse themselves alone for about ten minutes while exploring a toy or cradle gym. Ten minutes is a long time for a baby. Then new stimulus has to be introduced, or the old one moved to a different position, like the other side of the crib. Babies soon tire, and you must let them rest. Turn them over for sleep, change, or feed them according to their daily pattern. As we have said before, playtime should be a part of their daily schedule; it is part of their education.

Are you enjoying your playtime with the baby? Is the father entering into this?

> "I'm so busy I can't say I really play with the baby if by 'play' you mean sitting by him and continually picking up a toy he has dropped. If I happen to have a little time, I do. Otherwise, I just go to him when he cries."

You should, of course, go to him when he cries, but the baby also needs stimulating play. A baby learns through play. You don't have to sit beside the baby constantly; he can't concentrate for long periods. There should, however, be two or three short play periods with you or the father each day as a regular part of the baby's program. It can really be fun for both parent and child.

> "My husband and I take turns. I do most of the playing during the week. He does it over the weekend. Sometimes we do it together. That's the best way for us, I think."

> "My husband says he has no patience for playing with the baby with a rattle or a ring. When the baby is big enough to ride a bike or play baseball, then my husband says he'll play with him, but not now."

There are some parents who have difficulty relating to very young babies and are better with older children. However, a baby needs to have contact with both parents from infancy. Once the mother can demonstrate to the father the changes in the baby's development and their importance, the father may become more interested in the baby and find it easier to play with him with these simple toys.

Recognizing and Enhancing a Baby's Sense of Mastery

In addition to playing with the baby, you need to show approval of him. Your approval should be verbal and physical. Your tone of voice and facial expression should show that you are pleased, even delighted, with the baby's achievements. The baby then gets a sense of pleasure at mastery and a feeling of approval. If parents are quiet, objective observers, noting the achievement but not conveying their satisfaction, the baby does not feel approval or develop a sense of pleasure at mastery, which is necessary for a positive self-image. This approval is the earliest way in which parents can help a child establish the inner drive toward achievement which is necessary later on for school achievement. This is the time for the parent to begin to look for achievement and recognize it. The baby thrives on this recognition. It may mean the difference between a self-confident person who strives for achievement and one who doesn't try because he never experienced recognition while his personality was developing.

How do you signal to your babies that you have noticed what the baby is doing and like it?

"Oh, I pick him up and kiss and hug him."

"I don't say anything; I just watch. I guess I should say something. I thought he would not understand. But his father says 'Marvelous.' "

Many mothers say, "I pick him up and kiss and hug him," or "I say, 'You're the most wonderful baby in the world,'" or "I tell him that he's marvelous," and so forth. The response does not have to be vigorous body contact or lavish praise, but it does need to be recognizable approval. For young babies clapping or saying "Good" is enough. They understand tone of voice and facial expression, if not your exact words. Later, as they grow older, a nod, a smile, or a little pat—some signal the child understands—is all that is necessary. Even young children seem to understand that lavish praise is uncalled for and often insincere.

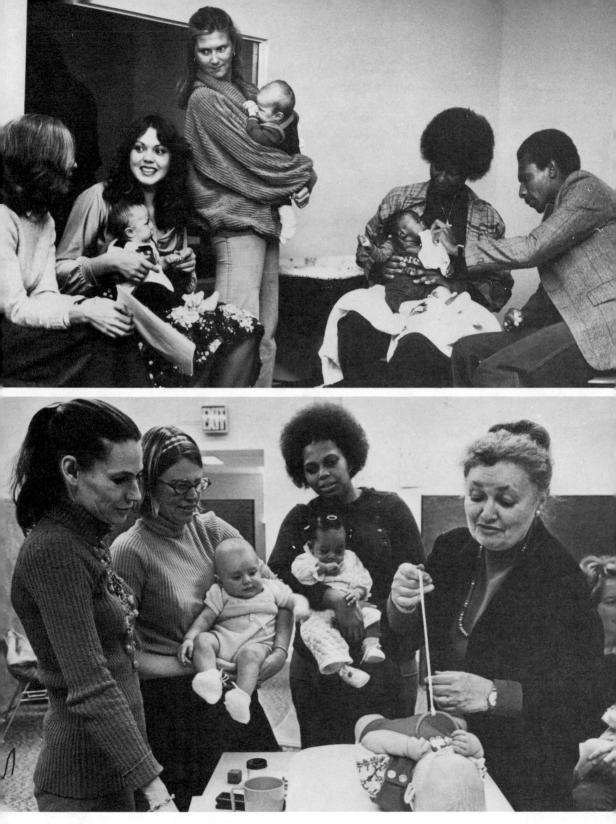

(Top) Parents discuss child-rearing topics with group leaders;
(bottom) Parents observe testing procedure at the Center.

Chapter Four

Age:
16 to 20 weeks _____

When the baby is lying on his back, his posture is now symmetrical, with his head facing straight up instead of to the side as formerly. The activity of his arms is more parallel; and he may clasp his hands together. When the baby pulls himself towards the sitting position while his arms are supported by the parent (see exercise described on page 18), he is now able to hold his head steadily forward without bobbing. When placed on his stomach, he can now lift his head well off the surface to about a 45 degree angle. In this position, he is also on the verge of rolling over. (Parents should be on the lookout for this development because the baby may roll off the bed or table.)

The baby now looks immediately at the red ring or rattle when it is offered; and her arms activate at the sight of the toy. When the baby is holding the ring, she looks at her hand, showing that she is beginning to know that her hand is part of her person. She will try to bring the ring to her mouth and her free hand to the middle of her body. She may look from hand to object. She may also begin playing with her fingers. The baby's attention can now be engaged by something as small as a marble, especially if it is a bright color, demonstrating her increasing visual acuity and ability.

At this age, excited heavy breathing represents a form of expression and the beginning of language. The babies are also beginning to laugh. They often vocalize and laugh in interactions with their parents. They are likely to exhibit a spontaneous social smile when approached by the parent or another familiar person. Babies are now ready to view the world from a more upright position; they can sit propped up for ten to fifteen minutes, two or three times a day. When the mother approaches with the bottle or other food, or goes through the routines preparatory to breast feeding, the baby may exhibit anticipatory behavior, such as sucking or mouthing motions or waving of the arms.

CUING IN: APPROPRIATE RESPONSE TO THE BABY'S NEEDS

We have discussed the new levels of development and how to utilize them to enhance the baby's progress. What we are suggesting is that you pick up "cues" from the baby. For example, when the baby is ready (that is, has reached the appropriate maturational level) to hold a rattle, the parent should be ready to supply it. In other words, the parent is patterning activities around the baby's demonstrated needs and developmental level.

Another example of this "cuing in" to the baby's needs, which you are all doing, is feeding. When the baby is hungry, she signals to you by crying or sucking her fingers. You then feed her either with the breast or the bottle. You respond to her need. This is sometimes called "demand feeding," but we prefer to think of it as a response or "cuing in" to the baby's need. "Demand" has a negative connotation. One can quibble about semantics, but a mother who feels she is **responding** to a need feels more positive about the baby than if she feels a **demand** is being made upon her.

How does your baby let you know she is hungry?

"My baby whimpers a little, then sucks her index and middle fingers. When I hear her, I get ready for the feeding."

"My baby never cries; he just looks around and kicks. Then I change him while I'm warming the bottle. The bottle is ready before he gets a chance to cry. I just can't bear to have him cry."

"My baby wakes with a loud, piercing cry, and nothing I do soothes him until he gets his feeding. There is never a warning. I'm in a panic, and I guess he is too until he gets at the breast. I've tried to change him first. If he is just wet, I feed him first. If he has soiled, I usually change him first, but his crying upsets me. I just wish he could wait a little."

You have all noted cues that you use to get the feeding ready and satisfy your babies' needs. Some of you have pointed out with some distress that the baby wants an immediate response. She puts you under intense pressure with her crying. Sometimes the baby even makes you a little angry because she can't wait.

Need for Gratification; Maturation and Basic Trust

It's natural to be upset when the baby cries violently and can't wait. However, parents must understand that not being able to wait is part of the baby's lack of neurological development. To be able to wait your turn is part of maturity. A parent can wait, but a baby cannot.

As baby's nervous system matures and as her needs are met, she learns to wait because she has established a sense of trust that her parent will meet her needs. The more often the baby experiences this gratification of her needs, the more secure she will become and the more she will develop a sense of trust.

If, on the other hand, a mother is inconsistent in her responses, the baby gets no sense of what actions on her part produce dependable responses, and she does not develop basic trust. This does not mean that the mother needs to sit with a bottle in hand ready in case the baby cries. It does mean that the mother has to have some idea of the baby's pattern and must arrange her day to suit it. For example, if you know the baby usually wakes for a feeding at 11:00 a.m., you should not plan to go shopping, visiting, or to the doctor's at that time without providing for the baby's feeding.

How do you feel about a baby's inability to wait? Does knowing that this is the result of the immaturity of the baby's nervous system help you cope any better with this behavior?

"I hate to hear my baby cry, but isn't always getting what he wants at once going to lead to a spoiled baby that always cries?"

"My husband thinks that babies need to cry to develop their lungs, and that it's bad to give in to them right away."

"I think a baby cries because he needs something and it's my job to find out what he needs. Letting him cry just isn't our style. Luckily, my husband and I feel the same way, so if one of us is busy with something or tired, the other goes to the baby."

There are people who say: "Let the baby cry, and she will learn that crying doesn't produce results. Then when she is quiet, give her attention." It is quite true that one can condition a child in this way; the baby will finally stop crying. But we are concerned about what this kind of conditioning may do to the development of the child's personality, her character development. There are several possible results of this kind of conditioning.

First, the child may become a person who trusts no one. We see these unhappy, suspicious people in our clinics all the time, and you have met them in your daily life. This type of adult is very hard to treat.

Another way an infant may cope with such conditioning is to become withdrawn, submissive, and inhibited, without the drive to accomplish anything or the capacity to enjoy life. You have probably run into such people. They just never seem to be able to get going. They may have talents, but they don't make adequate use of them. You feel like putting a fire under such people, but their fire was unintentionally, unknowingly put out long ago by parents who wanted to teach them not to cry when they were infants. To make it easier on themselves, the parents chose a way of dealing with their children that was inappropriate to their abilities and maturational timetables.

Another response the child can make to such conditioning is to become angry and hostile. This child grows up to be an adult with a chip on the shoulder, always ready to disapprove and be oppositional.

Of course, these are the extreme consequences of such treatment, but we see or read about such consequences all too often. Fortunately, most children somehow make it in life, in spite of parental errors. As parents, all of us make mistakes, but many of these mistakes can be nullified if, above all, we convey our concern and love to our children. Avoiding some of these mistakes by understanding how a child develops can make growing up and child rearing more mutually gratifying and help our children develop to their maximum potential. Parenting is not an easy job, but it is very interesting and can be very rewarding. Parenting should be considered a profession, not a chore that you endure until you can get on with the "really important things in life."

> "I have never thought of a mother's role in this way, and I feel a little bit uneasy. I'd planned to get back to my job as soon as I could. I felt that was the important thing I was meant to do."

> "I'm glad this has come up. I never thought of going back to work, but whenever I go out, someone asks me, 'What do you do?' When I say I'm a mother, they look at me with surprise as though that were not enough. Then they say, 'But besides that, what do you do?' "

> "Now I can see that all the little things a mother does are important and that my response can mean a lot to the baby."

> "Is there any cure for a person who grows up with a 'chip on his shoulder'? I hate to say it but my husband fits that description. Knowing his family, I can now see what must have happened. I don't want my baby to be brought up that way."

All of the people whose upbringing has led to emotional difficulties can be helped to some extent, but the procedure is often long and costly. That is why we are trying to help you bring up your children in such a way that you won't make the same errors that were made before.

Tuning In to Different Types of Cries

As we have said before, crying, in the beginning, is the baby's only language. We have to learn, therefore, what each cry means and how to respond to it.

Are you beginning to catch on better to what your baby is trying to communicate?

> "I think I have learned the meaning of a new kind of cry. It's not because the baby is hungry or uncomfortable, but because he wants to play with a certain thing. The other day, my baby screamed until the dog came over so that he could pet it."

That's exactly it. People are social beings; we like to interact with others. Babies have this same desire. Now you know that your baby is interested in the dog. The next time he cries when the dog is around, you can take him to the dog and not wait until the dog decides to come over.

Other babies may get bored and fussy, and just want to be picked up for a "chat" with you or for the opportunity to look at something **with** you. As the babies grow, your repertoire of things to do to interest them and calm the fussiness will increase. Sometimes you will have to go through a sequence of holding, walking, talking, playing, feeding, and changing the diaper. By this age, your babies are old enough to be amused with an object to hold and play with. The object may only be the cover of the vaseline jar or the pull cord on the shade or a favorite toy. Sometimes they respond to music. These are small things, but an understanding response on the part of the parent is very important in giving the baby the feeling that there is someone who tries to satisfy his needs. With practice, you will "tune in" better to your baby's needs and moods. As they develop, the babies' interests will change and enlarge, and you will be changing with them.

> "But what if you can't tune in to the cries every time? Some-
> times I get it right; sometimes it's my husband who does."

The fact that you are now beginning to know the different cries is very important. When the baby understands that you understand what he wants—even fifty percent of the time—it gives him the sense of trust and security that we have talked about. That basic trust is the earliest building block of character development. It forms the basis for all the baby's future relationships with people.

None of us can be perfect parents—I certainly was not one myself—and that is not what this program is all about. We are not trying to make you into perfect parents with perfect children. We are trying to help you understand your children better so that you can enjoy each other more. You know that in your adult relationships, the more a friend understands what you are saying, the more comfortable you feel. If you have had **some** conversations in which there was complete understanding, your relationship can survive a few misunderstandings. It is the same with the relationship between you and your baby. Sometimes, even if you don't understand what the baby wants but are physically there and comforting, the baby will be comforted and satisfied. We do the best we can to understand our babies. Our ability grows with practice, and the baby's sense of basic trust grows as well.

SPOILING AND ITS RELATION TO THE DEVELOPMENT OF BASIC TRUST

We have talked a great deal about picking up the babies when they cry and its relation to the development of basic trust. We are all aware, however, that the idea that you will spoil a baby if you pick him up when he cries is very ingrained in traditional child-rearing attitudes. We worry about "spoiling" our children by attending to them. Actually, what we're really doing is spoiling our children by **not** paying attention to them. This is an awfully hard idea for lots of people to understand. Maybe you think we dwell on it too much, but it comes up over and over again in various ways at different ages.

> "I would just like to go over the idea again to see if I got it right. If you pick up a baby whenever he needs it, he looks for that satisfaction. You feed him or comfort him so when you put him back to bed, he is satisfied. He gets what he needs; he doesn't get spoiled. When you pick up a baby that much, it's because he needs it that much, and that's not spoiling."

That's right. It is supplying the baby's need when he needs it. The baby who doesn't get what he needs when he needs it is the one who lacks trust and is never satisfied. It is very hard to reshape this kind of basic character structure. You have seen older children who are never satisfied, no matter what you give them. If you could go back in their life history, you would probably find that these were the babies who didn't get what they needed when they were very, very young.

You see it also in adults. For some people nothing is quite enough. If they have one kind of camera, they've got to have another and another—nothing is quite sufficient. These adults are really trying to satisfy with material things a need that wasn't satisfied in early infancy. These material things do not replace what was needed, so they are never totally satisfying.

Parents often buy their children enormous presents but spend no time with them. They don't give of themselves at all. They think they are giving to the child, and they can't understand why the child is not satisfied. Such parents are only substituting material things for themselves, for spending time with their children. Nothing should be given **instead** of sharing feelings and time with a child. There is no substitute for filling important emotional needs. Actually, children often enjoy small things—a spool, an eraser, or a small box—if it is something that the parents are sharing **with** them.

> "But my mother says it will spoil the baby to pick her up when she cries."

This topic comes up over and over again as relations and neighbors criticize parents for responding to babies' cries. There seems to be little understanding that until a baby is verbal, crying is his language, the way he brings attention to his needs. Trying to find out what the baby needs is the parents' job. As the parents become more accustomed to the type of cry, they begin to understand what the baby means and can satisfy him more quickly.

Consistent response to a child's needs enhances his sense of basic trust. The way a baby is spoiled is by inconsistency. When a need is satisfied sometimes and ignored at others, it makes a baby insecure. He doesn't get gratification consistently, and so he becomes very demanding in order to get a response. He learns that he must cry louder in order to be heard. This leads to a very aggressive, angry relationship between mother and baby, and the baby's personality will generally remain angry and aggressive. Other babies may only whine and cry. Still others give up easily and stop expressing their needs. These children will have little drive for success later on because they have had no experience of achieving satisfaction. None of these traits lead to healthy personality development. The babies who have been responded to appropriately are more likely to be pleasant, secure, and effective children and adults.

"You have been stressing the words 'appropriate response.' Does that mean that what is appropriate now may not be when the children are older?"

That is absolutely right. Since little babies can only cry, we must try to figure out what their cries mean. Toddlers can say a few words, and we need to learn to interpret them. A four-year old can sometimes express himself very accurately. A baby must learn to trust the people around him. Delay causes him great anxiety and teaches mistrust. An older child who has developed basic trust in his parents will believe them when they say "in a little while."

As the babies get older, we will talk about teaching the babies to delay, to learn that they cannot always have everything they want immediately. This process of delaying gratification must also be learned and is a part of healthy personality development. But it is the second step. The first step is to learn trust because one's needs have been responded to and gratified.

Have you noticed any difference in your babies when you respond to them quickly and when you let them cry?

"Well, I came from a family that believes it will spoil a baby if he is picked up any time he cries. But since I came here, I've been listening to you, and now my baby is a little doll. He is not a crybaby."

"My instinct is to pick up the baby. When I do, I'm happy and so is the baby. But when my mother-in-law is there, she gives me the business, and, although I still pick the baby up, I feel uncomfortable."

"You know, I get this from my mother too, about how she raised five children and she never picked them up when they cried. I don't say anything. I just can't tell her three of her children are in therapy, but it's true."

You are all in a difficult position. Perhaps you should tell your families that you understand that they mean well for the baby, and that you know they did the best they knew how in raising their children. But point out that new things have been found out about babies' development, and that you are trying to follow what you think is best for your baby. Tell them you mean no disrespect to them, and ask them to give you a chance to see if your way works.

Many people expect children to be able to do things that are beyond their emotional maturity and beyond the maturity of their central nervous systems. Explain that when the baby is older, you will be teaching him to be more self-reliant and less demanding. But also point out that you won't try to do this until the baby has reached the appropriate stage of emotional and physical development for it.

Fathers' Attitudes Toward Crying and Spoiling

In the last sessions, we have been talking with the mothers about different kinds of crying. Some cries mean the babies are hungry; others mean they need a diaper change; still others mean they are bored. The baby may just want a little company and a change of scene. Each kind of cry needs a different kind of parental response. The mothers feel that they are beginning to understand these cries and how to respond to them.

We have also been talking about the importance to the babies' personality development for their needs to be satisfied appropriately as soon as possible.

How do fathers feel about this? Are you beginning to tell the difference between the various kinds of crying your baby does? How do you feel about attending to your baby's cries? Do you think this causes spoiling?

"When I get home, sometimes everything is calm. Other times I can tell from my wife's expression and the baby's crankiness that it's been a bad day. I decide right then that my wife needs a break. I play with the baby. You know, I think he really likes to see a new face. He laughs, no matter what I do. But other times, in the night, I can't do anything, and it takes a long time to quiet him. Then I think I have spoiled him."

"Yes, those are the times that drive me crazy. Sometimes my wife and I pace around all night, it seems, and the baby keeps fretting. Then if we put her down, she screams."

"I was brought up in a large family. I remember that one of my younger brothers was always crying when I came home from school. For that reason, a crying baby seems a natural thing to me. I know that period will pass. I don't think of the baby as spoiled. I can see now that a large family has its advantages."

"My mother says those are the times to let the baby cry it out, but my wife can't stand it. She says you think it's bad for the baby, and then I have two miserable people on my hands. So I get up and pace around with the baby. I'm sure she's going to end up a spoiled brat."

Crying is the baby's only language at this age. She is telling you she is uncomfortable and needs something. If you respond to her cries and try to help—if only by being a warm human presence—she will begin to feel that the people around her can be trusted to help. Answering the baby's needs is not "spoiling" the baby. We do not "spoil" our children by attending to them; we spoil our children by **not** paying attention to them consistently.

Inconsistency is also hard on the baby. She can't understand why sometimes you help her and sometimes you don't. This confuses the baby—a spoiled baby is a confused baby. It is important for parents to be consistent in the way they handle the baby and for both parents to try to act the same. If it is always the mother who attends to the baby's needs and never the father, the baby may grow up feeling that only women are comforting. It is important for children to see both parents as loving and caring, so that later on they can also accept both parents as limiting and disciplining without resentment.

MORE ON ATTACHMENT

Attachement to Parents and Other Caretakers

While you are satisfying your babies' needs and establishing their trust in you, something else is happening. As the baby is beginning to have faith in you, she is also becoming more and more attached to you. She watches you as you move around the room; perhaps she cries now if you leave or smiles and coos when you return. If the mother is the main caretaker, she will be the first to experience this special recognition from the baby. But fathers can also have this experience if their attentions to the baby are as frequent and consistent as the mothers'.

How many of you have already noticed this special kind of response in your baby? Is the response to different members of your family different or the same? What evidence that the baby recognizes and is attached to you have you seen so far?

"**My wife and I both work. The baby is not really attached to anyone yet. How can we help her form attachments to us and the baby-sitter?**"

As we discussed earlier (see Chapter 1), I think your wife returned to work at the right time—before the baby was attached **only** to her. Now, you have to make sure that your caretaking is consistent, that you have one consistent baby-sitter, and that each of you have special times with the baby. For example, when you get home, you might play with the baby while your wife fixes dinner (or vice versa, if you are the cook). Then your wife might have her special quiet playtime with the baby before the baby goes to bed. Your wife might also give your baby the evening and morning bottles. It would also be good if you were both around most of the time on weekends. The routines of care are important; then the baby learns which adult fills which part of the daily caretaking.

"It sounds as though we'll be doing nothing but taking care of the baby and working at our jobs."

It is important that you give your baby as much attention as you can. Whatever sacrifices you and your wife make now will pay off later. After a while, you will be able to do more for yourselves; the baby will not always need so much attention. If you are consistent with your attention now, I think you will soon begin to notice signs of attachment. It may take longer, but it will happen.

"My baby is mostly attached to me, but she is also beginning to become attached to my husband. He gets home early in the evening, and they play together. She really sees and reacts favorably to about six people because all of our parents are around a lot, too."

But you noticed some difference in her behavior toward you? What did you especially notice?

"Yes, she has begun to cry when I leave the room, and she kicks and laughs when I come back."

The baby's strongest attachment is to the person who takes most care of her. She is most comfortable with that person because she is familiar with the way that person handles her and she feels secure.

Attachment to Places; the Implications of Moving

"Our baby is also mostly attached to me. She looks for me just to be sure I'm there. She'll respond to some people and not to others, as you said. We are moving soon. I wonder if it will bother the baby?"

Babies become attached not only to people but also to favorite toys and familiar surroundings. You may find that there will be a change in your baby, that she'll recognize the difference in the room. So it's a good idea to put the same things in her crib. Try to arrange her new room as nearly like the old room as possible. Babies like familiar things more than they like change. We introduce change to stimulate them and keep them interested, but they do not welcome complete or abrupt changes in their environment, such as a move to a new house entails.

Have you noticed that your baby is especially attached to some of her toys or to her surroundings?

"We noticed that when we moved. Our baby was terribly interested in two green pictures that were in her room, and she

kept looking for them. So we put them up right away. We were surprised that she seemed to miss them."

It was very sensitive of you to recognize that. It is always a good idea when one moves to get the baby's room settled first and make it as nearly like the old room as possible, with special things that have meaning for the baby in place.

"We often go away for weekends, and I find that the baby doesn't do as well in a strange place. Now, to make her comfortable, I have to take all her crib toys and some other things with us, and arrange them as similarly as possible to the way they are at home."

Having her toys in their familiar places makes your baby feel more secure. It is important to understand that this sense of security is easily upset just when it is beginning to develop. This attachment that we are talking about is as important as basic trust in a child's development. The baby who establishes an attachment and feels secure with one person and place will then be able to relate to other people and other places as well. Our experience has been that children who don't make close attachments do not grow up to be adults who can. One must experience attachment early in life. First comes attachment to one person, the primary caretaker. Sometimes, if parents share caretaking duties, the early attachment is to both parents almost equally or, in the case of working parents, to the baby-sitter and the parents. Later, the attachment enlarges to include relatives and friends and, in later life, to one's mate and children.

We will discuss the whole sequence of attachment much more fully in the future. An awareness and understanding of the child's emotional as well as physical development makes parenting an interesting and exciting job.

"Yes, and scary when you think how many mistakes you can make."

You will make some mistakes, and other people with influence over your children's lives will make mistakes. No one is perfect; we all make mistakes. But we hope to help you avoid as many of the common mistakes as possible. All of us have a certain tolerance and plasticity; we can recover from some mistakes. But you are correct in feeling that parenthood is a great responsibility. We agree with you. That is why our program exists: to give you support, and help you get more pleasure out of bringing up your babies.

MORE ON EXPLORATION

Now the babies are getting more mobile. They are beginning to spend more time sitting up. Some of them can even turn over. They are still interested in exploring things with their mouths, but now they

**Develop-
ment
from Oral
to Visual
Exploration**

are beginning to be more interested in looking at them. They peer closely at them, wave them in the air, and bang them against other objects. Soon, they will lose the toy over the side of the table or carriage. This will be more or less accidental at first; later it will be more purposeful. If the babies' central nervous systems have developed sufficiently, they will momentarily notice the disappearance of the toy and look for it. After a second or two, they will lose interest and explore something else. "Out of sight, out of mind" literally explains this stage of development. Some babies are also able to hold one small toy while trying to reach for another.

Have you noticed your baby beginning to explore visually? Have you noticed an increased interest in touching things or trying to manipulate them?

> **"My baby tries to put everything in her mouth. As I'm about to pull it out, she takes it out herself. Then the object is all wet with saliva. She looks at it and puts it back in her mouth, then takes it out again. Finally she begins to bang it on her table or whatever is near. She makes such a mess!"**

Perhaps it is a mess, but this exploration is your baby's earliest form of intellectual curiosity and should not be discouraged. Just try to have the baby do this in her play area, highchair, or playpen, where she can't make too much of a mess. Babies are not fastidious; they're not supposed to be. They will learn not to make a mess when they are older. Now is the time to be messy.

> **"My baby gets so excited when he holds the rattle, looks at it, and then makes a noise by banging it on the tray. He seems to be trying to see if he is the one that is causing the noise."**

You are right, and it is a great discovery for him. He should feel that you both recognize his achievement, too.

**New Ways
to Play
Utilizing the
Baby's New
Exploratory
Skills**

> **"Our baby seems to take great pleasure in dropping his toys and seeing us pick them up. I think he is trying to get our goat."**

Parents can utilize this level of development by playing the game of "Where Is It?" When the baby drops something, pick it up and say, "Here it is!" or "Here is your block or ball or doll," mentioning the name of the object. This game has many advantages. It utilizes the baby's level of development in motor and visual coordination. It also provides language stimulation, both in the words the parents use and in the child's communication of pleasure at finding the lost toy. It can be a happy encounter with the parents. Later on, the baby will become more adept and retrieve the toy herself if she can reach it, but, at present, it is the parents' job to retrieve the object.

Some parents begin to feel that the baby is dropping things purposely just to make them pick them up, just to "get your goat." This is a common adult interpretation of what the baby is doing, but it is mistaken. The baby is merely exploring space. She is only trying to solve the mystery of why a block placed on a table disappears when it is moved a little bit.

Have you noticed your baby trying to explore space? How do you feel about this new experience?

> "My baby has just begun to drop toys, and I have tried to stop her because I have a bad back and can't be constantly bending down to pick things up."

That is unfortunate because the baby needs to be able to explore. Perhaps you can attach a string to her toy and tie the string to the chair or carriage. That way you can return the toy by pulling on the string without bending down. That will also enhance the play a little because the baby will be able to watch the toy reappear. Or you can arrange for someone else to be around for this playtime. The game could be saved for the time father is home. It could be father's special game with the baby.

> "Why shouldn't we stop our babies from throwing things down and making a mess?"

We feel that this early exploration should not be thwarted because studies indicate that babies who have been thwarted at this age may give up and lose the drive to explore and study that is so important when they are in school. This early curiosity is the precursor of the curiosity and drive to explore that is so necessary to success in later learning.

This is not the first exploratory effort the baby has made. We have encouraged you to allow her to touch your face, your hair, your clothes. These were the beginning exploratory gestures. Now the babies are beginning to explore space.

Another game that enhances the baby's concept of space and language is "Up and Down." When the toy falls, the parent says, "Down." When the parent picks the toy up, he says, "Up." In this way, the baby learns the concepts of up and down. No one says that this kind of game is not tiring or that the parent will want to repeat the game as many times as the baby may need to repeat it in order to understand the ideas of solid space, empty space, and up and down. When you get tired, just give the baby a new activity; pick her up and take her to another part of the home, go out for a walk, or play another game. Incidentally, another good game for a child this age is "Clap Hands."

The whole idea is to understand that the baby is not malevolent. She is not trying to upset you; she is merely trying to understand the world around her, and she needs her parents' help to do this. This can really be one of the aspects of parenthood that gives parents the most fun and satisfaction. It is also fun when both parents share in these play experiences.

> "The baby is much more interesting to me now. I hold things up for him, and he reaches for things more now. He seems so happy when he gets hold of them, when he drops them and I give them back. It is fun. When I get tired or he gets tired, we do something else. It's no big deal to do that."

> "Our baby takes her rattle and smashes it against the wall. Sometimes she flings a toy, and it breaks."

This flinging she's doing is also experimenting, but the toys used in this experimenting should be sturdy, so that they don't break when they're dropped or thrown. Babies should be able to drop or throw things. Say "Up" when you pick the object up, and "Down" when she throws it down. The baby's really trying to explore space. That is a stage of development all babies must go through. It is a learning experience.

> "I thought maybe she was enjoying breaking it."

She doesn't know it's going to break; she just enjoys banging it. You have to give her things that are substantial, that are not going to break. It is a pity that so many toys are plastic because plastic toys tend to be fragile. Once all toys were made of wood and were durable. Plastic toys gained popularity because they were less expensive than the wooden ones. I don't think you can say that your baby is being destructive; it's just that the toys you've been providing break easily.

> "If we let her do this now, won't she grow up hitting things against the wall?"

No, this is just a phase of development. If you don't want your baby to hit the toy against the wall, move her away from the wall, and give her something she can bang her toys on. Demonstrate for her what she may do. It is the job of the parents to arrange the baby's environment so that it is not dangerous for baby, parents, or property, while at the same time allowing the baby the opportunity for exploration.

MOTHERS' CONFLICTS ABOUT WORKING

Most mothers have concerns relating to when and whether to return to work. Often conflicts develop between husband and wife over this issue.

> "Because we talk so much about the importance of the baby's forming an early attachment to one person, my husband said to me: 'That's it; you've got to stay home. No job is as important as giving our baby a good start.' I feel totally trapped."

"My husband thinks that these discussions are doing a great thing for women by showing how important mothering is. He's glad you think fathering is important, too."

"As you know I have to work. I feel guilty about not being at home, but your suggestions about how I can help my baby make me feel better."

It is very important that all of you have the opportunity to express your feelings about this subject. Our society is changing rapidly. It is widely thought today that the only meaningful work is outside the home. Society places little value on homemaking and child rearing. Many older women suddenly feel that they've wasted their lives; younger women are determined not to follow in their mothers' footsteps. This attitude ignores children's needs; it often ignores women's needs as well. The child needs a consistent caretaker in order to develop the appropriate attachment or bond for healthy personality development. Being a good mother is as important and worthwhile a job as being a good lawyer or a good doctor. We encourage those of you who can or want to stay home with your children to do so—and enjoy it.

At the same time, we know that some of you must work and that others of you will be happier if you work. A child will be better off with a good mother substitute and a happy part-time mother than a full-time mother who is unhappy or angry about being stuck at home. We are ready to help all of you, whether you work or not, to foster your babies' attachment and security and to meet your babies' needs.

Each of you must decide what is best for yourselves and your families; we are here to give you help and support.

"That is the best thing about these discussions, the support I get from you and the other mothers. It's good to be able to talk about these things and know I'm not the only one who is having a problem."

FEEDING

Developing Feeding Techniques; Avoiding Eating Problems

By now most of you have begun introducing solid foods. The babies' main nourishment, particularly protein, however, still comes from milk and will continue to do so for some time. The purpose of beginning solid foods now—cereal, fruits, vegetables, and meat—is mainly to get the baby used to eating from a spoon. By the time the babies are nine or ten months old, when more nourishment is derived from solids, they will have learned to eat from a spoon and will be able to do it well. By patiently introducing new foods, you will help them develop a taste for a variety of different foods.

Not all babies like a wide variety of foods. Some will only enjoy one or two cereals, one or two fruits or vegetables, and one or two kinds of meat. Some babies will eat no vegetables—only fruit.

Others like only vegetables and not fruit. This should not be a cause for concern. The important thing is not to force food so that feeding becomes a struggle and a battleground. A food that is refused at six months may be "adored" at nine months. If at first the baby does not like a particular food, a mother can always try to introduce it again later.

> "Some days my baby will eat all her meals well. Other days she will eat only one meal, or not at all. Usually, if she takes her first feeding well, I know it will probably be a good eating day."

> "Well, I'm not sure how the baby's going to eat until lunchtime."

Experiments have shown that, over time, a baby generally learns to take a sufficient amount of the right foods. In any one day, or at any one meal, he may not have a balanced diet, but in the long run he gets a balanced diet if this is what is offered to him. There are some who overeat and need some limitation. There are some that may eat well for a day or two and then have a day or two when they do not eat well at all.

Each mother has to learn her own baby's style and accommodate to it. It is important not to force a child of any age to eat. The best way to create an eating problem is to try to force a child to eat. When the baby eats, make a favorable comment like "Good" or "All gone." If he doesn't eat, remove the food without comment. The baby will know when you are pleased and when you are not. The important thing is not to make a big issue of eating.

> "I know that is right. I have heard it before, but somehow I feel so upset when the baby doesn't eat well."

You are worried about his health, but perhaps you also feel you are failing as a mother. In giving food to the baby, you feel you are giving love. When the baby doesn't eat, you feel that he is rejecting your love.

> "That's absolutely right. How did you know?"

That's a very usual feeling for mothers to have. It's one of the universal attitudes. But as we've said before, good care is not measured by the child's weight. A baby that doesn't eat a great deal can still thrive and make progress. Each child grows physically at a different rate and needs a different amount of food for healthy growth.

Different doctors recommend that mothers begin spoon feeding their babies at different times with different foods. Some advise starting with fruit; some with cereal. The doctor has reasons for his recommendations, and they should be followed, even if your neighbor is doing it differently. It is not important which food is started first; what is important is whether the baby is ready for it. The mother should realize that the introduction of each new food is an experiment. Her reputation as a mother and the baby's future do not depend on the baby's acceptance of each new food on the first try.

"Aren't there some babies who have special problems with eating? My neighbor's baby is on a special diet because he has celiac disease."

Yes, and there are babies that are allergic to certain foods, even to milk, but we are talking about the average baby. There are some babies that do have specific problems in food digestion and the babies' doctors should be consulted. When there is vomiting of an explosive kind, not just spitting up, or when the stools are loose and frequent, or the baby is colicky, the doctor should be consulted. But these situations are not relevant here because we are talking about ways of starting good eating habits and avoiding emotional problems centered on eating.

There have been reports recently concerning the deleterious effects of various additives, particularly coloring, in prepared baby foods. While there isn't complete agreement on this subject, it is a concern. For that reason, it is a good idea to read all labels on baby food containers carefully and make sure of the ingredients. If you study baby food labels carefully, you will see that a large part of any given baby food is water with some thickening substance added to give the food bulk. It may occur to some of you that you would prefer to prepare the food at home with a blender. You can always freeze some for use as needed. In this way, you will be more certain of the contents.

"My baby is one of those allergic ones. She breaks out in a rash from some mixed baby foods. So I can only give her simple foods, like pears alone or applesauce alone."

"I have something of the same problem. My baby doesn't get a rash; he gets cramps and sometimes loose stools from new foods. So I can't give him mixed foods, and I've started to give him homemade food. I just steam the vegetable, say carrots, and put it through a Foley food mill. You can use a blender if you have one, I guess. I make enough for several days, freeze it in the ice cube tray, and warm one compartment when I'm ready to feed him that food. It sounds like a lot of work, but it really isn't. I find it cheaper, and the baby likes the food better.

"It may be better because you know exactly what went into it. If it disagrees with the baby, you know just what to eliminate from his diet, and you're not stuck with a lot of jars of food you can't use."

After consulting the doctor, each mother has to do what is most convenient for her and agrees best with her baby. We get into set patterns of doing things sometimes and overlook the possibility of sensible changes.

> "My mother saw a kind of straw that fits in a bottle. Do you know the gadget I'm talking about? It's a straw inside of the nipple, so a baby can hold the bottle upright. At what age should babies be using this device, or should they use it at all?"

Yes, I know what you mean. This gadget is designed to hasten the baby's holding the bottle for himself, because he does not have to hold the bottle up to drink. It is also supposed to assist in diminishing the amount of air swallowed. It may do both of these things, but there are other considerations. One is that the baby does not have to be held for his feedings; he can feed himself. While this may relieve the mother, the baby may still need the closeness of being held. So one has to be sure the baby is ready for this independence. Second, it makes sucking easier and faster. Cutting down the sucking time may not be an advantage if the baby then needs supplemental sucking time with a pacifier. In some cases, therefore, it may force independence on the baby before he is ready for it. In others, it may make the mother feel that the baby has accomplished something he really hasn't. Some babies may enjoy the independence when they are older. Each mother has to evaluate the situation for her baby and his needs.

> "I had the feeling that my mother thought the gadget was great."

It may be great for children who dawdle and need the help, but it would not seem to be particularly necessary for children who take their bottles well.

Effect of Teething and Hot Weather on Appetite

> "What makes babies' appetites so erratic? One day my baby eats so well, and the next almost nothing but some liquid."

There are many factors which alter a baby's appetite. One of the most frequent of these is teething. Teething may make food intake painful. Another is temperature; some babies eat poorly in hot weather. Actually, babies respond very much as adults do. They too may prefer liquids to solid foods in hot weather or want only certain types of food. This should cause no concern if the babies continue to take in adequate amounts of liquid in their formulas, water, or juice, and get enough vitamins. On a cool day their appetites will return, and they will eat more if they need it.

Have others of you been noticing these changes in diet and amount of food eaten?

> "I notice a change in hot weather; my baby only wants to drink."

Milk is still the most important food for babies of this age. That's the food their digestive tracts can handle best. Usually, during the summer months there will be days when babies won't eat very much. If this condition lasts for weeks, or if the babies don't take their milk, then the doctor should be consulted. If they are taking their milk, some fruit juice, weak tea, or plain water with some sugar in it, then you don't really have to worry as long as the baby is active, contented, and developing well.

> "In the hot weather I don't take my baby out for long. I'd rather keep her in the shade. I heard from some mothers that it wasn't good to keep the baby exposed to the sun for any length of time, only two minutes or so."

Exposure to the Sun

That is necessary especially with blond or redheaded babies. Their skin is more sensitive to strong sunlight or even reflected light. In general, it is right not to expose the baby to hot sun for a long time. It is better to increase the baby's tolerance to sun gradually, in two-to-three-minute increments each day. The baby does need to have some sunlight in contact with his skin because the sun's rays help produce the natural vitamin D which prevents rickets. When the skin is tanned, it no longer permits the sun's penetration. The tan acts as a shield preventing the production of vitamin D. That is why it is a good practice to expose only a small part of the baby's skin at a time, so there will always be some untanned parts. We've all become "sun worshipers" and want to be suntanned. It is not the best thing for us. Blistering from a sunburn is very painful for a baby and can be toxic like any other burn. This is another reason for cautious exposure to the sun.

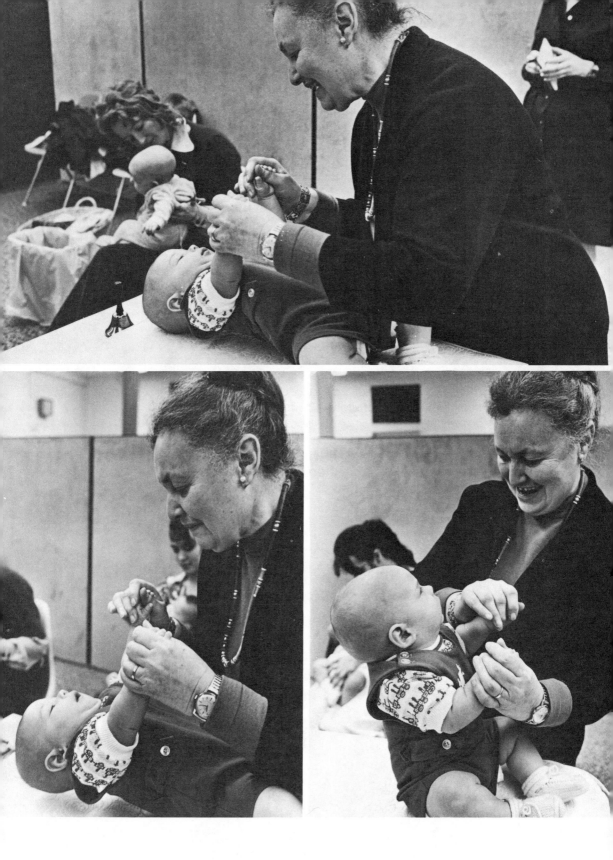

Five-month-old infant learning to pull self to sitting position.
(Exercise described on page 18)

Chapter Five

Age: 20 to 24 weeks _____

At the age of twenty weeks, the baby seems suddenly to make quite a leap ahead in development. She seems much more alert and competent. As the baby pulls herself to a sitting position (see exercise, page 18), there should now be no head lag. Once in the sitting position, the baby's head should be held steady and erect, not forward as a month ago.

When the baby is seated in a high chair, or on his parent's lap near a table, he may scratch the tray or table top. This is the beginning of manual exploration. The baby is also becoming more adept with his hands. When the baby is offered a small block close to his hand, he may make a sweeping gesture with his hand which may enclose the block. Parents may be surprised at the tentativeness of this grasp; but this is normal for this age. Practice with small blocks or empty spools of thread increases this beginning manual skill. If a second block is offered to the baby, he may look at it but will probably make no effort to grasp it.

When a rattle is held close to the baby, she may make a two-handed attempt to get hold of it. The same phenomenon may be observed if the parent dangles the red ring near the baby. The baby may now look momentarily for the block or the rattle when she drops either of them. All of these activities are indications of important developmental advances.

The baby's great achievement in language at this age is squealing. Some parents may be disturbed by squealing because they think it is a form of crying; but, in actuality, it is an important new vocal ability.

If the parent places a mirror in front of the baby, after a little staring, he will smile at his image. During the feeding, the baby begins now to pat the bottle which he will be able to hold in several months. (Breast-fed babies will do this when given a bottle of water or juice.)

About this age, some of the babies may recognize that there is a difference between their parents and others, particularly strangers. This "stranger anxiety" may cause them to stare or cry. This ability to discriminate familiar from unfamiliar people is a big developmental milestone (see discussion, below).

Because so many important developments take place about twenty weeks, there may be significant differences between babies of this age. Some babies may be turning over completely, some not at all. Some may have already discovered their feet and are putting them in their mouths. Some may grasp objects well; others are not yet able to do so. It is, therefore, important for parents to remember that each baby develops in her or his own way and at his or her own rate. Often a baby will advance in one area faster than in another; eventually, development evens out.

STRANGER ANXIETY

Some of you may now be noticing that your baby is aware of strangers and seems to cling more to you when they are around, or she may freeze up and look apprehensively at the stranger. Most of you are pleased that your babies have been very friendly and have not objected to being held by a visiting relative or friend. Now all of a sudden, for no apparent reason, the baby cries and won't leave mother. If you are not prepared for this stage of development, it comes as a great shock and may even be embarrassing if the visitor happens to be the baby's grandmother or the boss's wife. Have any of you had this experience yet?

> "Yes, it happened with my husband's mother. She lives on the West Coast, and she came to visit us for the first time. She was so anxious to hold the baby and hug her, but the baby just took one look and let out a scream. Poor Grandmother looked as though she would cry, so I had to comfort the baby and assure Grandmother it happened because the baby didn't know her. But it was upsetting. It took about half an hour of eyeing Grandmother and just sitting next to her till the baby finally let Grandmother touch her. Now they are friends. But it was tough there for a while."

> "Well, that happened to us with a visitor who claimed to know all about children. She practically grabbed the baby from my arms, and he cried, really yelled and kicked. She told me in no uncertain terms that there must be something wrong with my baby or the way I was bringing him up."

Yes, some people who do not really understand babies regard this behavior as an expression of an unpleasant disposition, crabbiness, or parents' failure to bring up the baby properly. However, this display of wariness towards strangers really shows that the baby has advanced in her development. She is beginning to know the difference between her mother and a stranger. She is just reaching the stage when she is able to see herself as separate from others. She has just recently learned that the appendage that holds the toy is her hand. She is just beginning to get a sense of **self** and a sense of **others**, a real milestone in her development. The problem is most apt to occur when the visitor rushes up to the baby, speaking loudly and over enthusiastically. The baby feels threatened and clings to "Mommy" or bursts out crying. Of course, if the visitor is a grandmother who is seeing the baby for the first time, or after a long interval, one must understand her enthusiasm and disappointment that her warm greeting is met with such a negative reaction. It is generally a good idea to warn visitors, especially someone like a grandmother who is meeting the baby for the first time, to go about making friends with the baby slowly. That way, the baby will have a chance to get used to the new person, and her initial reaction will not be negative. Tense social situations can often be avoided in this way.

"What is the best thing to do? It's been a problem for me because my son behaves that way with his Grandpa."

The best thing to do is to hold the baby close to comfort him and ask the grandfather to sit down a little bit away. Inform Grandpa that the baby is at a stage in which he is just beginning to recognize the difference between mother and other people, and that he needs a little time to get used to a visitor. Assure Grandpa that he is not at fault, that the baby's fearfulness or outburst of crying does not mean that he does not like him. Later, the baby may reach toward Grandpa and make his own overtures. The best thing is not to place too much emphasis on the whole episode. It is especially important not to communicate to the baby that you are displeased with him.

"What if there is a certain person the baby just can't take? Mine doesn't cry with anyone else but her grandmother, who comes quite often."

There are instances in which babies don't like certain people. For some reason that person arouses some anxiety in the baby. It may be the quality of voice, the facial expression, the person's size, the vigor of the approach, some characteristic which upsets the baby. The baby's reaction may last for some time, even several weeks or months. This is a difficult situation both for the baby and the other person, especially if the other person is a close relative. Sometimes it may even happen to the father, if he has been away for a while. It is painful for all concerned, but the baby needs to be comforted and exposed gradually to the other person from the safe vantage point of mother's arms or lap, or his carriage or crib, anywhere the baby feels safe on his own ground. When the baby feels secure, he will show interest in the new person.

"You answered my question. Grandfather is a very large, tall man, and he has a loud, booming voice. He's very jolly and vigorous. I think that's just what frightens the baby. Just what all of us like about Grandpa is upsetting the baby. I never thought

of it that way. None of us did. That's why we couldn't understand why the baby cries every time he sees Grandfather!"

Most problems occur because we don't understand things from a
baby's point of view, only from our own.

"My baby goes to everyone. He doesn't seem to have any fear
of anyone. Should I be expecting this to change?"

Yes, most babies pass through this stage at around five to seven
months. Here again it is important to remember that each child is
different. They will all pass through this stage on their own
timetables.

SEPARATION ANXIETY

This brings us to another situation in which baby cries and the mother
is puzzled and annoyed. That's when mother leaves the baby alone
for a moment to answer the doorbell or telephone, go to the bathroom, or attend to some chore in the house. The baby cries; the
mother can't understand why. This happens because the baby has
not reached that stage of development when she can separate
from the mother; she can't bear to have her mother out of sight. We
know that mothers are ready to separate from their babies long
before the babies are ready to separate from them. We all know
about the physical stages that lead to walking; we know the baby
has to turn over, sit, crawl, stand, and then walk. We accept this
gradual process. However, the stages in separation and individuation are not as well known. Our understanding of this area of development has been acquired rather recently, largely due to the
research of Dr. Margaret Mahler in which she was able to delineate
the process of separation in normal children.

"That is something I never heard of, and I have been upset
because I can't leave the baby alone a minute. As soon as he
realizes I am not there, he cries, and it's driving me up the wall.
What are the stages we should expect?"

For about the first six months of life, the baby needs to be in very
close proximity to the mother (or to caretaker) and can barely
discern that she is separate from her. As the baby's central nervous
system matures, she begins to become aware of her own body. You
have seen this begin to happen in the way the babies are now
looking at the toys that are holding and at their hands. Gradually,
when the baby drops her toys, she begins to look to see where they
went. Later, she finds her feet and puts them in her mouth. These are
signs that the baby is becoming aware of the extent of her own
body. Then the baby realizes that she is separate from her mother
and very much in need of her. Shortly after this, she begins to
recognize that strangers are different from her mother. She may
even feel that a stranger will take her from her mother. When the

baby has reached this level of development, she cries when mother leaves, even for a minute.

For mothers this may be a great nuisance. It is annoying if it is regarded as improper or naughty behavior on the infant's part. Instead, if you understand that this behavior is a stage in development which will pass as the baby matures, you will find it less annoying. For the baby, it is very frightening when she cannot see her parent because what cannot be seen does not exist as far as the baby is concerned. This is also why babies of this age do not look very long for toys they drop. Their central nervous systems have not yet developed to this level of understanding. They must learn from positive experience that their mothers will return. At this age, babies do not yet have the capacity to remember people or objects. This comes with experience. The pathways carrying messages to their brains have to be developed so that these events will register.

"How much time does all this take?"

It will probably come as a stunning surprise to most of you that it may take some babies until they are three years old to separate fully from their mothers. Some can do it earlier; others take even longer. The average age is around three years.

When babies first begin to crawl and walk, they leave their mothers momentarily but come right back when they discover how far away they have gotten. As they get older, they travel farther. Studies have shown that the distance is proportional to the baby's age. Mothers say: "Well, she runs away from **me**. Why can't I leave **her**?" The baby knows she is coming back to you, but she doesn't yet know you will come back to her, and she can't get along without you. When the baby is more competent in her motor skills, and when she is verbal, she will begin to understand that you will come back, and that you do exist even if she can't see you. When a child can say "Mama" and talk about "Mama," this helps her hold the image and memory of mother, and mother continues to exist. When the baby has achieved this understanding, then separation and individuation can take place. So you see, separation has its stages, just as physical development has. If a parent understands these stages, coping with them is easier. Then, the baby's crying is not interpreted as "bad behavior" but as part of her immaturity, her "babiness." This understanding can help the parent have less of a feeling of being "trapped" by a demanding child and more of a feeling of being needed. Understanding that you are fulfilling such a need is one of the satisfactions of parenthood.

What have you been doing if the babies cry when you leave them? How do you feel about the baby's crying in this kind of situation?

"I just decided I couldn't stand the crying, so I usually turn on music, carry the baby with me, or put him in the back sling as I do my work. He seems to enjoy that much more than being in his crib, and I'm happier too."

"Everyone used to tell me to leave her alone and let her cry. They said I was spoiling her by carrying her with me. But I don't leave her alone or with anybody who would let her cry. I thought it was interesting when you said that at this age babies don't know that they are separate from you, that it frightens them when they can't see or hear you."

That's right, it frightens them because they don't know you're some-where else and that you will come back. That's why what you're both doing is just fine. Taking the babies with you so that they can see you is the best way to cope with this problem.

"Oh, you hear so many different things. I guess you have to decide: 'This is the way I'm going to do it.' Everyone went through that business about 'Don't pick the baby up because it'll spoil him!' I'm going through it now. All my friends say, 'Let him cry, and he'll get strong lungs.'"

There was a time when the baby needed to cry to inflate her lungs, but that was when she was first born. She had to cry to get her lungs to function and, in the first few weeks of life, to keep all of the lung expanded. But that is not needed at this age. The advice you've been given is a misapplication of what was **physiologically** impor-tant early in infancy but is not **psychologically** correct now.

"The hardest thing is the fact that my baby always needs to be where she can see me."

Yes, that's hard. It means that she needs to learn that you will come back. She has to have the repeated experience of your going and returning. She will then begin to develop trust in your returning. That takes time. Everyone knows the babies are not going to walk or talk the day they are born, but everyone thinks the babies know that you're coming back. Babies simply do not know this; it is something they have to learn by repeated experience.

"I think one of the hardest things initially is to learn to put your own needs second and to adjust to the baby's needs. The baby just cannot adjust to us."

It is very important for parents to understand their baby's helplessness and needs. When you realize that you are doing all these things because of your baby's needs, parenting becomes easier and can be more gratifying because it stops being a battle for control.

MOTHER'S NEEDS IN RELATION TO BABY'S NEEDS _____

Mothers in primitive societies seemed to be able to cope with their babies' separation problems in a more natural way than we in our complex society can. They carried their babies on their backs on papoose boards or wrapped in shawls or slings. When they worked in the fields, they put the babies down alongside them or, at least, near them. Whatever they were doing, the baby was close by. If the baby was not close to his own mother, then he was close to a mother-substitute in the extended family or tribe. In our society, the baby's need for close contact comes as a surprise and is an unwelcome aspect of parenting. However the baby's needs have not changed. We are just beginning again to recognize these needs. What should we, in our society, do? How can we keep our talented, educated, independent, sophisticated mothers from feeling that the baby is a burden and not a joy, and that they are "trapped" by their baby's needs?

Perhaps all this discussion about the baby's needs has given you a feeling that you are in for a long siege and that you are really trapped, and there is no way for your own needs to be met. Is that what you were thinking?

"Yes, that is just what I've been thinking. You talk about the babies' needs, but what about time off for the mothers?"

It is absolutely essential now that the babies have a more predictable pattern that each mother has time off. She may not be able to go off when the spirit moves her, but she can work out a system for having a regular afternoon or day a week when she can go out by herself, or with her husband or friends. Besides being a parent, she is also an adult with needs that have to be met. Parenting does not have to be servitude if one organizes one's life. There should be some arrangement made with an aunt, a grandmother, or a regular baby-sitter. Then the mother feels, "This is my time." Mothers can have time for themselves and still remain the primary caretaker of the baby.

"I do think that's terribly important, at least one day a week, and you can dream about what you're going to do on your day off. Sometimes it can be a whole day, sometimes it can be an hour, or half an hour, or half a day, but you must have that time, and taking it doesn't mean that you don't love your baby. I know I love mine, but still I need time off."

Doctors, lawyers, and carpenters all have to have time off. No one can do a good job twenty-four hours a day, seven days a week. There has to be some change of pace. Each mother has to know she can have a specific time when she can do what she wants.

Gradually, as the baby gets older, it is possible to include the baby in some of the things that a mother wants to do. Also as the baby gets older, the mother gets more time off because the baby begins to develop an interest in playing with his toys and exploring his world. He becomes less constantly demanding.

"I notice that the baby falls asleep after her bottle, so that's a fine time to have coffee and look at the paper. Then I know the baby's going to be up for a time, and I'm going to be entirely devoted to her. If I go down to the laundry or go marketing, I take the baby. If I'm going to the beauty parlor, I leave the baby with a neighbor or with her grandmother. That's every Thursday, and I don't feel in prison all the time. I really can enjoy the time I'm with the baby much more."

"I just keep wondering if there is something wrong with me. I waited a long time to have this baby. I've always wanted to be a mother, so I don't want to be away from my baby. If my baby needs me, that is what I am there for. That's very satisfying to me. When we go out, we always take our baby with us. We don't find that a burden or confining."

That is how you feel, and that is right for you and your baby. Some mothers have waited a long time to have a baby and are very happy to stay home with the baby all the time. They are also happy to go everywhere with the baby. If there is a place where the baby can't go, the mother doesn't go, and she doesn't mind. However, there are other mothers who need to have some time of their own—perhaps a short time each day when the baby can be left with a neighbor or relative, or a longer period once or twice a week when they can do things on their own like shopping, going to the beauty parlor, lunching with friends, or going to a movie, or when they can do something that was an important part of their lives before the baby came. They still feel they need this free time in order to be more patient with the baby and the baby's needs.

"If you are the kind of mother who needs time off, how can you make your time off fit in with the baby's needs?"

That has to be worked out carefully. It is important to have the baby cared for in the mother's absence by the same person on a regular basis, so that this substitute care becomes part of the baby's pattern of life. It is best to have the caretaker come to your house, rather than leave the baby in the caretaker's house, unless it is a house the baby has become very familiar with, like Grandma's or a neighbor's. The baby needs to get to know the person who takes care of him in the mother's absence. He needs to adjust to this person before the mother leaves. She can then leave the baby confident that he and the caretaker will get along.

"Every time I leave my baby, he cries, even when I leave him with my husband. So I have to sneak out. I hate to do that. Is it the right thing to do?"

Very often parents feel it is best to sneak out, but this will bring about a lack of trust on the baby's part. He will cling more to mother because he will be afraid she will sneak off again. It is best to say a formal good-bye quickly and casually and then to make the return greeting prolonged, happy, and enthusiastic. After sufficient experience with a happy return, the baby will be less upset when you leave. His protest at your leaving indicates his attachment, and that is good. It is appropriate for his age. He can soon be distracted by the caretaker.

"What about a mother's returning to work? When is the best time for that?"

Returning
to Work

In one of our earlier sessions, we talked about this and the difficulty of returning to work just at this period of developing attachment. Some of you are already back at work and have told us about your routines for establishing your baby's attachment to both you and the baby-sitter. This is a good time to discuss it further.

In view of the stages in a baby's ability to cope with separation, the baby needs a consistent caretaker until he can achieve his own separate and individual existence. For some babies, this may not occur until around three years. Other babies may be able to separate at two-and-a-half or earlier, and some will take longer. One must judge the right time for one's own child. The stages in the process are the same for all babies, but the timing—the maturational timetable—is unique for each child. A mother should feel that giving her baby this secure start in life is a worthy and important job, and society should support her in this undertaking.

"What if the mother has to return to work and just can't put it off until the baby is ready?"

This a very serious question and many families have had to make this decision. If the mother must return to work for financial reasons, or has a profession she can't or doesn't want to give up, then she has to make a serious choice regarding the baby's separation needs. As we have said, it is better for a mother to return to work before the baby is attached mainly to her. In this way, the baby forms an attachment to the caretaker, who should be a constant person in the baby's life. Secondly, the mother has to arrange her time so that when she is home, she really spends meaningful time with her baby. Just being at home or in the same room while she is doing admittedly necessary housework is not adequate for the baby's need. There have to be playtimes and caretaking activities that are done exclusively by the mother. This can in part make up for the time she is not there. The problem arises when the mother comes home tired and expects the baby to appreciate how hard she has been working and not bother her. Obviously, the baby cannot be expected to do that. He needs the mother's attention when she returns. If parents are aware of this, then the necessary adjustments can be made. When the mother understands the baby's needs, she will feel less irritation with the baby's clinging demands for attention. Remember: It's a good sign if the baby demands your attention; such behavior means that the baby is attached to you.

"Very soon I may have to go back to work. Is there something special in the baby's behavior I should be prepared for?"

A baby who has become accustomed to his mother's care and attached to her will protest at her leaving. After being without her all day, no matter how good the substitute care, this child will be fussy, his sleeping and eating schedules may be disrupted, and he may want to be held more. The mother needs to expect this and plan to spend a lot of time with him when she comes home. Children who have experienced too early separation won't let their parents out of sight for a moment without crying when the parents return. Parents should recognize this behavior as an expression of the child's need and not get angry.

"Is there some way to help the baby separate without excess anxiety?"

The most important thing is that the introduction of a new caretaker be gradual. The caretaker, whether it be a relative or a hired baby-sitter, should come to your home for a few days to watch your way of caring for your baby and then gradually take over some of your functions. In this way, the baby gets to know her and becomes accustomed to her way of doing things with him. During this time, you can absent yourself for short periods, then longer periods, until the baby accepts your leaving without too much agitation and begins to learn that you will return.

Many parents may not be able to find an appropriate person to come to their homes to care for their children. Another solution for children of this age is called "family day-care." This means care given by a qualified person in her own home. Regulations vary in different states but generally, licensed family day-care strictly limits the number of children who may be cared for by one person and assures a certain level of competence. Care in a day-care center is also a possibility, but we feel it is the least desirable alternative for babies of this age (actually, center care is rarely an alternative as few centers take children under two years of age). If you leave your child with another mother or in family day-care, the process of separation should also be gradual so that the child becomes familiar with the new caretaker, the new routines, and the new environment while the parent is still available for support. To make the transition, it is necessary to bring a few of the child's toys from home, especially favorite ones such as his blanket or teddy bear. In the long run, extra time spent at the beginning of different care is time well spent in maintaining the child's sense of security and well-being.

"But that may take a long time, a week or more."

Yes, it may, but the question was, "Is there some way to help the baby separate without excess anxiety?" This is the way to do it. For each child, the time it takes for such an adjustment varies.

"Does child care have to be all the mother's job? Can't the father help a little too? I'm not thinking of a fifty-fifty arrangement but just sharing a little of the responsibility?"

Naturally, the father can help and share in filling the gap. Some fathers work at home and can do a great deal. Some like to take over the baby's bedtime routine when they come home. Some can play patiently and happily with the baby. Some help with the household chores. Some mothers and fathers naturally and spontaneously can be very cooperative; others have to make formal and explicit assignments of roles and obligations. Actually, all of this ought to be discussed and agreed upon well before the baby arrives. But even if it has been, new parents find it very hard to comprehend how many time-consuming jobs taking care of a baby entails, even under the best circumstances, with the most contented baby in the world.

Therefore, some reasonable adjustments have to be made. It is not an impossible situation. A little understanding of the baby's and the parents' needs will make it easier.

"Until I had the baby, I thought I'd go right back to my job. But since it is not a financial necessity, and it can mean so much to the baby to have me home, I've decided to stay home."

"I never for a moment thought of going back to work until my baby was in school. I have had enough of the business world."

"Well, we need the money, and I've been planning to return to work. I am a teacher, and I like my work, but I am going to postpone returning to my job as long as I can. The baby needs me, and I enjoy taking care of her."

"I had to go back to work because my husband lost his job. I'm a nurse. My husband took care of the baby in the morning. In the afternoon when he went to school, he left him at the baby-sitter's house. I took him home at six. He cried a long time, and for a few weeks he would not eat at the baby-sitter's house— only when I took him home. It was very hard. Now my husband is working again, and I am home. It is much better that way."

Your baby had already become attached to you, so that leaving him with someone else created a trauma for him. Sometimes one cannot avoid that, but I am glad that things are better now for your baby and your family.

"I went back to work when the baby was about three months old. It's tough. My husband and I devote all our time to nothing but the baby and our jobs. But I think the baby is forming an attachment to us and the baby-sitter."

It is hard work to meet the demands of both a baby and a job successfully. The development of attachment takes time. The baby's attachment to a full-time baby-sitter is different from his attachment to his parents, but it can supply the security and feeling of trust so important to healthy development. The most important thing is to have a consistent caretaker that you and the baby like. It is not always easy to find such a person, especially one who shares your ideas of child rearing. If you work part-time, it is sometimes easier to find a good caretaker. A grandparent or other relative may be available to baby-sit on a regular basis. Sometimes one can arrange something with a neighbor who also needs a similar service on a regular schedule.

Baby-Sitters

"I don't work, but I like to get out one or two afternoons a week. Do I need the same baby-sitter, someone the baby knows, each time?"

It is important that the baby-sitter be known to the baby and come regularly. It is very difficult for the baby, if there is a different baby-sitter each time. Some mothers put the baby to bed before the baby-sitter comes and then leave. If the baby wakes to find a stranger, this can set up a long period of difficulty in getting the baby to sleep on subsequent nights. The baby is anxious that mother may be away again when he wakes. This sort of interference with the development of a baby's basic trust and separation is avoidable. But once it has occurred, it takes a long time to undo. How are you all managing?

"Well, I'm lucky. My mother lives nearby, and she loves to baby-sit. The baby is quite happy with her. She knows his whole routine."

"I have to take our son to my mother-in-law's house. There are other people there, so he is entertained. But when I get him home, he is irritable. I think he gets overexcited, and my mother-in-law doesn't handle him the way I do. She knows how to take care of children. She has had plenty of experience. But it's just different."

"I have a neighbor across the hall with a baby our baby's age. We are in each other's apartments all the time, so my baby knows her and her baby. We both need to economize so we exchange baby-sitting services. If it's at night, either my husband or I sit in her apartment, and she does the same for us. It works out okay."

"The landlady is my lifesaver. She is fond of the baby and has had nine of her own, so she is glad to help me out. She seems to know just how to handle my baby, too."

"I've tried using the student nurses at the hospital across the street. Their schedules vary so much that now I have two sitters. That gives me a 'back up,' and the baby likes them both."

"I just haven't been able to find anyone, and I don't think the sitters available are worth the money. Besides, we like taking the baby with us."

Each of you seems to have found the solution that suits your needs, but each solution is different and that is to be expected because each baby and each family situation is a little different.

Nowadays we have another type of baby-sitter available to us. This baby-sitter is not human; it's electronic. I'm talking, of course, about the TV, and we should take some time now to review its advantages and disadvantages as a baby-sitter and stimulus.

TV as a Baby-Sitter and Stimulus

Many parents have reported that their babies are just fascinated by the TV screen. With babies this age, TV provides the stimulation of exciting movement and sound, and it's fine for a few minutes. But it is not good as a constant diet. It is not something to put the baby in front of while you do chores, no matter how quiet it keeps the baby. The quieter the baby, the better mother likes it. But the electronic companion is not a substitute for human contact and stimulation. If the baby is exposed to TV for too long a time, either he is bombarded with too much stimulation, or he gets bored with the device, turns aways from it, and is alone in the room without mother's stimulation of speech, touch, and involvement.

One also must think about program selection. The tone of voice, manner, and gestures used by some of the puppets in **Sesame Street** are frequently imitated by young children. Constant exposure may give a speech model which is not the one you may wish to foster in your child. It is true that children can parrot letters and numbers earlier after seeing **Sesame Street**, but whether this really helps them to learn concepts is still in question.

Also, a mother may leave her child watching a pleasant, harmless program, stay away a bit too long, and return to find the child looking at something frightening, unpleasant, or violent. There have been no reliable studies of the effects of violent programs on children, but violent programs clearly are bad models of life. For the older child who is verbal, there is, in some children's programs, a very subtle but definite teaching of deception. One need only watch these programs occasionally to see that much of what is supposed to be humorous is really detrimental to the teaching of reality in life and the difference between right and wrong.

"Then what options are left to the mother? What relief can she have for a few minutes while she tends to something urgent?"

There may be short intervals of judicious use of TV. The mother's intervals of time for herself come as the baby begins to be stimulated by appropriate toys which he can manipulate himself in a safe place close to mother. Of course, she can always use nap time and after the baby's bedtime for things she needs to do. Mothers must understand that "bad" days, when the baby is restless and needs her undivided attention, are not going to last forever. On some days, the baby is striving to reach a new and more mature level of development. Trying to do this gives him a feeling of disequilibrium. Being understanding and patient are a big help to the baby. This attitude will make it easier for the mother as well because she will not be adding her agitation to the baby's.

APPROVAL

Recognition of Approved Behavior

Now that the babies are more competent and can do more sitting, reaching, and holding, they need to be given the message that their progress is being noted and approved. It is common practice for parents to take approved behavior for granted and to comment only if they disapprove. The most important thing, however, is to let the baby know when you approve of her behavior. The human animal has a built-in need for recognition. This need should be fulfilled early in the baby's life. The baby understands approval very well. For example, when a baby takes her bottle well or takes a mouthful of cereal, and the mother acknowledges this by saying "Good baby," a smile spreads over the baby's face.

When the baby plays with a toy appropriately (for example, shakes her rattle), responds when mother enters the room, pulls herself to a sitting position, or turns over, the parent should recognize this accomplishment in a clear, positive way.

Human beings learn best when they receive approval. Most of us would agree with this statement. Our experiences with children tend to verify it, but it has also been demonstrated scientifically. Experiments have shown that children who have been doing poorly in school begin to do better and behave better when given appropriate approval.

Have you begun to show approval of your babies' accomplishments, and how do you do it?

"Well, there are lots of things the baby does that please us, but I thought she was too young to have our approval really mean anything to her. I noticed that she grinned when I smiled at something she did, but I didn't attach any significance to it."

"I think my ideas are a little like that too. When I told some of my friends my reactions to what my baby did, they said that I was making too much of her achievements because all babies do similar things. So now I just kind of keep quiet."

It seems that some of you have been inhibited in your natural expression of appreciation of the baby's accomplishments by comments of people whose notions about babies are not in keeping with what is best for the baby. But the point you should bear in mind is that you want to let your baby, not other people, know you like what she is doing.

There are also many parents who are pleased by their baby's developments and proudly point them out to someone else, but make no comment to the baby. The baby needs positive reinforcement for her successes. That's how she learns that she is successful. She needs to know that her achievements please you. Then she will be pleased with herself and will try to evoke this response from you again. She will have an incentive to work for success.

The drive to achieve is a very important element in personality development. If a baby does not get positive response, she loses incentive for success and gets no sense of satisfaction from achievement. If this lack of recognition persists, this child will have difficulty in working to achieve during the school years. Such a child will have passed a critical period when she could have learned this drive for achievement. That is why it is so important to recognize all the little bits of developmental progress. The baby learns the feeling of success, and the foundation for further incentive to achieve is established.

You may notice that no mention has been made of praise or adulation; all we have been concerned with is simple recognition. It is not necessary to "go into ecstasy," unless you feel that way, and it's natural for you to express yourself in such terms. One doesn't have to say, "Oh, you marvelous baby!" Just "Good" and a smile or pat will do.

> "Well, I try to show my approval by a smile; my husband does too. I think the baby is getting the message because he tries to repeat whatever we smiled at."

> "I pick my baby up and hug and kiss her whenever she does anything I think is cute and makes me happy. Is that wrong?"

There is nothing wrong in hugging the baby if you feel moved to do that. However, it should not be the only way of showing recognition for what the baby does. A smile or a "Good" will be enough. The baby will get the message that you approve from your facial expression and tone of voice.

> "Some people tell me the baby will be spoiled by being praised. He'll think he always has to be praised."

We are not talking about praise, we are talking about recognizing the baby's accomplishments so that the baby will get the feeling of approval for achievement.

There are some people who feel constant recognition of this kind causes the baby to think that she can do no wrong and will "spoil" her. As we have said before, "spoiling" does not come from reinforcing the child's positive development but from inconsistency in attention to her needs and achievements.

> **"Won't a baby need to be reassured all her life then? Won't she grow accustomed to such recognition and need it all the time?"**

That is what happens to the baby who doesn't get consistent reassurance. The baby who gets consistent reassurance develops self-esteem and doesn't require constant reinforcement. She gives it to herself. The baby who has never had consistent recognition is never certain of herself and is constantly seeking recognition from others. Perhaps you know adults who constantly need to be told that they are doing a good job. No matter how well they perform, they never feel that what they have done is good enough.

> **"Well, I always thought that kind of reaction was just modesty and good manners, but sometimes it has seemed a bit much."**

No, such behavior is more likely to be caused by insecurity, which has its origin in a non-responsive, non-approving atmosphere during infancy.

DISCIPLINE: SETTING LIMITS

Just as it is important for the baby to know that you approve of certain things, she must also learn what is not acceptable. She must be protected from danger. The baby must learn not to touch electric outlets, the hot stove, or a plant that may fall on her. To teach what is unacceptable, the parent should consistently and firmly say "No," remove the baby from the forbidden activity, and immediately give an alternate activity from which the baby can derive loud and clear approval. This must be done consistently and firmly, but not angrily. In this way you are teaching "limitations." Do not expect that the baby will get the message the first time. There will have to be countless repetitions of the situation before the baby learns. Each baby has a different learning rate. Some may learn in a month; others only after several months.

Has your baby reached the stage of development where she is ready to learn some discipline? How have you been handling the problem? Have you found that instead of approving of your baby's activities, you are saying "No" more often?

> **"I guess I do emphasize the 'No's.' If the baby is doing something that I don't like but that isn't harmful or dangerous, I just let it go. For example, when he is touching something like a cup of hot coffee, I say 'No' or something to stop him. But if he bangs a spoon—well, I just let it go."**

"It bothers me when my baby bangs with a spoon; it makes too much noise, and I say 'No.' "

Actually, banging against the table with the spoon is an accomplishment for this age. If the baby is making too much noise, you can put a napkin or mat on the table. That will cut down on the noise considerably. Also, the change in surface will produce a change in sound that will be of interest to the baby.

"I thought the baby banged because it bothered me, so I say 'No!' "

That is a common misconception. The baby does not intend to annoy you. In most cases, she is just showing off a new achievement.

"Well, how will she learn to stop? What is the way to teach her?"

The process of learning limitations goes through stages just as learning to walk goes through stages. We all know about the stages connected with learning to walk and accept them. The stages of internalizing limitations and restrictions are not so well known. The baby should be limited and given an alternate, acceptable outlet for her activity. However, at first, she may persist in going back to the forbidden activity and look to see if mother will stop her again. At this stage, the baby should not be expected to have learned. She may smile coyly and try to evoke a smile from mother. Mother, however, should unsmilingly and firmly remove the baby from the forbidden object or activity. In the next stage, the baby may go up to the object, say "No" to herself, but still touch it. However, she still relies on the mother to remove her because she still needs the parent's help to do what she is learning is acceptable. Finally, the baby will get to the stage when she can go up to the object, say "No," and not touch it. At this point, the baby should get recognition for her achievement in self-control. She is then at a stage when she can also sometimes find an alternate, acceptable activity for herself. A few children can achieve this by three years; others may take longer. Also, it will depend on the attraction of the object in each given case.

"It seems that this is not an easy process. Does it come naturally with age?"

This is a process that develops only with parental help. No one says it is easy. But once the process has been achieved, the baby is on the road to establishing conscience mechanisms. The growing child will be able to discipline herself according to the standards set by her parents and the cultural values which her family holds. Helping the baby develop self-discipline is one of the big jobs and great opportunities of parenthood. When the child has learned this, it is a tremendous satisfaction to both parents and child, and sets the pattern for all self-discipline later in life.

"I never realized there was so much to it. My husband and mother think if you tell the baby to stop, she should—and right there and then, too!"

"That's the way I was brought up. When someone said 'No' to a child, it meant 'No right now, this minute.' The child was supposed to do as she was told immediately."

Some parents have been brought up to think that if you say "Stop" or "No" to a child, she should do so immediately. If she doesn't, she is a bad baby. In fact, the younger the child, the less she is able to respond at once because her central nervous system has not matured sufficiently. Responding to verbal instructions is learned behavior. The message must go to the brain, be processed and understood, and then directed back to the arms and legs involved in the activity. It's a more complicated process than most of us realize. It takes time for a child to develop the appropriate pathways in the brain.

This process is not completely developed in some children until they are seven or eight or nine years old. Something stimulates a baby to want to reach for something, and that message goes to the brain. That stimulus has to be discharged by some activity; it can't just stop. That is why the baby should be given an alternate outlet or activity until she learns how to deal with such situations. The child's response is not a matter of being good or bad, obeying or disobeying. It is a matter of anatomical and physiological development—that is, maturation of the central nervous system. This is not generally understood, and that lack of understanding gets in the way of establishing good parent-child relations and good character structure.

"When I limit my baby in any way, my mother says: 'Let him be! He is only a baby. When he is bigger, he will learn to behave. Now let him be!' Is she right? Is that what you mean? Is that the thing to do?"

It does not help to let a baby do anything she wants for a long time and then begin to set limits. It is better for the baby to learn to cope with limitations gradually, according to her developmental capacity. There are many parents who for some time let a baby do anything she pleases. Then one day, the parents decide they have had enough and come down on the baby like a ton of bricks. This is not logical or effective. In fact, it is counterproductive.

These two areas of child rearing—appropriate recognition and consistent appropriate limitation—are vital to the development of a healthy responsible personality. When these areas are not handled properly beginning in early life, they may become the nucleus around which develops a maladjusted personality who becomes the school dropout or delinquent. That is why we make such a point of these two topics in our discussions, and why we will be discussing them again in many frames of reference.

"Well, what stage are our babies in right now?"

It varies a little with each one, as you know, but in general your babies are or will be soon at the stage where they recognize your approval by your smile or tone of voice. They are beginning to recognize, too, what you mean when you frown or use a disapproving voice. In other words, they are beginning to recognize the difference between these two kinds of behavior on your part, but they are much too young to control their actions.

"Are they really beginning to tell the difference already?"

Yes, they are just beginning this process and they need your help: first to learn what is approved and disapproved, and then how to control and adjust their own actions. They also need your help in learning to accept alternate outlets when what they want is not acceptable. You will help them along this pathway, and finally they will be able to say "No" to themselves and find another activity or plaything. You will find, however, that children sometimes need help in selecting alternate activities, even as teenagers. Learning self-discipline goes through many stages of development during the whole period of childhood.

"At what age can a child look at something she knows is not allowed and say 'No'?"

That may take what seems a very long time to you. It varies with each child. A few babies begin to get some understanding by eighteen months; most take until three years or longer. If you are consistent and patient, your child will be a bit closer each day to achieving that level of development, the beginning of conscience. When she has arrived at that level, she will begin to internalize "No"—and your values.

"How long does it take to teach a child not to touch just one thing she shouldn't?"

That depends on the individual child and how consistently the parent handles the situation. With some children the learning process must be repeated a hundred times before the lesson becomes fixed in the child's mind; with other children it need be repeated only ten times. How long the process must go on varies with each child and each situation. Every child has his or her own maturational timetable, and learning what not to do depends on that.

"How do you indicate to a child that you don't approve of what she's doing but still love her?"

When a child is older and more verbal, you can make the distinction between the child's actions and the child herself. You say, in effect, "I don't like what you're doing, but I like you." Our babies, however, are too young to understand this verbal distinction.

Our babies are now at the very beginning stage of this understanding. The biggest clue our babies now have to your attitude is your voice. They sense the attitude inherent in a particular tone of voice—that is, the "meaning" of the tone, as distinct from the words spoken. Also, as you hold them, they can sense whether you're angry or comforting, soothing, and pleased—and they can feel the difference between the two attitudes. In the same way, you communicate your state of mind—whether you're tense or relaxed—when you feed your baby.

At this age, the babies are also beginning to be more visually discriminating. They are able to see that your eyes are set back and that your nose protrudes. They are also beginning to see your facial expression, and they can sense your approval or disapproval from it.

In addition, the baby can detect your attitude from what you do. For example, when you are feeding the baby and she spits the food out, you wipe it off and let her know you don't like what she's done. Then, when she takes her food well, you say, "Mmmmm, good." These small actions and others like them give the baby a clear idea of how you feel about what she's doing.

THE "ANGRY ALLIANCE"

How Babies and Parents Upset Each Other

We have tried on the whole to emphasize the positive things that parents can do to help the babies develop healthy personalities. There are times, however, when things do not run smoothly, and you get angry at the baby. You lose patience and scold the baby or handle him roughly. This often happens when you have planned to do something while the baby is napping. Then, for some reason, the baby does not want to nap. Maybe you were in a bit of a hurry to get something done, and you put the baby down a little bit too soon. The baby protests. You get angry, go to the baby, and scold him. Then you put him down firmly and leave. The baby protests again, and you repeat your previous responses—only this time a little more forcefully. If you "win," and the baby finally goes to sleep because he is tired by this time, you remain upset. The hassle has diminished your satisfaction in your own planned activity. The baby's basic trust in a loving, need-satisfying mother has been damaged a little as well.

On another day, the baby is teething, or some food has upset him, or he is entering a new developmental stage, and his physiological equilibrium is disturbed. For that reason, he is fussy and hard to soothe. You want him to play quietly with a toy or sit quietly in his high-chair while you do something in the kitchen. But he cries and constantly interrupts you. Your voice and your way of holding him show your annoyance. The baby senses mother's anger and disapproval. The baby gets worse, and the mother gets more tense. Pretty soon both mother and child are angry.

When this kind of interaction becomes frequent, it may become the pattern of the parent-child relationship. This we call an "angry alliance." Does this sound familiar to you? What experiences of this kind have you had? How have you reacted during them?

"I consider my baby very good but I must confess we do have some 'bad days,' especially if I am expecting company and want to get a little more time in the kitchen. I guess I do hurry a little, and the baby feels the difference and gets fussy. When I simmer down, she responds better."

"That's happened to me a lot, especially if I'm hurrying to get the baby down for a nap so I can keep an appointment. I have a feeling that he just gets fussy in order to keep me with him. I feel myself getting angry, and I begin to wonder: 'Gee, why did I want this baby so much? Life was so simple before he arrived.' Then when I'm away for a while, I miss the baby so much that I can't wait to get back home."

"Most of the days were like that at the beginning. I just hated to be with the baby. Then we got a routine going, and things have been going along pretty well, except for some days. On those days my husband comes home and finds me in tears and the baby crabby. My husband is more patient than I am. He gets us both calmed down."

The Baby's Need for Gratification

Interestingly enough, the parents' needs are the same as the babies', but parents rarely recognize this fact. The adults' central nervous systems work just the same as the babies'. If the parent plans to do something special while the baby is asleep, and the baby interferes with the plan the parent is frustrated. All the messages going up to the brain ("bake a cake," "do the laundry," "read the newspaper," "pay the bills") are stopped by the baby, and the parent has no outlet but anger at the baby because the baby has frustrated the parents' plan.

When the baby has a need for some activity (to touch some forbidden object, put his hands in the cereal, or touch a TV dial), the parent stops him. He is frustrated and persists or cries until the parent diverts the baby's stimulus for activity toward a substitute, acceptable activity. The baby needs a substitute outlet for the stimulus to his central nervous system. His need to complete the planned activity is just the same as his parent's need to carry out his or her plans. The difference is that the baby is an infant. The pathways for postponement in his central nervous system are not yet developed. He needs an immediate outlet; the parent has to find the substitute gratification for him.

The adult, however, should have matured enough so that his or her postponing mechanisms are developed. Thus, the adult, not the baby, is the one who has to postpone gratification of a plan and find an acceptable substitute. A mother can do this, for instance, by comforting and diverting her baby. Sometimes if she relaxes and realizes that she can always carry out her other plans later, the baby relaxes and goes off to sleep. She will find that adaptability pays off in the long run.

Have you ever thought that you and the baby share the same feelings and react in the same way to frustration?

> "No, I never thought that. I find I'm too concerned with how the baby makes me feel and not concerned enough about how the baby feels."

> "Maybe what we are trying to do is make the baby fit in with our own needs rather than trying to meet the baby's needs."

> "Sure, that's it. When I was going to have the baby, everyone said: 'Now just don't let the baby run your life. Get back to your normal routine as soon as you can.' I guess I'm trying to do that, and the baby is too young to be ready for it."

Part of the difficulty that some mothers have with postponing their own gratification may go back to their own childhood and upbringing. It may be that they were brought up with the philosophy that immediate gratification of an infant's need meant "spoiling." So these mothers did not get satisfaction at the appropriate time and are still striving for it. Also, they have been so thoroughly indoctrinated with the idea of not "spoiling" a child that they are having a hard time unlearning that lesson.

Teaching Delay of Gratification

> "That's exactly it. I'm petrified of bringing up a spoiled brat. I'm determined that mine won't be one."

Some mothers think that a baby whose needs have always been met quickly will expect such a reaction all his life and will never be able to tolerate anything but instantaneous gratification. That would be true if we did not also teach the baby to tolerate delay. However, this teaching of delay must come at the appropriate time, when the baby's central nervous system has matured sufficiently. The baby must have had enough satisfactory experience with his environment to trust that his needs will get attention before he can learn to tolerate delay.

> "Well, how does one arrange to have a baby tolerate delay?"

All right, let's take the feeding situation as an example. At first, the baby cries violently when hungry and quiets down when the bottle is thrust into his mouth. That is his first form of gratification. His crying gives the new mother a sense of urgency, and she responds quickly. As he gets older, the baby may whimper a little and can wait a bit before starting to howl. He is maturing, and he is less insistent; he is learning to wait. Later, he may begin to cry for his feeding, hear his mother making certain familiar noises which he has come to associate with the arrival of his food, and quiet down and wait. If she takes too long, or his hunger pains become very strong, he may cry again. The mother can also try to soothe the baby with her voice as she prepares his food. He learns that her soothing words precede the feeding, and that his needs will be met. This is the beginning of postponing gratification. It must come gradually in accordance with the baby's developmental level. Later, when the baby is sitting up in the kitchen and can watch his mother prepare his food, he learns to wait a little longer. Then as the baby becomes more verbal, one can say, "Just a minute, I'm coming," in a friendly assuring manner. As the baby gets older that "minute" can be extended. Each mother learns what her baby's level of tolerance is, and she gradually teaches him to wait a little longer before she satisfies his need.

"How long does it take a baby to get to the stage when he can tolerate delay?"

The timetable for this level of maturity is different for each baby. Some learn early. They have good experience with their parents. They know their parents keep their word, and they trust them. Some babies are apprehensive; they do not develop trust as quickly. This apprehension may be due to their particular endowment, or it may be the result of inconsistent responses on the part of the parents. Some days the parents respond immediately and other days they take a while to respond. It takes these children longer to learn to trust their parents and, consequently, longer to tolerate delay.

"What happens to the baby whose mother does not respond to him when he needs it?"

The baby whose needs have hardly ever been responded to promptly is the one who grows up impatient and unable to wait for gratification. This is the person who can't wait to be served in a restaurant, can't wait in traffic, or can't wait for solutions to problems. In some cases, people who cannot tolerate any delay of gratification become "sitting ducks" for the kinds of doubtful enjoyments that seem to afford a large degree of instant gratification—for example, alcohol or drugs. These people, of course, constitute extreme examples of what happens to the baby whose needs are hardly ever met promptly; there are many degrees of reaction up to that point.

"At what stage do you think our babies are now in their ability to wait for a bottle?"

They are about ready to recognize some of the sounds you make in preparing food for them. If they can see you, they are beginning to know what you are doing. They can be quieted by your voice when you say, "Here comes your lunch," or "I'm getting your bottle," or "Here comes Mommie." They don't exactly understand the words you are saying, but they do understand that food is coming.

Have you noticed your baby behaving in a way that indicates that he is waiting for you or that he understands what is going on?

> "Yes, I think the baby isn't as shrill in her cry, and she seems to be able to give me a warning cry and then wait a little."

> "Mine isn't up to that yet. He shrieks till I get there, and sometimes he can't quiet down right away. He needs a good bit of soothing."

> "Well, mine can wait what seems like a few seconds—maybe even a minute—if I talk to her all the time while I'm on the way over to her. The waiting time is very short, though."

Of course, infants and children have no real sense of time, and a minute may seem very long to them. Adults have to be aware of that. A child does not really learn to wait and postpone, in the sense that adults understand those ideas, until he is verbal, usually around three years of age or later. One of the measures of our maturity is how long we can postpone gratification. One of the first things children are taught in nursery school is taking turns, waiting to get what one wants. Entry into nursery school coincides with the maturational level at which most children develop the ability to learn to wait.

> "Well, I guess adults' expectations are a little out of line. I'll have to explain this at home because everyone gets on me when I say, 'The baby can't wait and must be tended to first.'"

> "Do these babies really know when we are angry with them?"

Yes, they can feel the displeasure of the parent, and it can create the same angry reaction in them as it does in you. If such an "angry alliance" gets to be the pattern of the relationship between parent and child, the seeds have been sown for the development of an individual who responds with anger all the time. A crabby, angry baby may grow into a crabby, angry adult. This is what all parents want to avoid.

Except for those few children who seem to have a genetic endowment for hyper-irritability, most babies respond to patient and consistent attention. It may be harder with those few children who seem to have a genetic disposition for hyper-irritability, but even they can be helped to overcome their innate tendency.

> "If you get into this angry pattern with your child, can it be overcome?"

The longer it goes on, the harder it is to undo. It takes many hours of therapy and great expense to undo what need never have happened if the parents understood their children's developmental needs.

"I've noticed that if I am patient, my baby relaxes, and neither of us gets upset."

"Well, I've had that feeling of frustration once in a while, and my husband has too. I guess both of us want things to go on just as they did before the baby arrived, and we have had trouble adapting. Being able to see what's behind our reaction makes it easier to cope."

We must recognize what is happening. Instead of being childish, ourselves, we must wait that little bit extra and show that we are more grown-up than the baby. The whole process of growing up is developing the ability to delay gratification. We help the baby develop that capacity by teaching him to tolerate more and more delay, according to his maturational level.

"My baby cries as soon as he wakes from a nap. It's happening more and more every day."

He cries when he wakes up because he is hungry, and he wants something to eat. He's trying to tell you that he wants something. There are some babies who want the bottle or breast immediately, just as some people want coffee immediately on waking and others are able to shower and dress first. We all have certain innate tendencies. Each mother has to know how to adapt to her baby's style. She can't expect the baby to adapt to her; the baby is not adequately developed for that. We are not taught enough about child development. We think, "We're going to get married and have children, and the children are going to do just what we want them to do, just like dolls." And, when the babies are very, very tiny, mothers can do just what they want to with them. But as soon as the baby begins to develop and to assert himself, the mother is surprised and disappointed.

"Yes, that is exactly the way I'm beginning to feel. I'm beginning to wonder, 'What happened to my sweet little baby?' He cries, and he's not as quiet as he was. He is not minding. There is something wrong with him."

He is crying only because he can't say: "Mother, please come here. I'm lonesome; play with me," or "I'm hungry," or whatever his message is. Crying is his only way of speaking.

"My baby always cries so loud even when there isn't anything much wrong. Why is that?"

Babies of this age are not yet able to modulate their cry in proportion to their feelings or needs. A mother must remember that the volume of the cry—and some babies cry more lustily than others—is not necessarily in proportion to the need. Loud crying should not be viewed as a crisis or as a fit of anger.

"You think a mother should get to the baby at once anyway, even if she knows that?"

Yes, she should respond to the baby as quickly as she can. But, if she understands the meaning of the cry, she doesn't have to race to the baby with her heart pounding as though a catastrophe had occurred.

"Well, I'm still doing that. I'm almost in a cold sweat till I see that the baby is okay."

Most parents go through that to some degree, but in time they get to know their baby and they become more secure. So does the baby.

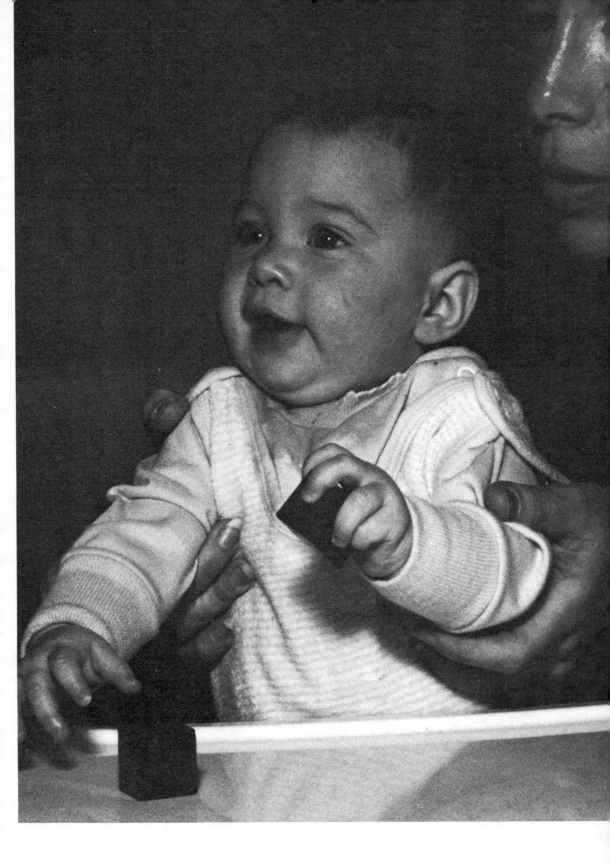

Six-month-old infant holding one block
while reaching for another, as mother looks on.

Chapter Six

Age: 24 to 28 weeks _____

_____**HIGHLIGHTS OF DEVELOPMENT—TWENTY-FOUR WEEKS**

When the baby is lying on his back, he holds his legs up and extended. He is now more likely to roll over on his stomach by himself. When the baby pulls himself to the sitting position (see exercise, page 18), he lifts his head higher and sits much straighter. Most babies should be able to sit propped up for about thirty minutes at a time now; and some babies may enjoy doing it even longer.

When seated in an infant seat or high chair, the baby may now begin to grasp a block or cube in a **palmer grasp** (cupping an object against the palm of the hand and then closing the fingers around it) and will hold it longer. While holding one block or spool, the baby will reach for a second and will also look at a third, if it is presented. This shows the baby's greater awareness of several objects presented at the same time.

Babies will now hold onto a rattle or ring for a long time and will usually bring these objects to their mouths. This kind of oral exploration is of developmental value and should not be discouraged by the parents, unless the object is dirty or dangerous. When the babies drop the rattle or block now, most will look for it momentarily.

Babies should be beginning to make sounds and spontaneous vocalizations in response to parents' conversation. They should respond to loud noises or a bell being rung near their heads by turning towards the sound. (If the baby consistently shows no response to such activity, the parent should consult the baby's physician to make sure there is no hearing deficit and that this lack of response is only due to lack of attention or immaturity. After colds, the baby's ears should be examined to make sure there has been no infection which can cause hearing impairment.)

Many babies of this age now recognize that there is a difference between their parents and strangers. This is age-appropriate "stranger anxiety."

By now, most babies are beginning to grasp their feet; they are, therefore, beginning to become aware of how far their bodies extend. When a mirror is placed in front of the baby, he is likely to smile or vocalize, although he does not yet really recognize the image as himself. At this age, babies are just beginning to be aware of themselves as separate individuals apart from the mother.

COMFORTING

"Tuning In" to the Baby's Needs

We've been talking for a while about mothers' feelings of frustration. Part of this frustration results from the baby's need for comforting, which the baby expresses by crying. If a mother "tunes in" quickly to the baby's need and makes the baby happy, the mother is satisfied and gets a sense of accomplishment. If she can't comfort the baby, then both mother and baby are unhappy and frustrated.

In the early stages of infancy, the babies' needs were simpler. They needed to be fed, changed, burped, put into a more comfortable position, or rocked. If you fed or rocked them, they settled down. Now the babies are older, and their need for comforting is more varied and complex.

Have you noticed that your babies need different kinds of comforting now?

"My baby needs more than just to be picked up. She wants to do something, like look out the window."

Some mothers feel that feeding is the biggest comfort there is. How do you feel about that?

"It depends on what's bothering my baby. Sometimes she's hungry, sometimes she has gas, sometimes I think she's bored. She wants someone to talk to or a little music. There's no one answer."

"There's a special game I play with my baby. I hold his feet and push his legs; he bends his knees until his legs are over his abdomen. This game seems to comfort him a lot. Even if he is angry and I do that, he calms down."

"My baby likes motion. We jog around a bit. Then I put him in the infant seat, and he watches what I'm doing."

You are finding new things that you can do with your babies. It is good that you are finding other diversions besides food. The need to comfort or entertain oneself by eating can get started in one's personality at this early period. Thinking of other diversions for your babies is important to their development and can make caretaking more interesting as well.

Now that the babies are older, they should be spending more time propped up in a sitting position. In this position they can see the world about them instead of just the ceiling and the mobiles over their heads. At first babies will be comforted and satisfied by sitting up alone. As it becomes less novel an experience, they will want something more.

They are also becoming interested in the things around them and are beginning to reach for objects. If they can't reach the object, they cry to have it put in their hands. They may also cry when a toy falls out of sight and become calm again when it is retrieved.

Some of the babies are teething and put things in their mouths to soothe sore gums. Others put things in their mouths to explore them orally. The babies are also at the stage when they may just stare at a toy, looking at it from various angles. The act of holding on to something is satisfying; small dolls and stuffed toys or toys with projections to hold on to are good for this purpose.

Some babies like vocal comforting—being talked to or sung to. Some still need to be held closely and walked or rocked. Others need to be taken outdoors where the air and the variety of sights and sounds keeps them from being restless, sometimes even soothes them to sleep.

Some like squeaky toys or jangling keys or music boxes. Others like toys that produce noise when moved. Babies seem to derive a great deal of satisfaction from moving and controlling such a toy. A cradle gym put up across a crib or playpen can also be very stimulating and satisfying. Here again, the baby's satisfaction is derived from her ability to manipulate the device.

The introduction of these new devices for comforting your baby does not mean that the babies are through with the stage of being comforted by feeding, changing, burping, and rocking. It does mean, however, that something new is often needed. This need for more variety is a sign of progress and shows an advance in development.

> "Sometimes trying to comfort the baby becomes a burden. For instance, he often wakes up crying. Instead of taking the bottle I bring him, we have to walk around a bit or go look in a mirror."

Of course, now the baby's need for comforting is making more of a demand on mother, but discovering new stages in the baby's development also adds interest to mothering. Finding new ways to comfort the baby gives the mother the satisfaction of knowing that she understands her baby's needs. As we have said before, you will not be able to understand and respond perfectly every time. The important thing for the baby is that her parents are available, paying attention, and trying to satisfy her need. This responsiveness increases the sense of trust and attachment, which are still the fundamental issues of personality development.

TOYS AND PLAY

Most of the babies have been given many toys, some of which may now be just right for their age. A brightly colored cradle gym, suspended across the crib or playpen, can be very pleasing to the

Appropriate Toys and Equipment

baby. A playpen is not essential; it is not useful very long and takes up a good deal of space. A blanket can be spread on the floor, and the baby can roll safely on it and reach for toys. A playpen is, however, a safe place to put a baby. A mother can still see the baby, but the baby is out of the mother's way.

A baby who can sit up can be placed in a jump seat or high chair so she is out of mother's way but still in sight. Too often a playpen is used as an isolation unit, and the baby is left unstimulated too long, especially if the child in question is a "quiet baby."

The way all pieces of equipment are used for the baby is important. The main objective should not be to isolate the baby, but to keep her safe, happy, and stimulated. They should also allow for development of motor and learning skills.

What toys does your baby enjoy playing with most now? Have you noticed that your baby is interested in some new kind of toy? What is it?

> "I have one of those balls that have hand grips. She holds on to it and also chews it."

> "My baby plays in her playpen a lot. She can play in it for hours. She has a cradle gym with two yellow rings and a Humpty Dumpty. When she kicks the cradle gym, it makes a sound."

Does she seem to get a sense of achievement out of playing with the cradle gym?

> "Yes, she does. She kicks it and plays with the rings."

I see your baby has a sponge toy. What else does she like to play with, or does she just like to play with the one thing?

> "She also has a doll and an elephant. But the sponge toy is her favorite because she can squeeze it and get it to make a noise."

She likes that because she can make a sound with very little effort. Many toys are hard to squeeze. She can also put it in her mouth and chew it. It is a very satisfying toy for her.

When the babies were little, we gave you a red ring. That's one of the best toys for the baby now. The baby can use it for teething; she can drop it and pick it up; and, if you hang it up, she can pull on it. It can also be attached to the side of the crib or the carriage so the baby can learn to pull it back after dropping it. Babies need little things they can play with and manipulate, and the red ring can be used for a long time.

> "My baby has a little toy with red feet. Every morning when I go in to him, he has the feet in his mouth. The toy keeps him company constantly."

Well, he has already found a way to entertain himself.

> "What about those great big stuffed toys that everyone brings the baby as presents? Some scare my baby. One of them, a red clown, he really likes and looks and looks at."

Sometimes a baby becomes enamored of a large stuffed toy and likes to have it in his crib or playpen. At this age, it is more important for the baby to have small toys he can learn to hold and manipulate. A small rag doll, a squeaky toy with appendages that the baby can tug, poke, squeeze, and put safely in his mouth without having parts of it come off are best.

It is part of the fun of parenting to look for the right toys. Some mothers enjoy making wool or rag dolls themselves or cutting sponges into interesting shapes. Colored plastic measuring spoons make excellent toys. There are many things about the house which are fun for the baby. For example, an empty vaseline jar with safety pins inside makes a satisfying toy for the baby to shake and make a sound which he can control. Make sure, of course, that the lid of the jar is screwed on tight.

> "I've tried that, and it has been more of a success than any expensive toy my baby has. He also loves to play with an old white sock of his father's which I stuffed and embroidered a face on."

THE FIRST STAGE IN DEVELOPING A SENSE OF MASTERY

Now the babies are beginning to reach for things; they often miss what they're after, but by next month they will be more successful because their hand-eye coordination will have improved. Because they need the satisfaction of reaching for an object and getting it, they may need some help from the parent. This satisfaction in being able to reach out their hands and get what they want is the first stage in the development of a sense of mastery. This is a very important developmental step and should be recognized by parents with approving words and gestures.

Parental Satisfaction from the Babies' Responses

By now the tremendous anxiety about feeding, burping, changing, and getting the schedule working should be diminishing. It should be possible to have more fun playing with the baby. The father can share in this. He may even be the one who finds new playthings for the baby or devises new ways in which both parents can enjoy the baby's progress together. Comforting and stimulating aren't just a mother's job.

> "I get a lot of satisfaction from finding the right thing to comfort the baby with, but my husband says I work too hard at that. It doesn't really make that much difference to the baby; if I leave him alone, he will quiet down."

But it does indeed make a lot of difference! By your comforting at this early stage, you are helping the baby develop into a person who has a sense of security and trust in the people and the "world" around him.

A child who does not develop this sense of basic trust can become whining and cranky. He may also become very quiet. A quiet child, often mistaken for a "good child," may be depressed. Perhaps when the baby's father understands this, he will get more satisfaction out of finding ways to comfort the baby himself, and then he will form a closer relationship with his baby. If you both feel you are doing something important, then it isn't viewed as a nuisance. You are helping your child's personality development.

> **"My baby is doing something now that I love: sometimes she will do something and look for my reaction, my approval. She does that naturally, and I get very excited. It makes me feel that I am important to her and that she trusts me and wants my approval."**

Your baby is beginning to look for your approval quite early, and it's very good that you noticed it.

> **"I haven't noticed anything like that yet."**

Each baby develops on a different timetable. Your baby may be doing the same thing soon, or maybe she's doing it already and you haven't noticed. You have to be very, very perceptive to notice a baby's glance for approval at this age because it is quite subtle. Later on, it will be more easily noticed. It is very important to acknowledge this development and to reinforce it.

FATHERS' FEELINGS ABOUT THE BABIES' DEVELOPMENT AND CARE _____

We have not met with the fathers for nearly two months and you have probably noticed many changes in the babies during that period.

> **"You are right. My baby has increased her activity considerably; she is much more interested in moving around and so on."**

And what do you think about that?

> **"I was glad to see it, because I was concerned that she would end up as a halfback for the Giants. She eats so much; but if she exercises, she will gradually reach the right size. She is heavier, but she doesn't seem to be as sluggish."**

Some babies have a tendency to be heavier than others even without eating a great deal. Others remain tiny even if they eat more than most babies. Each baby is unique. Each starts out with certain endowments and an individual maturational timetable. The initially large child may turn out tall and thin, and the thin baby may become heavier as an adult. We can't tell in advance. Usually there is a family pattern, but this pattern is not always a reliable predictor of the future.

"My baby is creeping, but he doesn't sit up. He is mostly doing physical things."

When you say he doesn't sit up, you mean he doesn't pull himself up to sitting? It is too soon for him to be doing this; most babies pull themselves into a sitting position around eight or nine months. However, your baby does maintain a sitting posture when you prop him up and that is all that one should expect at this age.

"I think my baby is stabilizing. She doesn't seem as nervous and insecure as she was. She's calming down. She does have occasional fits when she goes haywire and seems very angry."

I am glad to hear that your baby seems less nervous. You have had a special problem because of her digestive disorders. She may still have periods of abdominal discomfort because of this. A baby like this needs more comforting than others—and much parental patience.

"I don't think that's the problem. She just doesn't know how to behave. She just doesn't respond at times."

Perhaps she is not responding as fast as you would like her to. There is a reason for that. All babies have a basic insecurity. We are all born with a basic anxiety because we don't know what's coming next and whether there will be anybody to take care of our needs. As babies, we are totally helpless. Our infancy and dependence on the parent last very much longer than they do for other animals. Maturity involves the development of a sense of security, and that takes a long time. So, if you expect a great deal from the baby now, you are bound to have disappointments because she can't make those quick responses. Some babies make more demands on their parents than others; it depends on what kind of nervous system they were born with. Some are very easy going; others are more irritable and have a lower frustration tolerance. None of these babies is old enough—that is, their central nervous systems are not well enough developed—to make the instantaneous responses parents would like and expect. For example, you have seen me ring a bell at the side of the baby's head, and you have seen how long it takes for the baby to turn to the sound of the bell. She cannot turn at the fast rate of an older child.

"When do they begin to make that quick response?"

Children do not achieve those smooth, quick responses and reflexes until they are eight or nine years old. It takes a long time for the nerve endings to make all the proper connections in the central nervous system.

"Oh, my goodness, that's a long time."

You are all laughing with surprise. Just how long it takes this kind of maturity of the central nervous system to develop does usually come as a big surprise to most parents.

"Okay. Even if her responses will develop slowly, will she always be querulous?"

That goes away. You help the baby get over this querulous response by soothing her when she needs it, rather than being angry and impatient. It is not easy, but she is so much better that you must have been doing a good job.

"Yes, she is better now. The trust is starting."

Yes, it is, and that is very important. It is a good feeling for both parents and baby.

"My baby's very active; he needs a man right now."

Do you find this unpleasant, or are you pleased with it?

"I'm very pleased, but I can see what a hard time my wife has all day."

It's good that you realize this. Sometimes fathers have no idea how much a mother has to do to take care of a baby, and this sometimes makes mothers feel overburdened. It is good to let her know you understand this.

Do you all feel you are getting to know the babies better? Are you getting a feeling of attachment for them? Are they becoming attached to you?

"I think that the longer you are exposed to the infant, the more you get to know her. That's the case with me. I spend most of my time with the baby on weekends because there is only about half an hour between the time I get home and the time she goes to sleep. I don't want to play too much then because she just gets hyper. Nonetheless, I feel that I know my baby and that she is attached to me. I don't have any yardstick to judge by, but I believe that's the case."

Good! Some fathers don't feel attached to their babies at all because they are not with them very much. Other fathers do have a chance to do a great deal with their babies and enjoy doing it.

Is there any special function you perform for your baby that you especially like doing?

"Yes, I gave her baths before she outgrew the sink. That was something I did regularly. I don't know if she associated it with me or not."

Did you enjoy doing that?

"Yes, I did. Now I give more general assistance: help out with certain feedings, help put her to bed, play with her. Playing is the main thing I do with her."

Playing is an important way to relate to your babies. What kind of games do others play with their babies?

"Mainly 'Boo, Who Are You?' and bouncing her on my lap or lifting her in the air—things that enable me to maintain my mental image of myself."

Another version of that game is "Peekaboo." You know that when you play "Peekaboo" with a baby, you have to remain in view. Just covering one side of your face with your hand momentarily is enough at this stage. If you hide completely, the babies will think you've gone, and they will become upset. When you are both on the bed and you get down to hide, the baby has to be able to see enough of your body to know you are still there.

"I push the carriage and the kiddie car around a lot. We get down on the floor together, and the baby watches TV in bed with us. I feed him in the mornings and at supper time too."

At this age, another game to play is "So Big." You play this game by raising the baby's hands way above her head and saying "So Big." After a couple of months, the babies will follow the parents' demonstration of the game and will raise their own arms above their heads. In the meantime, they enjoy watching the parents do it.

Do any of the fathers have any special duties that you help your wives with, any special part of taking care of the baby that you take responsibility for?

"We trade off on sleeping late on weekends, which we couldn't do when my wife was breast feeding. I get up and give him a bottle on Saturday mornings so that my wife doesn't have to get up. The baby wakes up at six-thirty no matter what time he goes to bed."

"My wife is still breast feeding so it's hard to help in that way. I watch him for a couple of hours while my wife goes out."

Have you been able to arrange your lives so that both of you can go out and leave the baby with somebody?

"No, we don't have anyone to leave her with. We have to take her wherever we go."

"We are lucky. My father-in-law can sit for us now."

"We have neighbors across the hall, and we take care of their child when they go out. They do the same for us, but it's not often."

Finding the right person to leave the baby with is difficult when there are no family members or close friends. Sometimes a student nurse can sit on her night off, or an older teenager who lives nearby. However, it is something that needs to be worked out. You are grownups, and there are some places that you want to go that are not appropriate for the baby. Besides, you do need time off **together** once in a while.

Sometimes, one or the other of the parents feels neglected because of the baby. Sometimes fathers feel that mothers are too wrapped up in the baby and are not paying any attention to their needs. Sometimes dinner is not ready or a shirt is not ironed. The wife may be worn out when the father gets home. Mothers, on the other hand, sometimes complain that fathers are so entranced by their babies that they ignore their wives. They never remember their birthdays, only the babies'.

Are any of you having these feelings?

"To tell the truth, yes. That was the way it seemed to me at first. My wife was only concerned with the baby. But now that I'm getting more involved with the baby myself, I'm not so concerned about how much attention I get. Still, once in a while I'd like to feel I'm special too."

"I still feel my wife spends entirely too much time with the baby. We never have time to ourselves until after the baby is asleep for the night, and by then we are too tired ourselves."

"After my husband gets home neither he nor the baby seems to know I'm around except if they need something."

"I don't mind that. It gives me time to get dinner. Then we put the baby to bed together and have dinner together. However, when I think about it, the baby seems to take up an awful lot more time and needs me more than I ever thought she would. It takes a lot of arranging for us to have time together."

"When will the baby be able to do without so much of my wife's time, our time?"

What you are asking is when can parents expect the baby to be able to separate from them and not need so much attention and contact, so let's discuss that.

FATHERS' FEELINGS ABOUT ATTACHMENT AND SEPARATION _____

The mothers give us the impression that the fathers think that the babies should not still need to be so close to the parents and that the mothers are being too attentive, making the babies used to more attention than they really need. Is this a fair statement of how the fathers' feel?

> "It is a fair statement, as far as I'm concerned. My wife and I are constantly battling about the attention the baby gets. My parents, who come often, also feel that we are, as they put it, too lenient with the baby."

> "No, I have found that either I don't notice the crying as much, or the baby is crying less. She is happier and crying less—and needs less attention."

> "How long does this whole period last? How do you hurry it along?"

The babies need to have their parents available for a long time, and how long this "long time" will last will be different for each baby. Ideally, the parents should not separate from the baby before the baby is ready to separate from the parents. Parents get very annoyed if the baby cries when they go out of the room. Sometimes they scold the baby. But the baby does not know you are there if she cannot see you.

> "But why is that? The baby sees us go into the other room. He must know we are there."

His ability to integrate that experience has not matured in his central nervous system. Those associative tracts require use, experience, and the development of memory before the baby can understand that. This takes time, for some babies not until they are three years old.

That's why the "Peekaboo" game is important. It does two things: It shows the baby that when you disappear, you also come back; and it's the beginning of teaching a baby to be able to be without you, however momentarily.

But the whole process of learning to separate takes a long time. We all know about the babies' physical development—that first they learn to sit up, then to crawl, then to stand, and then to walk. We know that sequence, and we expect the babies to learn to walk in stages. Attachment and separation have a life history too. At first, the babies cannot tell the difference between themselves and the parent or whoever is taking care of them; they really don't know the difference between themselves and another person. Then, they begin to realize that they are separate from the parent. But they still need to be with the parent a great deal. This is the stage the babies are in now.

> "That means you can't leave the baby at all?"

That is not necessarily so. It does mean that the baby needs to get used to another person, the father or another caretaker, and to develop a sense of security with that person too.

PARENT SUBSTITUTES: BABY-SITTERS

If babies have a number of different people taking care of them (such as babies in an institution who have different attendants every eight hours and different caretakers for vacations and days off), the babies can never form the kind of attachment or relationship that will enable them to relate well to other people. That's why we stress the baby's need for a consistent caretaker, whether it is the mother, father or someone else. That doesn't mean that you have to be tied to the baby for three years until the baby can separate, but you should leave the baby for short periods at the beginning and leave her only with someone with whom she is familiar, someone who is a good substitute for the parent.

> **"Once we had an emergency and left the baby with a trained nurse who knew how to take care of babies. But the baby didn't know the nurse and was so weepy and hard to manage when we got back."**

Good parent substitutes are very hard to come by, and you're better off not leaving your baby with somebody who is a poor substitute and not a "mothering" person. By spending time with your baby during these early months, the baby's attachment to you is developing. By now the babies may also be used to the grandparents. Gradually they will get used to other people.

More on Stranger Anxiety

> **"Why do some babies seem to be able to go to other people at first, and then begin to cry at the sight of every stranger?"**

As we have already discussed with the mothers, some babies begin to show stranger anxiety when they are about six or seven months old. That's when they really begin to notice that other people are different from Mama and Papa. Sometimes Grandmother, who was a frequent visitor for the first six months, goes away for a week or two. When she comes back, she's regarded as a stranger. The baby cries, and Grandmother gets very upset. The same thing may happen with an aunt, a family friend who has not seen the baby for a while, or with a new friend. This reaction indicates that the babies have learned to tell the difference between the people who are close to them and those who are not. It shows a new level of development, which should please you but may need to be explained to the relative or friend.

From the way you are all nodding and smiling, I can see that you have all had these experiences. We even have them here in this setting. Most of the babies pass through a period when they suddenly regard me as a stranger. Sometimes they get over it quickly, and other times it takes a week or two. It's a very normal reaction.

"My boss and his wife are coming for dinner next week. The baby was great the last time, but do you suppose he'll pull this 'stranger' bit this time? It will be hard to explain."

I think now that you understand what is going on—that the reaction is a new stage in development—you will not have any difficulty explaining to your boss and his wife. Other people may feel that the baby is badly behaved. The parent has to be the baby's advocate and explain his situation to others. A parent who is sensitive at this stage helps instill basic trust in the baby by not scolding or handing the baby over to a stranger before the baby feels secure or shows an inclination to go to the stranger.

"Well, what happens when parents don't understand or know about all this?"

If the baby doesn't have basic trust in her parents, she won't develop basic trust in other people. That baby will be very difficult and may cry a great deal. If the baby establishes basic trust in the parents, then she looks upon other people with trust. Children are then able to separate from their parents much more easily. The process starts right here and now, and that's why we are talking about it. Just about now you are beginning to feel that you can leave the babies because they are older and should know that you are in the next room. But when you leave them, they don't know if you're coming back. That kind of separation is very difficult for them; many will be three years old before they are able to separate happily.

"Well, what about the present trend of sending babies off to nursery groups earlier and earlier?"

We look upon nursery schools and day-care as being rather difficult for children who are under three years old. You know it is even harder for children to separate from the parent in unfamiliar surroundings. This is quite different from being left at home with a familiar sitter. Some children are able to accomplish this at eighteen months; some not until they are three and a half, but the average age at which this happens is around three years. Then the child can walk away from the parent and stay in another room all by herself and not be upset. If, once in a while, you find a child crying all of a sudden because she doesn't know where you are, that shows that separation anxiety is still present. That's the reason we have to be careful about who takes care of the baby and when the change is introduced. A new caretaker has to be introduced gradually. I don't think parents should be made prisoners to their children, but, at the same time, parents should bear the baby's need in mind.

"Well, what did our parents do? Did they stay with us all the time?"

Some parents did stay with their children; others thought they were "liberated," so they didn't. I recall a common kind of incident years ago. A mother would go marketing and leave her baby sleeping in the carriage outside the store. When she came out, the baby would be screaming and frantic. The baby had awakened and felt deserted, a very traumatic experience for the baby. Some parents didn't realize how the baby felt and would be angry with the baby. Other parents would come out and soothe the baby. Then, as now, the parent's behavior depended upon whether she felt embarrassed because the baby was crying, or whether she was really sensitive to the baby's needs.

It is best to wait for the baby to separate from us rather than to attempt to separate from the baby. The process of separation goes through various stages, and one must handle it differently at each age. It comes up when a mother has to (or wants to) take a job. It comes up again when the parents want to take a vacation, and it comes up when you think the baby is ready to go off to nursery school. We'll discuss separation many times because it is such an important and sensitive topic.

MOTHERS' REACTIONS TO FATHERS' PERCEPTIONS OF THEIR ROLE _____

It was evident from our Fathers' Night meeting that the fathers each have different ways of relating to their children. In our society, infants are cared for mainly by mothers or other female caretakers. The father's involvement has been minimal in the actual care of the baby. His role is mostly to be the provider of food and shelter for the family, and often this role leaves him little time to spend with a baby. In spite of this traditional concept of the father's role, some fathers look forward to coming home to feed, play with, teach, and help the development of a new baby.

In our group this seems true especially now that each baby is more competent, can sit up more, and is beginning to show more of his own personality. Some fathers come home with a desire to help in sterilizing bottles, doing the laundry, even marketing if mother has been unable to get out. This is probably the ideal father's response from the mother's point of view. That way, the mother can share the joys of child rearing as well as the more tedious tasks with the father. Other fathers may view their role differently.

How does your husband view his role now that there is a baby in the family? Does he seem to have time to be a parent? Is the father's role in child raising causing any conflict between the parents?

> **"My husband seems to make time for the baby. He was so anxious for a baby. He seems to come home only to see the baby. Sometimes he forgets to greet me, but I don't mind. The baby needs his attention too."**

> **"My husband always calls to see if I've had time to market and if he can bring anything home. That's a big help."**

"In our case the situation's different. My husband works very late, and the baby is asleep when he gets home. The only time he has with the baby is early in the morning. Sometimes he gives the baby her first bottle."

"My husband works so hard at his job. He feels that's his part and it's enough. All the rest he leaves to me. He expects me to do everything, just as I did before the baby came."

"My husband says he can't handle babies. He feels that when the baby is five, he will start to become more involved."

There are fathers who can't participate in caretaking and playing with their children. They see their role solely as providers and the mother's duty as child rearing. In addition, some want their wives to greet them at the door with a smile and with a well-prepared dinner ready on a beautifully-set table. Even though there is a new baby in the household, they want everything just as it was before the baby was born. They cannot understand why their wives cannot function in the same way they used to. In fact, these men are often jealous of the attention that the baby gets and see a well-prepared dinner and neat house as attention to themselves. Sometimes these fathers, remembering usually their teenage years, recall homes in which their own mothers performed these almost-superhuman tasks, and they expect the same of their wives. Others come from homes where their mothers had a great deal of help and could wait on their fathers, even though there were small children in the family. This situation is not the usual one in our society now, but the memory of it is still there.

"My husband couldn't care less if he comes home and finds the house in a mess and dinner not ready. He would just as soon go out and get us a Chinese dinner. It makes me feel a little guilty, but I know that I will do better when I have the baby more settled. My husband comes from a family that's very easygoing."

"My husband is not like that; his situation is entirely different. He has two jobs, and I have to be sure that his dinner is ready when he gets home at five o'clock so that he can eat it quickly and go to his other job. He would be very angry if the dinner wasn't ready, and I understand that; but it does put a lot of pressure on me just around dinner time when the baby begins to act up. But my husband is helpful too because he does the marketing on his way home. The only time he can play with the baby is for a little while before he eats."

Yes, just around dinner time is when most babies do begin to "act up." Now that they are able to sit up a little in an infant seat or high chair, they sometimes quiet down when they are watching you in the kitchen and you talk to them as you work. Then they don't have the sense of rejection. When you are not tense about the situation, they relax too. Babies are very sensitive to mothers' tensions. Some mothers resort to backpacks. In that way, their hands are free, but the baby is with them and doesn't feel isolated.

> "My husband came from a family where there was a great deal of help, and he expects everything to run just as smoothly in our family. His family was very autocratic, and that is the way that he understands child rearing. What can I do about that because that is not the way I want the baby to be brought up?"

Different parental attitudes toward child rearing can be a source of much friction. We hope these sessions will be of some help to you both. Sometimes the conflict is difficult to resolve, and one must have special professional help with it.

It is important for both parents to try to talk objectively about their expectations of each other, now that there is a new baby in the household. Parental roles should have been discussed and settled before the baby came, but even if they had been, no parent really understands beforehand how much time and attention the baby will need or how difficult it becomes to take care of the baby and still do the household chores. Usually, the parents have to agree on a new set of priorities once the baby has arrived and they discover just how complicated meeting the demands of both baby and household can become.

There are also parents who have difficulty relating to infants but are able to assume the parental role more easily when the child is older and more verbal. When this is the case, it is difficult for the caretaking parent. It creates an added burden to try to explain and show off the baby's developmental achievements. Some parents, especially mothers, resent this attitude, and some of this resentment is reflected in their treatment of the baby. Some of the pleasure to be gained by sharing with the other parent is lacking. However, if the mother understands her husband's make-up (or vice versa), other helping roles can be found. It is also likely that a reluctant father will pick up some of the mother's enthusiasm for the baby's achievements. Most babies enjoy playing with their fathers, and this enjoyment usually becomes mutual, even before the baby is talking.

> "We can't wait until the time when the baby grows up and talks and does more things with us. We'll be more 'tuned-in' then. We are both too old to cope with an infant."

> "My husband is the patient one. He loves babies. Though I am enjoying the baby now, I'll be happier when she is older and can talk."

Most of us develop our attitudes toward parental roles by the examples we have had as we grew up in our own families. There are some fathers who see their role as managing the family situation. Those men were brought up in an autocratic environment, and they are passing on that heritage in their own families. If such a man happens to marry a woman whose past experience has been the same, she will be able to cope with this situation. If, on the other hand, the mother comes from a less autocratic family, the situation can be painful. Adjustments will have to be made on both sides, but the problem is not insurmountable.

"That sounds like us. By being patient and trying to under-stand, we are managing to cope. We did need help. Talking here helps, and then we go over things again ourselves."

There are fathers who are much more "motherly" than some mothers. The mother may regard the father as much too fussy, much too anxious about the baby. She may feel that he interferes too much in her role as a mother and gives her the feeling that she is not taking good care of the baby. He is the one who jumps up first and attends to the baby during the night. Maybe this is just the father's nature to be anxious; maybe his father behaved in this way. Some fathers regard their wives as inefficient, so they try to take charge of the household. If fathers, however, do things for the baby naturally and uncritically, it is very helpful; but if they are critical, then they can cause friction and undermine the mother's self-esteem.

"My husband is extremely fussy. He never seems to be happy with the way I do things, but he doesn't think that it is his role to help. He comes home at night with his work, and right after dinner he sits down to do it. If I need some help with the baby, he acts as though I were imposing on him."

That attitude must seem unreasonable to you, and I can understand your feeling. But let's look at the matter from the father's point of view. If a father still has the pressure of work to do at night, one can perhaps understand how he may find it trivial and annoying to be asked to mind the baby, so that mother can get clean diapers from the laundry room. He may think, "Well, she's been home all day; she could have arranged to have her laundry ready for the night." The father is annoyed because he feels the mother is adding to the pressures on him.

But this is a situation that can be worked out. This same father may be happy to play with the baby when he is ready. Perhaps he could be encouraged to play with his child for a few minutes before dinner. That may be the moment for the mother to make a quick trip to the laundry room.

"Oh yes, on his own time my husband plays with the baby and shows her things, but he doesn't regard helping me as part of his role."

Indeed, in most cases, it takes a lot of insight to find a successful way to interrupt someone who is absorbed in something. You have to learn what things antagonize the other person, and just how to behave to get the desired response.

"What about the father who feels he has to have his exercise and outings, just as he used to before the baby came?"

There are some fathers who stay little boys themselves, who feel that they should not be expected to assume the responsibilities of being fathers. They want to go on with their bowling, tennis, or sailing without making any accommodation for the fact that there is a new baby in the house. This can be very annoying to mothers who feel that they need more help and expect fathers to share the responsibility of child rearing.

On the other hand, it is necessary for most of us to have some exercise or playtime which is relaxing and healthy. As men's health is statistically more vulnerable, it is probably best that their athletic activities be continued on a regular basis as a health measure. Perhaps men unconsciously feel the need for this exercise as a way to preserve their health, rather than as a way to get out of chores. Women may have to take a broader view of their husbands' needs. By the same token, mothers also need to arrange for some free time when they can do something that is relaxing for them. As a matter of fact, both parents come back to their parenting roles more able to cope with and enjoy the baby when they have some time for themselves.

"That helps me understand my husband's point of view. I guess I should get out more myself."

Perhaps we need to take a more objective view of what is going on. Few parents, whatever their antecedents or character structures, are unconcerned about their children, but each individual has a different way of showing this concern. All of us have preconceived notions of what to expect from a baby and what to do for a baby. No one realizes how time-consuming child rearing is. Most of us do not know what the timetable for the baby's development is and what the baby is going to need at each stage of development. As parents learn this together, and we hope we are helping you do that in these sessions, they begin to get a great deal of pleasure in seeing the development of their baby. With knowledge and understanding, parents can enhance their baby's development.

Being a good parent takes patience, consistency, knowledge, and, above all, a sense of humor. Sometimes fathers who spend little time with their children do not consider things that mothers worry about as very serious. They sometimes joke about them or dismiss them as trivial. For some mothers this is a great affront. They say, "Well, you haven't been with him all day." While this is true, the father has been putting up at work with a great many things that he has found very trying. When he discusses these problems with

his wife, she looks at them differently and often makes some suggestions. To each, the other's job may seem easier; for each the
other's perspective can often be helpful.

ABILITY OF MOTHERS TO ADAPT TO ADVANCES IN BABIES' EXPLORATORY BEHAVIOR

Just as mothers have begun to feel comfortable about their babies'
schedules and understand their behavior and needs, the babies go
on to a new level of development. The new level at this age consists
mainly of increased interest in exploration. The babies are now
beginning to reach for things. They like to push things over the sides
of their high chairs, and they are able to hold something in each
hand. They sometimes grab hold of things that they shouldn't touch,
such as the draperies, plants, or cups of hot coffee. This new exploratory behavior is also a sign of motor development and improved
eye-hand coordination, which needs to be dealt with appropriately
and not considered a nuisance.

The parents should make sure that the baby has small things that she
can hold in her hand and explore by looking at them, by throwing
them down, by tasting them. When she reaches for the thing that
she should not have, the baby should be taken away and given
something that she can hold so that her exploratory needs are met.
When the baby is able to hold two small objects, one in each hand
and look from one to the other, she feels a sense of mastery. This
activity should be recognized by the parent with some verbal comment such as "Good" or "Nice."

It is important that these early attempts at mastery be recognized
because recognition helps the baby develop initiative and self-
esteem. Parents should, therefore, get into the habit of reinforcing
an infant's sense of mastery by recognizing the achievements no
matter how small they may seem. While this advancement in
development is harder on the parents, who must keep a closer
watch on the baby, it should also give them pleasure. It is satisfying
to see the smile of a baby who has reached out and grasped
something that she wanted. If the parent then smiles and vocalizes
something pleasant, the baby recognizes the approval and
responds positively.

Have you noticed any of these developments in your baby? How
have you been responding to them?

> "I have been noticing that I am more irritable with the baby. I
> guess I got used to having him sleep, and now he wants to
> play more. When I carry him around, he gets hold of the
> venetian blind cord or a plant. It has been making me angry. I
> think it is a nuisance—not an advance."

I really think it helps parents to understand that this reaching and
grabbing is an advance in development and a necessary step in

maturation. Give the babies something to get hold of that won't be dangerous or annoying, so that they can use this newly developed behavior to advantage. From now on, child rearing will require more creative thinking and stimulation on the parents' part. It will demand more thought, but most parents will find that this produces more fun for them.

> **"My baby reaches out and pulls my hair when I am feeding him. Sometimes that hurts."**

Babies often do reach for their mothers' hair; it is especially tempting to reach out and touch long hair. The babies do not know that they are hurting you. The baby should be allowed to explore his mother's hair and touch her face; this is how he gets to know who she is and what she looks and feels like. The mother can hold her hair so that the baby just gets the ends and pulls against her hand instead of against the hair in the scalp. Sometimes a baby uses a patting gesture to explore the mother's hair or face, and the mother likes this.

As parents, we must tolerate a few patterns of behavior that we don't particularly like because they fulfill a baby's need for development. Some of us may tolerate some of these better than others do. The important thing is to allow as much exploratory behavior as possible and safe.

Games: The Need for Appropriate Challenge and Achievement

This new level of development makes new kinds of games possible. Parents can hold out toys that the baby can reach for and get hold of. It is important for the child to get a sense of achievement and parental approval. The toy should, therefore, be held so that the baby has to make a little effort to get it, but not so far away that the baby cannot reach it and gives up the effort. It is also important for cradle gyms and other such toys to be placed in a position that is conducive to appropriate challenge and achievement rather than to frustration. The baby will also enjoy holding a dumbbell-shaped rattle in his hand and shaking it while holding something else, such as a block, in the other hand. The baby enjoys the achievement of making noise by shaking or banging. Parents should take pleasure in this achievement as well and let the baby know they are pleased. To the adult the banging may be an unpleasant sound, but to the baby it is a great joy and achievement. Sometimes children make an unexpectedly loud sound with their toys and frighten themselves. Then they need to be soothed. Sometimes another object can be substituted, or a towel or diaper placed on the surface the baby is hitting to deaden the sound.

Babies of this age also enjoy the tinkling sound of a bell, which they are now able to grasp and bang but not actually ring in the normal sense of that word.

It is good to have a time each day in which either father or mother or both participate in this kind of play with the baby. This activity is fun for parents and also important for the babies' sense of achievement.

"Our baby is starting to do these things. Now my husband, who had thought that the baby was just a lump and a chore, gets real pleasure in sitting by him and playing with him while I get supper."

For babies, play is really learning. It is through play experiences that they learn most about the world around them. How do you feel about it when the baby drops something on the floor? We have talked before about how tiresome this was to many of you. Does it help at all to understand that the baby is exploring space?

"Yes, it does. I've tried to do what you said. I say 'Down' when the toy falls and 'Up' when I pick it up. Yesterday she said 'Uh, Uh.' I like to think she was trying to say 'Up.'"

She probably was trying to say "Up." Eventually the babies will learn these two words and the concepts that go with them. You are really teaching through play, and, as we have said before, the activity can always be changed when the parent gets tired. There's no need to get a backache!

"I understand now that this kind of play is important, but my mother tells me that it's ridiculous. She thinks that I should teach the baby not to throw her toys on the floor by letting them stay there."

It's hard to disagree with a grandmother, but sometimes it has to be done. We understand now that this exploratory behavior is important to healthy cognitive development. Research experiments have shown that this exploration becomes the stimulus for learning. If babies are thwarted at this age, they lose interest in exploration now and in learning later on in life. Therefore, what seems like a nuisance to parents now is really the cornerstone of learning and intellectual growth. That is why we encourage you to enhance the baby's exploratory behavior. Perhaps if this were explained to the grandmother, she would understand our point of view.

___VOCALIZATION: THE NEED FOR REINFORCEMENT BY BOTH PARENTS

At this time, in addition to greater development of manual ability, there is more vocalization. The baby is making more babbling sounds like "ah-ah," "mah-mah," or "dah-dah." The parents should repeat these babbling sounds so that the baby realizes the parents are pleased. This approval encourages the baby to try again. When he makes a sound and hears it repeated by the parent, he begins to have a sense of verbal communication because **his** sounds mean something to the parents. If the parent speaks to the baby so that he can pick out the sounds, the baby may try to make other sounds, too; this is the beginning of conversation. It is important also to speak with modulation in tone and rhythm. While the baby may not understand anything of what is said, he feels the pleasant tone of the parent's voice and has the sense of being attended to and recognized. Very often he will smile and gurgle in response to parental speech.

This kind of vocalizing back and forth should be done many times during the day. The mother can call to the baby from across the room, but sometimes she should be closer to the baby so that he can see her mouth move, meet her eyes, and respond to her smile. This activity is fun for fathers, too, and they should be encouraged to participate in it. Babies are very sensitive to sound, and they can tell by the tone of voice whether the parent is pleased or displeased. Sometimes a loud voice can make them cry. Parents have to be sensitive to this and learn how to talk to their babies.

> **"You talk about having a conversation with the baby. When my friends hear me talking to the baby, they think I am silly because the baby can't understand me, and they make me feel self-conscious."**

We know now from research that the babies who are talked to and stimulated by speech are the ones who speak better and perhaps earlier. Speech is something that has to be taught. If a child were never spoken to, he could make sounds, but he would not learn to speak a language. The earlier one begins to stimulate a child with speech, the better it is for the baby; it doesn't matter if the baby understands the communication or not. Research has shown that babies babble in the same sounds in all cultures, but by six months they begin to make only the sounds of the language they hear around them. Communication through speech is not only necessary in itself but also as the foundation for learning to read. Children with limited vocabularies—and limited experience in verbal communication—have greater difficulty mastering reading and written communication.

> **"After I say something, my baby looks at me for a long time, and then I see his mouth curl up as he tries to make sounds. Sometimes he does, and we smile at each other. It is great fun. Sometimes when I am in the corner of the room and I talk to him, I can see his arms and legs wave, and sometimes he makes a sound or two."**

This is just what we are talking about; that is the kind of stimulation we think the baby ought to be getting.

> **"My husband is home very rarely, and he has a big, booming voice. Sometimes the baby cries when he talks to her, and that upsets him, of course."**

That is upsetting, but if you can explain to your husband that the baby is sensitive to sound, he will learn to use a softer tone with her.

As she gets more used to him, she will then not be frightened by his usual voice. She needs to get better acquainted with her father and to develop a sense of trust in him. If a father is away for long periods of time, it is normal for the baby to be apprehensive. The father should be reassured that he is not doing anything wrong; the baby simply needs to get used to him.

"In our family it is entirely different. The baby sometimes responds to me when I talk, but she responds much more to Daddy when he comes home. This makes me quite jealous. I talk to the baby all the time."

Sometimes it's necessary to just say a little bit to the baby and give the baby a chance to talk back. Some mothers talk to their babies all the time; they talk at them without allowing the baby a chance to reply. Maybe this is what you were doing in your anxiety to get the baby to talk.

"That may be so; I'll have to see if I do that."

"I have some of the same feelings. The baby responds more to my husband, whom he sees so little, while I'm home with the baby all day breaking my neck to take care of him."

It's natural for a mother to want her baby to respond to her and to feel a little left out if she senses that the baby responds more to the father. Really, it is just a different response, not a better one. The father hasn't been there all day, so he brings some novelty and new stimulation to the scene. This is really a good thing because a baby needs to be attached to both parents, but the baby should be allowed to respond to each in his own way.

Some babies take longer to respond than others. Each baby has his own timetable. All the babies will develop these abilities but at different times. It is our job to understand that timetable. When we do, it is very satisfying to both parent and baby.

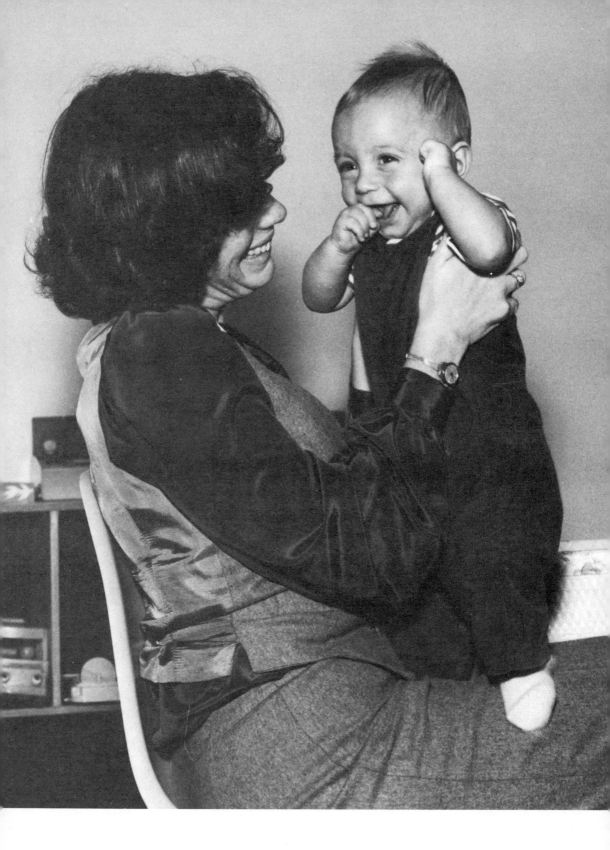

Seven-month-old baby
enjoys bouncing on mother's lap.

Chapter Seven

Age: 28 to 32 weeks _____

When the baby pulls himself up from the supine position (holding onto the parent's hands), he is now able to maintain a sitting posture briefly by leaning forward. When placed in a sitting position, the baby may not need as much propping and can sit for longer. In this posture, he can begin to take solid foods more easily.

When held in a standing position, the baby now has the ability to bounce a little. While fun for parents and child, this activity should not be overdone because babies should not stand until they can pull to a standing position by themselves. Some may be doing this on their own when on their parent's lap which shows physical readiness for standing.

At this age, the increasing competence of the baby's hands is noticeable. Most babies now use a **palmer grasp**. They can grasp objects like a bell by the handle with one hand and bang it or shake a rattle. The baby can also hold a block and put it in her mouth while holding a second block in the other hand. She may even study the blocks a moment. This ability to hold two things at one time—more than momentarily—is a big developmental advance.

The baby may even transfer an object from one hand to the other. The baby's use of his hands should be encouraged and should be part of playtime—i.e., handing a small block or spool to the baby and recognizing his achievement of holding two blocks or transferring a spool from one hand to the other. Not all babies will be able to do this at the beginning of the seventh month, but they should reach this stage by the end of the month. When the red ring is dangled beyond the baby's reach, he may try to grasp it. If he does not succeed, he will probably give up trying. Parents can stimulate these developments by engaging the baby in play with small blocks and the ring.

Vocalization is now progressing from the "mm-mm" sound in crying to babbling sound like "ah-ah," "mah-mah," "dah-dah." Parents should listen for these sounds and repeat them to the baby. This is another area for playful interaction that stimulates speech and provides fun for the parent and child.

The baby may reach out and pat his image in the mirror. This is always a fun experience for baby and parents, though the baby does not yet recognize himself. The parent can say, "That's baby," or say the infant's name. Eventually, the baby will get to know his name and associate it with his image.

DEVELOPMENT IN RELATION TO FEEDING

Exploration with the Hands

Now that the babies are taking semisolids and sitting up for their feedings, they are beginning to use their hands to intercept the spoon. For some mothers this poses a problem or becomes a nuisance because it delays the feeding. Reaching for the spoon is normal behavior and is part of exploration. If it impedes the feeding, it is sometimes helpful to give the baby something else to hold in his hands such as a bottle cap or even another spoon to play with.

How do you feel about the baby doing this? How do you deal with it?

"My baby is always putting his hands in his food, mooshing it around, and making a mess. He makes me very angry at feeding time. What should I do?"

Well, you can see from what I have just said that exploration of food with the hands is a normal part of a baby's development. If it bothers you, hold the dish away from the baby so that he cannot touch it and give him something else to hold. If he still reaches for the food, help him to fill the spoon and get it to his mouth. A few babies may be ready for this. It may simply satisfy him to be able to experience this once or twice, and then he will gladly go back to banging the spoon or block on his high chair tray. The important thing is not to get upset or angry. Try to use each new stage of exploratory development constructively according to the baby's ability.

"When can babies begin to feed themselves?"

Some babies, even at this age, can assist the feeding by putting their hands around the spoon, which is guided to the mouth by the mother's hand. In this way, early self-feeding may be started with the infants who are ready for it. Each mother can find out on her own whether her baby is ready. No matter what technique is employed, the feeding should not become a battle between mother and child. The atmosphere at feeding time is much more important at this period than the quantity of food consumed. In the long run, the food consumption will be enhanced by a pleasant atmosphere at mealtime. Eating will become an enjoyable experience for the baby. He will not begin to use food to establish his autonomy. Eating problems can have their inception at this very early age.

"If I let the baby help me feed him, it will take forever."

It may seem forever, but actually it will only take a few minutes longer. The baby may then learn to feed himself early, and you will have more free time in the long run. Really, feeding time should be a relaxed, enjoyable period. It should not be rushed.

"I just can't stand the mess the baby makes when he eats. I am sorry, I know I am wrong, but I just can't stand it."

Mothers are often annoyed by the messiness caused by the child's attempts to grasp the spoon or food. Messiness, however, is a normal part of infant feeding; that is why we have bibs. It is not necessary that every drop should get into the child's mouth or that the child's mouth should be wiped after each insertion of the food. This is very annoying to the baby. A baby's mouth should be wiped at the **end** of the feeding.

"These are some of the things that are so hard to get used to."

There are some things about raising babies that are more difficult for parents to do than others. One must bear in mind how the baby feels about it. You seem to be concerned only with how **you** feel about it. Would you think it pleasant to have your mouth firmly wiped after each mouthful, to have your hands constrained while you were eating? It is important to try to understand how the baby feels and how things appear to the baby. Then it is possible for adults to modify some of their thinking.

Nutritional Value of Different Solid Foods

Babies often show a preference for certain foods and refuse others. Some mothers are very upset when the baby refuses vegetables that the pediatrician has recommended. Some babies prefer fruit to vegetables, and some prefer vegetables to fruit. These foods are really interchangeable in their nutritional value, and it makes very little difference which is eaten. Other mothers become very upset if the baby will only take one kind of cereal. Some babies, now or perhaps a little later, will prefer to pick up dry cereal in their hands and feed themselves. Some babies prefer chicken to meat; others do not like either chicken or meat. Some like liver; some do not. Some like the commercial mixtures of meat, vegetables, and cereal; other babies prefer the single varieties. Some prefer food that is ground up and prepared by the mother herself. Some babies like cottage cheese, which is a good protein substitute if they do not like meat. The important thing is for the mother not to get tense and anxious about the variety and the quantity of solid food consumed at this period. As we have said before, the babies' main nutrition is still derived from milk; they do not need a wide assortment of food. What the baby is learning at this time is how to take solid foods from a spoon and to get pleasure in this achievement.

How do you feel you are getting along in helping the babies learn to eat food from a spoon?

"My baby takes his milk well, but he only takes a very small amount of cereal and a few mouthfuls of fruit. Then he turns his head away and doesn't want any more. What should I do? My mother says I must make him eat, or else he will never be a good eater."

This is your mother's point of view; maybe this is what she learned when she was bringing you up. It is our view, based on recent research, that whatever the baby takes, and takes willingly, is fine. He probably takes just what he needs.

As we have said, a baby's main nutrition still comes from his milk. If he is forced to eat, then he will resist even more, and a real feeding problem will be created. Feeding should not become a battleground between parent and child.

"If a baby is allowed to eat only what she wants to eat, will she ever learn to eat other foods?"

She will learn to eat other foods, but in her own time. Perhaps you are presenting foods that she doesn't particularly like now, but that doesn't mean she won't like them later. However, if the foods are forced on the baby now, she may despise them for life. There are many children who grow up liking very few foods until they are able to make their own choices. If they are healthy, and if no issue is made of their eating, they will turn out to be good eaters. I think all of us can think of a food that our parents tried to make us eat. They thought it was good for us or that it was good discipline to make us eat it even if we didn't like it. Some of us still don't like that food. What we are trying to do is prevent the child from developing that kind of attitude about food.

"I still remember the spinach scenes—no spinach, no dessert. I vowed I'd never do that."

"Won't the babies get anemia if they only drink milk?"

That used to be common before babies were given other foods in the first year. For those few infants who refuse solids, the baby's doctor can prescribe iron supplements and vitamins. That is a fairly unusual situation. We are talking about the gradual introduction of solid food and not forcing the baby to eat the foods he doesn't happen to like at first. We are stressing keeping the feeding period a pleasurable time and not making it a contest between parent and child.

"I don't want my baby to get too fat. If you let a baby have just what he wants all the time, won't food become the main interest in his life?"

If the parents only show approval when the baby eats his food, then he may indeed eat more to get approval. We are not advocating overdoing the approval if the child eats. Also, we are not recommending that a child be forced to eat something that he doesn't like. The parents have to respond to each stage or phase of development in an appropriate way.

CHANGES IN THE BABY'S SCHEDULE AND THEIR SIGNIFICANCE

Most of the babies are getting onto a schedule, and mothers are getting used to the schedule. Then suddenly, the babies seem to go off schedule and seemingly inexplicable changes in routine occur. The baby who had been sleeping through the night now wakes once or twice. The baby who had been taking two-hour naps suddenly wakes after half an hour. Such changes are usually very disconcerting. At first, the mother may be angry because the change in routine interferes with her plans, or she may be alarmed and decide that she is failing, that all of her good work has been for naught. However, if the mother thinks the situation over, she will find that there is usually a reason for this change in schedule.

"What makes these changes? I think the baby and I are going through such a period now."

There are many causes for sudden changes in a baby's routine. Such changes occur most often when the baby has been taken on a visit, or when there are new people in the house. Sometimes such a change means that a tooth or an illness is coming. Perhaps the mother herself is under some stress and is unconsciously conveying that to the baby. Perhaps the baby is being overstimulated prior to a nap time or bedtime; perhaps the baby has arrived at a new stage and requires less sleep. As the length of the day changes with the seasons, there may also be changes in the babies' biological clock in response.

Sometimes a baby who has been eating well will suddenly manifest little interest in food. This is not occasion for alarm but for an assessment of the situation. Perhaps the baby has become tired of the menu. Perhaps the mother is a little hurried when she's feeding her.

Have any of your babies been changing their schedules? Has this bothered you? What have you done to help yourselves?

"You just put your finger on what is bothering me. I had my baby on what seemed like a comfortable schedule for us. Then he started cutting teeth, and now he wakes at night. I don't know whether to go and comfort him or let him cry it out, so he will know that he has to sleep at night. Some people tell me if I go into him when he cries, it will set up a bad habit and I'll never get him to sleep all night again."

Waking in the night happens very often during teething. The baby cries because he is in pain. He may have clamped down on a painfully swollen gum. He needs to be soothed. When you go to him, he learns that you are reliable and will try to help him. That supports the baby's basic trust. At the same time, you are meeting his physical need by rubbing his gums, giving him something to bite on, or applying some medication if your doctor has advised it. A baby who has once established good sleeping patterns will return to them.

> "The same thing happened to me when our baby had a cold. He would wake when his nose was stuffy and he couldn't breathe. I went to him and wiped his nose, gave him some water to drink, and put the vaporizer on. When he was better, he gradually went back to his regular sleeping pattern."

> "We've had trouble with eating. The baby was always a good eater, but now she takes some feedings better than others. What should I do?"

If you do not try to force your baby to eat, she will eat well again when she is ready. She is passing through a phase of not being as hungry as before. Perhaps you have conveyed a bit of your anxiety to her, thus adding to her unwillingness to eat. Food should not be made a cause for conflict. If her nutrition really suffers, your pediatrician will be able to tell you what supplements she may need. But such supplements are rarely needed.

> "My baby used to take two long naps during the day, and I looked forward to that because then I could get my work done, or rest, or read. Now he takes a long morning nap but a very short afternoon nap. Is that going to go on?"

We have to remember that the babies are getting older, and that they do not now require as much sleep as they used to. This varies with each child, of course. Some will still need two long naps; some will drop the morning nap and continue with a long afternoon nap, or vice versa. Each mother has to adapt to her own baby's needs. Actually, the longer period of being awake allows more time for play and interaction with the parents. Now that they can sit propped up in their carriages for a longer time, they can be more stimulated by the sights around them. When they get tired, they can be put down flat for a nap. When the babies are taken out in the carriages, you can do your marketing and at the same time point out to the baby items of interest such as a car, a dog, another baby. These can be fun times, a growing amount of time to be enjoyed and used profitably.

> "I thought my baby was changing his sleep time when we came back from a week's vacation. He was at Grandma's and had a great deal of stimulation, but after a few days at home alone with me, he soon went back to his old pattern."

We can see from what has been said that most of these changes in patterns are temporary, but some signify a change in level of development. Now that the babies are beginning to move to new levels of competence, mothers need to adapt to these changes just when they have become comfortable with the previous patterns.

_____ INDIVIDUAL DIFFERENCES IN MOTHERS' ENJOYMENT OF BABIES

Mothers usually disagree about which phases of mothering give them most pleasure. Some mothers have always looked forward to dressing the baby in pretty clothes and consider that the most pleasant part of mothering. Others are more satisfied if the baby takes her feedings well; this is especially true of nursing mothers. Still others enjoy bathing the baby; some even teach their babies the rudiments of swimming during bath time. Others find each new exploratory advance very exciting and try to anticipate what is coming next. They proudly relate each one of the baby's exploratory achievements; they wait for the fathers to come home to show off the baby's achievements. Other mothers are most interested in the baby's speech development and make special efforts to get communication going and to help the baby make understandable sounds. Mothers can derive pleasure from progress in any one of these areas, but it is especially nice to be able to enjoy your baby in more than one way. Your pleasure communicates itself to the babies and enhances their self-esteem and sense of well-being.

What phase of taking care of your baby do you like best?

> "I had to laugh when you said that some mothers only thought about dressing a baby up in pretty clothes, because that's the way I visualized taking care of a baby. I didn't know there were such things as burping, bathing, cleaning up dirty diapers, entertaining and amusing a baby. I've learned a lot, and I now find that I am excited by other things. As a matter of fact, I am beginning to enjoy all of the things that I do for the baby. Does that mean I am not discriminating enough?"

On the contrary, it would seem that you are learning how to enjoy all phases of mothering.

> "I am not like that. I really like taking the baby out all dressed up and having people say, 'Oh, what a pretty baby.' "

That's a very normal attitude; there's nothing wrong with it. That's why we pointed out that different mothers get pleasure out of different aspects of baby care.

> "I guess my husband and I get most excited when the baby jumps up and down on our laps. You pointed out that the babies are able to hold a little of their weight now and support it, but my baby seems to be ready to stand up and climb all

over me. She doesn't want to sit down. Should I encourage this?"

If the baby pulls herself up, you should not stop her, but you should not encourage it. This is something that the baby will develop on her own. You should, however, encourage her to play with small objects, such as a rattle or block. She will learn to stand on her own as her central nervous system develops. Fine motor coordination will not develop, however, if she is not encouraged to hold and manipulate small objects. She cannot do this on her own or without her parents' assistance.

"Perhaps we are so pleased with this stage of development because we see it as a preliminary to walking, and we are anxious for her to walk—to be more active."

You and your husband are active, athletic people, so you are pleased that the baby is becoming more like you. Just remember that she will learn to walk when she is ready, and that she should be allowed to achieve this on her own maturational timetable. You are lucky that your baby's natural endowments seem to be matching yours.

"I can't wait for the baby to talk. That seems to me the most important part of being a parent, and each time she makes a noise that sounds like something, I get very excited. Do you think that I could be overstimulating her speech?"

If you talk to her all the time and are never quiet so that she can reply, you may be hindering her speech development. However, if you imitate her sounds and give her a chance to respond with another sound, then you are stimulating the development. It is very good to talk to the baby as you dress her, feed her, and do your chores, but stop every once in a while to see if she will make some kind of reply to you.

"That's really what I do, and it is such fun!"

Several of you have expressed enjoyment of different aspects or phases of your babies' development. You probably recognize that the baby is beginning to exhibit traits that suit aspects of your own personalities. This is very nice. It is important to remember, however, that each baby is an individual, not just a duplicate of the mother or the father. Some aspects of the baby's personality may be very different and should be appreciated and respected. When there is a big difference, it can cause difficulties. An active, noisy toddler can be upsetting to a reflective, quiet mother; a shy, quiet baby can be a puzzle to a hearty, outgoing father. Differences or similarities in the temperaments of parents and children will become more apparent as the children get older. For that reason, we will talk more about the topic later. For now, it is good to recognize that different parents appreciate and enjoy different aspects of their baby's development. Everyone does not have to be the same.

We have talked in previous sessions about a parent's need for some time off from child care, the use of baby-sitters, and the necessity of using the same substitute consistently so as not to disrupt the baby's development of basic trust. But we have not really discussed the practical instructions the parents should leave with the sitter. Whether the sitter is a relative or not, a teenager or an older woman, she should have a phone number where the parents can be reached in case of emergency. The telephone number of the baby's pediatrician should also be readily available, as well as the address of the nearest hospital emergency room. It is also a good idea to leave some money (about $5.00) tacked up where you have the list of emergency services, so that the baby-sitter has the taxi money to get to the hospital or the pediatrician without delay. Actually, it is a good idea to have taxi money available at all times, so you yourselves are not unprepared in an emergency.

Besides these emergency instructions, it is important to review that portion of the baby's daily routine that the sitter will have to cover. The baby-sitter should know which are the baby's favorite toys and which ones she goes to sleep with. The parent should also discuss the kinds of things that comfort the baby when she cries. The parents may want to ask the sitter to call them if there is any difficulty which the sitter doesn't quite know how to cope with. At that point the parents may be able to give the sitter some advice, or they may wish to come home earlier.

Parents should not anticipate that there's always going to be trouble when they go out. Usually everything goes very smoothly. You must, however, be prepared for the unusual situation. Parents need to feel comfortable that the sitter can handle difficult situations as well as routine ones.

By making these suggestions, we hope to help you feel more comfortable when you leave the baby. Emergencies are rare, but it's better to be prepared.

> "I've been leaving a telephone number for the sitter, and that makes me feel easier. I hadn't thought of taxi money. That's a great idea."

> "You talk about instructions for the baby-sitter. Suppose the sitter is your mother or mother-in-law? How can you tell her what to do, even if you know her way isn't yours?"

That's a situation that requires tact. But you should use tact with all baby-sitters. You can remind your mother gently where you keep all the baby's things, in case she needs them, and leave her a list or schedule of the baby's routine, just as you would for an "ordinary" baby-sitter. I can't believe that she wouldn't want to know how to reach you or the doctor if she needed to. She will probably admire you for your forethought in providing this information. She won't necessarily take it to mean that you don't trust her. You'll get her cooperation if you remember to say and do things tactfully when she's involved.

> "My mother is very glad to have everything written down because she is just as much of a worry wart as I am."

> "My mother-in-law thinks I'm 'kooky' anyway, so she expects me to write everything down."

> "When you mention all the precautions to take before going out and leaving the baby with a baby-sitter, it frightens me. Do you think it is better to stay home with your baby all the time, or take him with you, or what?"

Many parents have qualms about leaving their babies even with the best of baby-sitters and feel better when the baby is with them. For these parents, perhaps it's best to take the baby with them whenever it is possible. However, there are times when parents, no matter how devoted they are to their babies, must have time to do things together. Usually this involves going some place where it is not appropriate to take the baby. It is important for a good marital relationship to arrange to do things together as frequently as possible, on a weekly or biweekly basis, depending on the family setup, and leave the baby home with a competent caretaker whom he knows and trusts.

SPACING OF CHILDREN

Spacing of children is a topic that arouses a great deal of discussion and evokes many different responses. For some people there are religious reasons why the spacing of children is not considered a matter of choice, but something that should be accepted as nature provides. If one holds such views, we do not wish to interfere. It is a matter of the parents' personal lives and an issue that they face for themselves.

There are some parents who feel the issue should be decided entirely by the financial situation of the family. They want to give each child the very best they can. They feel they should not have more children when they can afford to have only one, or that the second child should not arrive until they can afford that child. This, too, is a valid consideration in spacing children.

Other parents feel that the physical health of the mother is endangered by having children too close together. In some cases, the mother's physical condition demands a long interval between children, or there may be physical reasons why the mother cannot have a second child.

Still other parents feel it was a mistake to have had their first child so early in their marriage. They feel that they were not prepared for raising the infant, so they want to postpone having a second one until they are better prepared. Some may even decide not to have any others at all.

There are parents who want to have their children very close together while they are young and vigorous and able to take care of them. They look forward to a long period of married life in which there are no new babies, so they will be able to have all the fun and do all the things they think they miss when they have babies to care for. On the other hand, some women who marry later in life may feel that they have only a limited amount of time in which to have healthy children.

Some parents feel that their living conditions are too crowded and they have no room for a second child. They do not feel prepared to make changes in their living arrangements, so they postpone having another child. All of these are valid solutions to the important question of spacing your children.

How do you feel about having another child? Perhaps you have other ideas.

"The only thing that is stopping us from having another baby is that we cannot afford one. We are just managing now. We want to give this baby the very best start in life we can, and we feel that having another baby would detract from what we could provide for the child we already have. That's our only reason for putting off having another baby."

"I think that when babies come, at whatever time nature decrees, one can always manage to support them somehow and give them the very best one can. I don't think financial reasons are the only consideration."

"We were married a long time before we felt we were able to afford a baby. We wanted one very much. We had no idea how expensive a baby would be, how much time he would take, but we are loving every minute of the experience because we had many years of our own personal pleasures and are now ready to devote ourselves to our baby."

"I'm afraid our reason for not having another baby soon is purely materialistic. We have an apartment that we like, and there is just room for the three of us. Having another baby would mean moving. We are happy the way we are at the moment. We may change our minds later on, but this is the way we feel now."

"I always thought that I would like to have all of my babies close together so that, as you say, there would be many years when I would be free of child care and when my husband and

I could lead the lives that we had planned. Now that I have my first baby, I see how much work babies are, and I'm not sure that I am ready to have another one right away."

"I feel just the opposite. I feel I'm just in the swing of learning how to take care of a baby and that I'd like to have another one while I still have all the equipment together and the routine fresh in my mind. That way I won't get rusty and have to learn all over again."

"I had to have a cesarean section, and I think I'd like to wait a while before going through that again."

All of the considerations you have mentioned are important. Each family has to decide for itself what is right for it.

Perhaps we do need to ask, "Why have another child, anyway?"

"Because that's a natural thing to do. Otherwise, why marry?"

"I wasn't anxious to have a baby, but my husband wanted one so badly that I thought that would be the right thing to do. Now, I'm not sorry. We might have another."

"We think we should have another child as a companion for our first one. That way, he will always have someone to play with later."

"Well, we had our baby because we wanted one, because both of us love children, and that is why we would have another."

That is the best reason for having a baby—because you want one, you want to be a parent, and you love having children. To have a second child just for the sake of the first usually is not the best idea. One cannot assure the compatability or companionship of siblings.

Assuming the timing can be controlled—and these days that's one of the things many parents wish to, and can, control—how much time should elapse before you have another child? Let's talk about that.

When birth control was first practiced in this country, and planned parenthood was started, two years was considered a good interval between children. It was thought that two years gave the mother ample time to recover from the birth process and also provided a suitable breathing space in which to give the baby a good start in life.

Now, we think that three years is the appropriate interval between children. Our reasons are not related to financial, physical, or religious considerations, but rather to the effect of a sibling on the first child and of the first child on the second.

When a baby is one year old, he still needs pretty constant attention from the mother. Having a new baby at this time would deprive the first child of the mother's very needed attentions. Also, the needs of the first child would make it difficult for the mother to attend to the second child adequately.

At the age of two, the child is not yet verbal and is just beginning the process of separating from his mother. He is just beginning to understand and test his own autonomy. Also, he is not yet toilet-trained. The period from two to three is very crucial to development in many areas—individuation and separation, toilet training, and speech. The child's development can be set back by the demands of a second child, especially if the parents are not aware of the first child's needs.

However, when the first child is about three years old, he has already achieved a certain mastery. He can express his feelings and understand communication. He has learned to eat by himself, he is almost completely toilet trained, and he is able to play in a separate room and even separate from his mother for part of the day at a nursery school or play group.

When a child is able to do this, he has become an individual with a sense of his own resources. At this point, it may be easier for the first child to adjust to a new baby. In addition, the mother has more time to devote to the second child without provoking intense sibling rivalry, although there is **always** some of this.

For these reasons, we feel that the most appropriate time to have a second child is when the first child is more able to accept the second child as a pleasant companion and a source of new interest. Three years is not an absolute age because some children mature more rapidly than others and may be ready for the new brother or sister at two-and-a-half years of age. Other children may not be ready until three-and-a-half years of age.

Each family has to assess its own child and its own situation. In his book **The First Three Years**, Dr. Burton White also points out that three years is the appropriate spacing interval for children. He raises the issue of the effect on the second child of a jealous older sibling, exerting influences which are not good for the development of the second child's personality. These are all-important issues that need to be considered. There is no absolute and final answer for everybody. Each family has to make its own decisions. Nonetheless, the effects of one child upon the other constitutes an important consideration and one that you should think about seriously when deciding whether to have another child and when to have it.

Some parents say, "I want to have another child soon because I want to have a playmate for my first child." This is not a good reason to have a second child quickly. Perhaps you can already see there are other considerations to be taken into account. You should have a second child, not as a companion for the first child, but because you want another child. The second child should be wanted as much as the first child and should be given as much attention as the first.

"I want to have four children. If I waited three years between children, I would be very old by the time my fourth child arrived. Waiting such a long interval between children would make having four impossible."

We are not saying that you **must** wait three years between children; we are saying three years is the ideal interval. There are certainly a number of circumstances which make a shorter interval desirable. However, if you know what is involved, especially how the first child can be affected by the second, you will be more understanding of the first child's needs. The mother who has children closer together must be prepared to have greater demands made on her than she expected with the first child. If one understands what is going to happen and does not become impatient, then one can deal with the situation. One must expect that at any given moment the children may have important yet conflicting needs. Handling this demands great patience, not to mention stamina.

"I understand exactly what you are saying because there is only a year between my two children. My first child is very timid and clinging and never seems to have enough of me, while my second child seems to be able to manage much better. Perhaps I know how to handle her better than my first baby. Having them close together is very difficult physically and emotionally. Had I known more, I would have made a different choice."

"I want to return to my career. If I take three years between children, I will always be just getting back into the swing of things in my work when I have to take time out to have a baby. So, I think, I would like to have all of my children close together and have their care settled. Then I'll go back to my work and know that I can keep at it without taking time out for maternity leave."

This is an entirely individual decision that a mother has to make for herself. What we are talking about is what would be ideal for each child. We are concerned with each child's development and the parents' understanding of what is good for his development at different ages.

It is possible that if a mother understands what is involved, she could manage to have children closer together and raise them well, providing she had sufficient help. Mothers and fathers have to make these decisions for themselves. If they understand the effects close siblings can have on one another, parents can make the appropriate adjustments in order to provide the children with what is best for them.

"If parents postpone having more children, by the time they have their second or third, they may be too old to be able to enjoy the children. They may find them a hindrance to their lives and resent them. Whereas, if they had the second child when they were younger, they might not feel that way."

This is a serious decision for the father and mother to make. But we are talking about what is best for the individual child. Certainly, if parents are going to resent having a child, they shouldn't have one. Children are to be loved and enjoyed; they should not be considered a burden that has to be endured. The whole object of our sessions is to help parents get the most pleasure from their children's development and to understand how to enhance their development, so that they can profit by what they have learned and be proud of their achievement as parents.

"I am enjoying every minute of my baby's waking time. I enjoy everything that I see him do, and I wouldn't want to give up any of these joys. If I had two children that were close together, I feel that the joy I am deriving from my first baby would be greatly diminished. As a matter of fact, both my husband and I so love this baby that we are wondering whether we could love another child as much, and whether it would be fair to this baby and to us to have another."

This, too, is an individual decision. It is not a decision that other people can make for you. Many parents are often worried about loving the first child. Usually that love develops. It also develops in the same way for a second child, particularly if the parents do not feel strained and harrassed and are able to enjoy the developing personalities.

INCREASED MOTOR DEVELOPMENT

Use of the Legs

As you are well aware, your babies are getting much more active. They are turning over; some can get to the sitting position alone; they are using their hands much more competently. You will remember that months ago we described neurological development as progressing from the head to the feet. Now the development has reached the legs. The babies are beginning to use their legs. Therefore, they need more room to kick while on their stomachs. They need space in a playpen or on the floor to make the transition to crawling. They need space now to use their legs.

Many of the mothers have been keeping the baby in a carrier or sling on their backs while doing the housework in order to keep the baby close to them but at the same time giving themselves the freedom to do their housework. This was useful when the babies were not mobile, but it may hamper the child's development if it is continued too long and interferes with her exploratory behavior and muscular development.

How much freedom of movement are you allowing your baby?

How do you manage to give the baby room to move and still keep her safe? Are you still using slings?

"I still use a sling when I'm in the kitchen or when I go marketing. I don't want the baby underfoot, but he still needs to be near me. At other times, he is on the floor or in his bed or in a high chair."

The sling, or pack, still has its uses, but you must decide whether it is hampering the baby's development because he now needs more room for movement and exploration. Even in the kitchen, a corner can be fenced off so the baby can have more freedom of movement.

"That's just what I did! You just get a flexible gate, stretch it, and fasten it across a corner of the room so that the baby has floor space, is in sight, and yet is out of danger. My husband set such gates up in the kitchen and living room."

"My baby's increased activity has been bothering me a lot because I'm afraid he'll fall off the bed. He doesn't like the playpen because he can't brace himself on the pad, and there just isn't that much space in my apartment to put a blanket on the floor or set up a gate. We're still in one room and haven't been able to get a larger place yet."

The lack of space in city apartments does make providing the baby with ample room for exploration difficult, but babies must get the chance to use their legs and start to crawl. Would it be possible to rearrange the furniture in your apartment so that at some time each day your baby gets a chance to exercise his legs? It is a nuisance, but then you can return things to their usual places. Perhaps a friend or neighbor who has more space would not mind it if once in a while you spread a small blanket or pad on her floor to give the baby a chance to move about.

"But isn't it dangerous to have the baby on a drafty floor? In my apartment the floor is so cold."

Of course, it is not good for the baby to be down on a cold floor. Wait until the room is warm enough, and place the baby on a thick rug or blanket. A bath mat will also do because the baby isn't going to go very far just yet. If the floor is always cold, place the baby on a firm bed, and watch her carefully.

"I've been noticing that the baby moves around his crib a lot on his stomach, but I was afraid it was too early to put him down on the floor. Now I see that perhaps I was holding back his development."

Yes, it is very easy to make that error. Some parents unconsciously do it because they want to keep the baby on their laps and under control. The more active the baby, the more work for the parent. Other parents make the mistake, as you say, because they don't realize the baby is ready for this stage of development. That's what these sessions are about, helping parents learn to "tune-in" to the baby's development at the right time. Sometimes babies get ahead of us and are doing things that were not anticipated for their chronological age. This happens because the babies' maturational timetables are more rapid than expected. Things like that keep us all on our toes. That's why we need to observe and interpret a baby's needs and level of development.

> "I guess I am the impatient kind that 'jumps the gun.' I have been putting my baby on my bed and on the floor, and he just remains in the same place on his stomach, like a lump."

Don't be discouraged; you just happen to be ahead of his developmental timetable. One of these days if you put something interesting down in front of him, he may be able to make a move toward it by kicking his legs and waving his arms. He will do this when he is ready. We have said many times before that babies usually follow the same sequence of development, but each has his or her own timetable for maturation.

LANGUAGE AND COMMUNICATION

While it is important to allow the babies freedom to develop their legs, it is not necessary, at this age, to spend time helping the baby to stand or encouraging walking. The baby will develop the ability to walk when his central nervous system matures and he is ready.

What is important at this age is the stimulation of language. A baby will make sounds spontaneously; these sounds will not become language unless the baby hears language. We have all heard of children brought up in the wild, without human contact, who could make all kinds of sounds and could communicate pleasure and displeasure, but who could not speak a language.

As you know, crying is the baby's first language. Her cries differ to express different needs and moods. From the cry comes the first language sound of "m-m-m." In the next stage, the repeated babbling sounds like "ah-ah," "mah-mah," and "dah-dah" are produced. Some of the babies may now be progressing to single syllable sounds like "dah," "bah," "kah," and "mah." Production of these single syllable sounds represents an advance in development because these sounds will later be used as the names for things, the first "words." Babbling shows the baby's experimentation with vocalization. The single syllable sounds form the foundation for the baby's understanding of vocalization as language. For example, the baby will eventually be able to associate the particular sound "dah" with "Daddy" or "bah" with "bottle."

When you hear a syllable sound, you should face the baby and then repeat the sound. Perhaps at first the baby will only look at you intently and not make the sound again. The next time you hear the syllable, you should repeat it again and show your enjoyment by your voice and expression. Pretty soon the baby will begin to respond by repeating the syllable with varying intensity, and you must do the same. Then you can offer other distinct sounds for her to repeat. As we have said before, the parent's repetition of the baby's sounds gives them importance for the baby and forms the beginning of a conversation. This kind of communication is great fun and something that both parents can enjoy. Fathers like to participate with the baby in this way.

Have any of you begun doing this yet?

> "I find it very hard to repeat a syllable or talk to the baby at all, because sometimes he looks at me as if he is surprised, and I feel so silly when I don't get a response."

Perhaps you are expecting a mature answer; looking at you is your baby's response. He is processing this contact with you. If you speak to him often and consistently, he will have sounds to process and store for future use. When that part of his central nervous system relating to speech production is sufficiently developed, he will make a response of some kind. This is a milestone in his speech development and a "red-letter day" for you because it was your stimulation that helped evoke the response.

Perhaps we all feel a little silly "gooing and aahing" to a baby. But if we realize that it serves a very important purpose in the teaching of language, we will lose some of the self-consciousness which causes us to feel silly.

> "I've been trying to talk to the baby, I think, since the day I brought her home from the hospital. I just can't wait to hear a sound back. Her father tries, too."

You are on the right track, but, in your enthusiasm, you may be bombarding the baby with too much speech. Why don't you concentrate on just a few syllables like "ah," "dah," "mah," or "by"? Say them in a lilting voice, and then wait for the baby to make a sound back. Or say "Here's Dada" whenever Daddy comes in, so that the baby is not overwhelmed. Also, your baby's maturation may not yet have reached the level of making distinct sounds. Continue talking to the baby, and one day, when the baby is ready, you will hear a response that you can recognize.

> "My husband is better at talking to the baby than I am. He seems more patient and isn't self-conscious, but I enjoy watching the interaction between them."

It is nice when there is some area where the father has some special impact on the baby. Unfortunately, it does not happen often enough. It is good that you appreciate this, but it should not stop you from talking to the baby, even if your husband seems to get a better response. It is normal for babies to respond differently to father and mother because they do things in different ways.

"Repeating syllables sounds to me like baby talk. I speak to my baby when I want to in the way I speak to adults. Is there anything wrong in that?"

If there is enough speech, and you say the same thing repeatedly, the baby eventually will talk. Speaking in long sentences without reinforcing individual sounds is not in tune with the baby's level of development. If the baby is only able to say "Dada" and you respond by saying, "I can't understand you; speak more distinctly," there has been no reinforcement for the baby. She will not know that her speech experimenting has been recognized, and she will not be encouraged to try again. Thus, the process of learning to talk is slowed down. Some children like that may not speak until they can more closely imitate the adult. But why delay the process and lose the fun of helping the baby build up her ability to speak? Of course, the way a parent speaks to his or her baby will vary depending on the parent's personality. We are only suggesting ways in which speech and the parent's enjoyment of it may be enhanced.

"I always wanted to say 'Dada' and 'Baba' back to the baby. It seemed the most natural thing for me to do, but I was afraid I was being too pushy with him and trying to move him ahead before it was time. Some friends made fun of me, too. It helps to know that speech should be stimulated and that my natural inclination in this area was right."

Parents often have the right inclination but are, unfortunately, inhibited by the opinions and criticisms of less-informed people. It is a shame this happens so often. So, if you have feelings or ideas about a child-rearing topic which others disagree with, we want you to feel free to air them here.

Need for New Toys

Up to this point, the baby's toys have consisted mostly of a stuffed cuddly toy, the red ring on a string, a cradle gym, and a rattle. They may be tiring of these toys and need more stimulation.

"Yes, it seemed to me that the baby was bored with his cradle gym, so I just unstrung it and changed the position of the dangling balls and rings. Now he gets all excited when I put the gym across his crib."

That was a very perceptive and ingenious thing to do. Something else you can do is use the ring on a string to stimulate reaching or pull it across the floor in front of the baby so he may be stimulated to try to wiggle after it.

"My baby seemed uninterested too, so I brought out a lot of new things I had put away. I thought he would be very excited, but he seemed unhappy and didn't know what to make of them."

It sounds as though you overwhelmed him with too many new things. He probably would have responded better if you had added only one new toy. Although the baby may not be as enthused as before about an old toy, he still has an attachment to it. Old toys should not be taken away entirely. If the new toy is right, it will be accepted and may even displace the old toy. The parent must keep the baby's level of interest and development in mind.

"My baby used to be pleased with just looking at a stuffed toy in her crib. Now she struggles to reach it and wants to pull it or put it in her mouth. Isn't that unsanitary?"

The baby needs to play with her toys in a familiar way. For the most part at this stage that means putting them in her mouth. So it should be allowed. Try to get stuffed toys that can be washed; those made of terry cloth or a plastic that can be wiped clean are best. Babies become immune to the bacteria of their own homes. While toys need to be clean, they do not need to be surgically sterile. As you may have noticed, we wash all the testing materials after we test each child, but we do not sterilize them.

Babies need to be allowed to investigate the various aspects of their toys on their own. They need to touch, taste, throw, smell, pull, and manipulate them.

That brings us to the kind of new toys which may be good for your babies now. Soft toys that are small enough for them to manipulate, that have appendages and projections that they can hold on to—small rag dolls or animals, for instance—are eminently suitable right now. Babies the age of your children are also intrigued by a "roly-poly" that moves when touched.

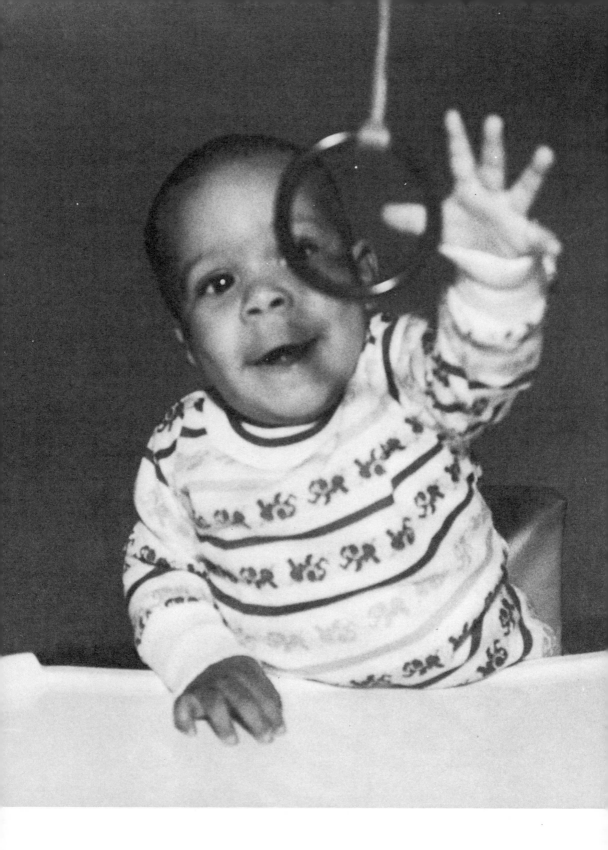

Eight-month-old baby reaching
for a red ring dangled from a string.

Chapter 8

Age: 32 to 36 weeks

The baby can now remain in a sitting position unsupported for long periods. Some babies may try to reach the sitting position on their own, although they may not fully succeed. The baby may be able to stand briefly when her hands are held, though standing should not be encouraged unless the baby can achieve the standing position on her own. Until she can stand on her own, she is not ready for standing for a prolonged period, even though she may be able to bear her weight when supported. When allowed freedom in the prone position, the baby may pivot her body around in a rudimentary crawling motion.

The competence of the baby's hands is increasing. When presented with a marble-sized pellet, he may rake it in using a modified **palmer grasp**; but he still is not capable of a **scissors grasp** (a grasp in which the thumb is opposed to the index and middle fingers). The baby can now hold a cube or block in each hand with a firmer grasp and retain both while observing a third cube. While holding a block, he may pay attention to a cup that is offered, although he may not reach for it.

The baby's vocalizations should now be clearer, and the baby may make single-syllable sounds, such as "dah," "bah," "kah," and "gah." Parents should repeat the syllables the baby says so she gets a sense of communication and approval from the parent.

The baby is now more playful. Most of his play consists of biting or chewing toys. To be safe, toys should be too large to swallow but small enough to be grasped by the baby. The baby will also be reaching for more toys. When the red ring is dangled from a string, the baby will persist in reaching to grasp it. Parents should hold the ring so that the baby is able to grasp it and gain a sense of mastery. This exercise can make a good game and provides an opportunity to express pleasure at the baby's achievement.

EXPLORATION ON THE FLOOR

Now that the babies are beginning to be placed on the floor, they are making preliminary crawling motions. Some are even able to cover some distance on the floor moving in this way. They are entering a new stage of development which leads to new ways of exploring. They are going to be noticing small objects on the floor. They will inspect the blanket or carpet on which they are placed. They will finger the design and texture and will invariably discover a crumb or particle that the mother was unaware of. They will most likely put this into their mouths. Because these activities require more vigilance, many mothers may be reluctant to allow the baby to make the transition from the lap, the sling, or the high chair, where they have more control, to the floor. This new developmental stage requires a new adjustment on the parents' part, and this adjustment may be difficult at first.

The baby should be allowed space to move about on the floor. The area on a rug, mat, or blanket should be circumscribed so that the mother is sure the baby will be safe from picking up pins, tacks, pills, or other dangerous items. Things that the parents themselves may not notice are often almost immediately discovered by a baby.

How do you feel about putting your baby on the floor? Have you done it yet, or are you already doing it consistently?

> "I'm afraid to put the baby down because the floor may not be clean and he may pick up dangerous things. As you said, having him on the floor makes me a little nervous."

Putting the baby on the floor is a great concern to many mothers, but the dangers of doing it can be limited by keeping the baby on a blanket or mat. Of course you can't go away and leave the baby there; he requires watching. The baby should be put on the floor for short periods when the parent or other caretaker can devote undivided attention to the baby. Then the baby can be picked up and held, or put in his high chair or carriage for another activity.

> "Our floor is always cold, so I let the baby crawl on the bed, but he gets to the edge in two seconds. Isn't this a good time to use a playpen? It's several inches above the floor, it's fenced in, and you can be sure the mat is clean before you put the baby in. You can leave him and feel he is safe."

A playpen does have the advantage of being above the draft on the floor. The area of exploration is limited, and parents have a feeling of security about the baby when he is in the pen. However, it is a very confined space for the baby and takes a lot of room in a small apartment. Also, playpens are expensive and useful for only a very short period in the baby's life.

> "I agree that playpens are too confining. Also the mat rumples

up, no matter how it's fastened, and hampers the baby's ability to crawl."

As we have said before, playpens have an added disadvantage for a baby. Once she is in the playpen, a baby, especially a quiet baby, is apt to be left alone too long without parental stimulation. Making sure the baby doesn't develop the feeling that she's been left alone is really the most important consideration from our point of view. That consideration leads us to another aspect of exploration.

At this stage, the baby's locomotion may not get her very far, but she will wiggle and try to reach a toy placed a few inches from her. Now that the baby is moving, you should take care to provide stimulation for this ability. As the baby becomes more proficient at moving, the toy may be placed a little further away, but never so far as to discourage her. When she has taken hold of the toy, she may utter a sound of glee, or smile and gurgle. The parent should reinforce this achievement with some kind of recognition—for example, smile or say "Good" or clap her hands, whatever comes naturally. However, the recognition must be obvious enough for the baby to understand that what she has done is an achievement.

In this way, the parent rewards the baby's exploratory effort and enhances her budding self-image as an achiever. As we have said before, this feeling of achievement and mastery is an important element in the baby's personality development and can have important implications for later achievement in school. Leaving the baby alone in a playpen does not give her this sense of mastery and recognition. Of course, if the parents sit by the playpen and attend to the baby, they can get excited with the baby over her accomplishments and enhance her sense of mastery. The playpen is useful as long as it is large enough not to limit movement, and as long as the baby is not isolated in it. For some families it may serve a need, but it is not a "must" for all families.

SETTING LIMITS AND THE BEGINNING OF CONSCIENCE

Now that there is more exploration, babies will inevitably reach for things which are dangerous: the stove, a knife, or an expensive ornament. In the last instance the danger is, of course, probably more to the ornament than to the child. In any case, such exploratory attempts have to be limited for the sake of safety. Now is the time to begin teaching the baby to accept certain limitations. These limitations should be few but consistent. The parent should say a firm but kind "No" and give the baby another safe object to explore. This substitute should preferably be the baby's own toy or cup if she was reaching, for example, for the mother's cup of hot coffee.

Have you yet encountered any situations like the ones I just described? How have you been handling them?

"This is very confusing for me because just a moment ago we

were talking about allowing freedom for exploration and now you are saying we must begin limitation."

Of course, how much exploration to permit and when to limit it is a difficult issue. The limitations are for the sake of safety, either for the baby or your possessions. They should always be firm and consistent; a substitute object or activity which can be approved should be introduced quickly. For example, if the baby is on the floor and manages to get near the corner of a tablecloth and is about to pull it and the dishes on the table over, he must be stopped. You may say "No," pick the baby up, and give him a napkin or a spoon to explore. Say to the baby, "Yes, you may play with this," and by your tone of voice convey your approval.

"When my baby touches something I don't want him to touch, I just move him away. Then he cries, and it gets me very upset. I feel so cruel, and yet I know it's not safe to let him touch certain things like a hot light bulb."

You don't need to feel so guilty; you are doing something that mothers must do. It is part of a mother's job to set limits. However, give your baby another object which he can explore. You will find that that will stop the crying quickly. If you make the substitution fast enough, it may not even occur at all.

"I find myself saying 'No' most of the day, and the baby doesn't pay attention. Sometimes I find myself screaming. I must be doing something wrong."

Just saying "No" is not enough; a substitute object or activity must be offered. Also, it's not effective to say "No" too often. The "No's" have to be limited to a few things and then consistently applied. Too often we say "No" when no real danger is involved. We turn off normal, safe exploratory impulses, which is not really what we want to do.

"I wonder whether the baby understands the meaning of 'No' now?"

The babies really don't understand the meaning of "No" at this age. You are teaching it to them by repetition of the word and the simultaneous limitation and change in activity.

It takes a long time for the baby to associate "No" with the particular activity. The length of time varies with each child's capacity and level of development—and the parents' consistency in limiting the baby. For some babies it may take a week or two; for others many weeks. For the baby, this is the beginning of learning to understand limitation. It is an important part of growing up and must be handled patiently and consistently.

Fathers, in our society, often have little time with their babies, but some time must be arranged so that they can enjoy the baby and participate in enhancing development.

Fathers enjoy watching children try to crawl and are very proud and pleased when they see this developing. Sometimes they may be a little impatient with the wiggling movements because they don't seem to get the baby very far. But if the father can be encouraged to spend some time watching the baby struggle to reach and finally get a toy, he too participates in the baby's achievement, and his approval adds to the baby's self-esteem.

Are the fathers beginning to spend more time playing with the babies and recognizing their achievements?

> "You are right about fathers having no time for babies. My husband leaves early and comes home when the baby is in bed. Only on weekends, if he is not working then too, he gets to see how far the baby has developed. He enjoys it when the baby sits in his lap and reaches for the rattle he is holding."

> "My husband thinks there is something wrong with the baby because she isn't crawling yet. He doesn't recognize that the baby is in the beginning stage."

> "My husband was like that too, but the other day the baby actually got to the doll he put down near her on the floor and was he so proud!"

Some fathers are not aware of the stages in development, and it seems strange to them that each new achievement takes so long. However, once they get the idea, they can be helpful in the recognition of achievement.

How are the fathers responding to the need for limitations? Are the fathers saying "No" frequently to the babies?

> "My husband has a very loud voice. When he says 'No' to the baby, it frightens her and she cries. Then my husband becomes annoyed."

Perhaps you can tell your husband that if he talks more softly to the baby and immediately gives her another object to play with, the baby will respond better and learn to accept limitations from him. It is very important to establish an acceptance of the father's limitations and for father to know how to limit.

> "My husband doesn't want to be the one to limit the baby. He sees the baby so little that he is afraid she won't like him if he says 'No.'"

That's a common attitude among parents. It makes for a great deal

Father's Role in Recognizing Achievement and Setting Limits

of confusion for the baby if only mother says "No" and father does not, or vice versa. Explain to the father that the baby will love him just as much and will develop, in time, a sense of security because both parents impose the same limitations. The baby will learn to accept limitations from both parents. If one parent limits and the other does not, it is a good way to set the stage for manipulative and delinquent behavior. It undermines the establishment of conscience development. We will talk about that in greater detail as the babies grow older.

> "I think my husband has a tendency to be harsh in setting limits. I think he hollers at the baby needlessly and gets impatient too quickly. He thinks I am too soft and that I spoil the baby."

This is a frequent problem because men were often severely disciplined by their own fathers, and they repeat that pattern. Perhaps we can help you best by discussing this with the fathers on the next Fathers' Night.

We must realize, however, that mothers can be just as harsh and strict as fathers. I have seen many families in which the father was the gentle, soothing one and the mother the harsh disciplinarian. Much of our parenting style reflects our own upbringing. We hope to show parents alternate ways that we feel are more constructive for healthy personality development and better parent-child relations.

Achieving a Balance Between the Baby's Need to Explore and Maintaining an Orderly Household

We have been talking about the babies' increasing mobility and their need for space in which to develop the use of their legs through moving and crawling on the floor. At the same time that they need space to crawl, they also need freedom to explore an extended environment. They need the experience of getting around the room and exploring. It's not a good idea, therefore, to have them always fenced in, although for safety's sake this is occasionally necessary.

We do recognize, however, that as the babies get more mobile, they can reach for things and pull them from their proper places. Some can maneuver to reach the lower shelf of a bookcase and pull out books and strew them over the floor. The baby's toys are now left in odd places, and adults frequently stumble over them.

In other words, the babies are beginning to make a "mess." If the parents are usually very orderly, this disorder may become a source of annoyance. Other parents are more relaxed and are pleased that the baby has reached this level of development. Although they may complain a little about the extra work, they accept it as part of their baby's growing up.

> "My baby is not going after books, but we have a tall plant that he makes a beeline for whenever I put him on the floor. It's an expensive plant, and he is destroying it by pulling off the

leaves. I know it's exploration, but I don't want the plant destroyed. I move him away, but he goes right back. It is a big tall plant which is too heavy to move and too large to be put up high. Besides the damage to the plant, I am afraid some-day he will pull it over on himself."

This is a difficult problem, but not an uncommon one. You want to save the baby **and** the plant. I would suggest that you never leave the baby unattended in that room. When he gets close to the plant and makes a gesture toward the leaves, indicate your disapproval by saying "No." Then, immediately give him some other way of discharging his impulse to touch the leaves. This will not only provide a distraction from the temptation of the plant, but an outlet for the baby's impulse to touch. The message "Reach out and touch" is already traveling along the pathways of the baby's central nervous system. You must help the baby find a substitute outlet. You might substitute a stuffed animal with long ears or tail that he could pull or touch. When he does that, the baby needs to be shown enthusiastic approval. By consistent repetition of this procedure, you will teach the baby to refrain from pulling the leaves on the plant. Your approval will become something pleasant, and he will prefer it to your disapproval.

"How long will I have to keep this up?"

That varies with each child. Some catch on very quickly; others need weeks of repetition. We began talking about this subject when the babies were approaching six months. At that time, they were just beginning to **recognize** the difference between approval and dis-approval. Now they are more ready to respond. Most of the babies at this age will stop, however briefly, when you say "No."

"Since the baby is moving about on a blanket on the floor of the living room, which is also the dining room and our bed-room at night, our house always looks like a mess. I am resigned to this, but my husband really doesn't like it. We always took pride in the way we kept our home. We are not fanatics, but we do like to keep the place neat."

It is very hard to keep a small apartment in the city neat when you have an active, curious baby who needs to explore and have room to play. When housing was less expensive and apartments larger, it was possible to have a playroom for the baby. The "parlor" or living room was kept sacrosanct. Some of us were brought up this way and feel frustrated when the baby interferes with our idea of a "well-kept house."

With a young baby, your priorities may have to change for a while. This period, however, will not last forever. If you look upon it as a period of advance in the baby's development, perhaps you will be less upset. We hope you will derive satisfaction from the baby's progress. Looking at the period in this light may also help your husband, relatives, and friends accept the situation more patiently.

"At first I thought it was fun to see things strewn around. Then picking up after the baby all the time began to get to me. Now I leave things around until the baby is in bed. Then it takes just a few minutes to straighten up. I put everything in a box in the corner. Then we have our living room as we want it for ourselves and company for the rest of the evening. It's a little more effort, but it works. My husband now helps put things in order and doesn't mind the mess as much as he did at first. He knows now it can be cleaned in a jiffy. The worse it is, the more he laughs."

"I guess I'm lucky because we have a large bedroom which we made into the baby's room. I keep him there for playtime. I don't care what kind of a mess he makes there. When he is in the living room, I hold him or have him in a high chair. I know this can't last forever; sometime soon the baby will want to get down on the floor in the living room. I dread that day because my mother-in-law was a great housekeeper, and my husband thinks his home has to be kept the same way. To him anyone who can't keep a house like his mother did is incompetent."

Each of you has to resolve this problem in a way that suits both the emotional and physical requirements of your family. However, everybody involved—and that includes your husband and your mother-in-law—will have to reorder some priorities to allow the baby to develop properly. Everybody has to remember that this is a stage that will pass. The length of time it takes to pass will, of course, vary depending on the baby's rate of development, but someday your home will be neat again.

THE DEVELOPMENT OF CONSCIENCE: A REVIEW

The Life History of "No"

Parents must realize that a baby's understanding of limitations and his ability to respond appropriately to "No" have a developmental sequence just as learning to walk does. Everyone accepts the fact that before a baby can walk alone, he has to turn over, sit up, crawl, stand, and walk with help. We also recognize that some babies walk by ten or eleven months while some do not until fourteen to sixteen months. Some of us may put a high premium on walking and try to coax a baby to walk earlier than he is ready to. In general, however, we know the sequence of the maturational levels that must be achieved before walking alone is accomplished, and we wait for the baby to achieve them in his own good time.

Understanding "No"—that is, internalizing limitations—also has a developmental sequence. Parents play a key role in helping this understanding to develop. The first step is to say "No" to the baby and remove him from the forbidden activity. It is equally important for the parent to provide another outlet for the baby's impulse by substituting an approved activity. This combined act of limitation and substitution has to be repeated consistently before it begins to take effect.

In the next stage of the baby's development, he stops and turns to look at his mother to see if she will say "No." The baby stops momentarily but will continue the activity unless the parent removes him and gives him an alternate acceptable outlet. Then he will go back and try again until he is certain his parent meant what he or she said. At first, the baby just can't believe that this loving parent who has provided so many good things will really deprive him of this gratification.

The third step of this sequence comes when the baby goes up to the object, says "No, no" to himself and still pursues the activity unless stopped. He still needs help in stopping; he has not fully integrated the "No."

Finally, when the baby has matured sufficiently and developed more self-control, he is able to go up to the object, say "No" to himself, desist, and find his own substitute activity. He has integrated the "No." This is the beginning of his own conscience mechanism.

> **"I never knew about that sequence or thought of conscience developing that way, but the process sounds like it is going to take a very long time."**

Yes, it does seem to take a very long time, just as learning to walk does, but the time it takes varies with each child's endowment and with the manner and consistency with which the parents respond. The process is usually accomplished when the child is about three years of age.

> **"We have a special problem because my husband has his office in the house, and there are many things in the office that are tempting for the baby to touch. When the baby is in there, we are saying 'No' all the time, and I don't want to do that. Do you think it is better to put the whole room off limits or continue saying so many 'No's'?"**

In such an instance, it would be less stressful to put the room "off limits." Keep the door closed and take the baby in for short visits. If one says "No" all the time, the baby soon begins to pay no attention. The "No's" have to be reserved for a few specific instances—situations which will be dangerous to the child or to your possessions—a hot stove or radiator, a sharp object, electric outlets (which should be covered), or lamps which can be overturned. Kitchen and bathroom cabinets should have safety locks. A special cabinet in the kitchen can be supplied with toys and pots and pans for the baby. Here he can explore and play safely.

Parents should decide together which things will be prohibited, and each parent should respond in the same way for the given situation. The number of prohibited things should be limited.

We will have further discussions about setting limits. What is important to understand at this point is that parents should start early, be consistent and kind, but firm in the way they say "No." Parents should not say "No" and smile because that gives the baby the idea that saying "No" is a game and that the "No" is not really meant. That way, the message is not clear, but ambivalent and confusing for the baby.

To be able to accept limitations is a very important part of a person's personality structure. The consistency with which the limitation is set and the mood in which it is done are very important.

> "It is very helpful to understand the stages the babies must pass through before they will be able to accept limits and control themselves. But I can see it's going to be quite a job."

It is a difficult job; no one said it was easy. But it will be rewarding. We all want our children to develop good conscience mechanisms and self-control.

Achieving a Balance Between Encouraging Play and Setting Limits

We have been talking a good deal about limitations. We must bear in mind that at this stage setting limits should not take up all of your energy. The main focus should be on helping the child use her new-found motor and mental development in a way that gives her a sense of mastery. Play is the child's "work," and the adult needs to assist in this "work."

We talked previously about new play activities and kinds of toys which the babies will enjoy and which will enhance their development. Play is also a way in which parents can communicate with their baby and a way for the baby to learn about different personalities. Each parent has his or her own style of playing with the baby. The baby learns to enjoy and expect a different way of doing things with each parent. Mothers often think that father plays with the child better and that the child finds playing with him more enjoyable. Actually the baby may enjoy the novelty of the father's presence because he has been away all day. It is not that the father plays **better**; he plays **differently**. Each parent is perceived differently by the child. It is important that the child makes this distinction and is able to make an attachment to both mother and father.

FATHER'S ROLE IN PLAY

"Roughhousing" and Overstimulation

Often fathers like "roughhousing" with the baby. This attitude seems to be rather universal, especially when baby boys are concerned. Fathers like to swing them by the arms and throw them in the air. Some babies chortle and seem to enjoy this activity, but most are frightened, and the chortle may not be a sign of joy. When the baby is swung by his arms, a dislocation of the shoulder joint may occur. Children should be lifted under the armpits to avoid this injury. When a baby is tossed into the air, he loses the feeling of support which he needs. Loss of the feeling of support can be very devastating to the baby. In addition, there is always the danger that the parent will not catch the baby in time or without hurting him.

Instead of this way of playing, fathers need to be encouraged to utilize the babies' developmental level, their new motor and mental skills. The baby can watch the father toss and catch some of the baby's toys. The father can topple the toys from a table or bounce them off his own head. Babies like all of these surprise activities because they add a new dimension to their experience, and their laughter is genuine and enthusiastic.

How have your husbands been playing with the babies? Have they been "roughhousing" with them?

> "That's exactly what my husband does. He throws the baby up in the air so high that I'm scared to death. The baby squeals. I think it is a squeal of fright rather than an indication of pleasure, but my husband insists the baby likes it. Besides, he thinks that is the way to make a man of him. Life, my husband says, is rough, so the baby must get used to rough stuff."

You will have to caution your husband as tactfully as you can against continuing this activity. Perhaps you can tell him that doctors do not advise this type of play with babies of this age. Frightening a baby early does not enhance his ability to cope with a "rough world." In fact, it may so impair his sense of basic trust that coping with life will become more difficult for him later on. This is a basic issue which we need to take up with the fathers on Fathers' Night.

> "My husband did something different. He hid behind the door and then came out with big loud 'Boo.' The baby was startled and cried. He hasn't done it since. He learned his lesson, and now he plays 'Boo' very gently, just touching the baby's forehead to his and saying 'Boo.' "

> "My husband is very gentle with the baby. Maybe because she is a girl and is petite. He is almost afraid to handle her. He thinks I'm tough with her."

> "My husband does something the baby likes very much. When he is pushing the baby in the carriage, every once in a while he will give the carriage a hard shove so it will go a little faster. He is close to the carriage and in perfect control of it when he does this so that there is no danger."

Again we see different types of engagement between father and baby. The important thing is for father and child to relate to each other on a level that is suitable for and not dangerous to the baby, yet in keeping with the father's personality and style.

All of our concerns seem to have been toward stimulating the babies. However, one must remember that babies can be over-stimulated. This makes them fussy and irritable. They may have trouble eating and sleeping when they have been overstimulated.

Some babies become overstimulated by visits to friends or relatives; others by too many guests in the house. Even loving grandparents can overdo things. Parental play that is too vigorous can also be overstimulating, as we have just pointed out.

As you get to know your baby's tolerance, you will learn to stay short of the point of overstimulation. However, if overstimulation occurs, it is best to take the baby to another room, preferably his own room, where he can be quietly held and rocked until he settles down. Then one can proceed with mealtime or bedtime. For some babies a bath can be a very soothing activity. A baby needs time and help to "wind down" after a period of play or other excitement.

Have you observed periods of overstimulation in your baby? If so, how do you calm the baby down?

> "I have that problem with my baby. My husband comes home just as I am about to get the baby off to sleep. Of course he wants to play with the baby, and I feel he should, but the baby gets all excited. When my husband has had enough play and wants to put the baby down to sleep, the baby is not ready. We have a hard time getting her off to sleep. Our dinner has to wait, and my husband gets annoyed and blames me."

It is right to let father have time with the baby. It needs to be pointed out, however, that the baby does get overexcited and needs time to wind down. Suggest to your husband that he could be the one who soothes and calms the baby while you prepare dinner. If you discuss this objectively without trying to assign blame, your husband will probably cooperate. You will have helped him to understand what is happening with the baby, and he will have an added role to play in the baby's day.

> "Should a baby be played with before bedtime? I always thought it was wrong. I have the baby asleep before my husband comes home."

It is easier to get the baby to sleep if there is no stimulation before bedtime. If that is the only time the father has to see the baby and they can enjoy each other, some accommodation has to be made. Some fathers play with their children for just a few minutes before they leave for work in the morning and then while they are home on weekends.

"My husband wants the baby asleep when he comes home so we can eat in peace and quiet. He says he likes to play with her on weekends when he is not tired and can be patient and when the two of them can be more active."

Parents have to adapt to the requirements of their own families. One needs to understand the basic principles and do the best one can. Parents can learn to recognize when the baby is overstimulated and what soothing measures are appropriate. It is important not to become frustrated and feel anger toward the baby or the person who is responsible for the overstimulation.

"How can you tell grandparents what to do, even if you know they are upsetting the baby and you will have hours of extra work getting him quieted down when they have gone?"

That's always hard. It depends a great deal on the grandparents' personalities and how well you get on with them. It is the baby's reaction which is really important. You can try to explain to the grandparents that the whole family will enjoy the visit more if they don't overdo the play. Any grandparent, reminded with tact, can recollect similar experiences with his or her own children. Overstimulation is not something new to this generation of babies. The nervous systems of our babies are responding to stimuli in the same way that the nervous systems of all babies have.

"Now I understand why our baby behaves so badly when we come home from a visit or a shopping trip during which we have tried to show him all sorts of things. We were so disappointed that he wasn't enjoying the outing, but I guess we tried to do too much too long."

Perhaps your baby is not yet ready for as much stimulation as you offered. It will be very satisfying to you when you learn just what is enough for him. In fact, this is part of knowing your baby. Knowing his capacity for stimulation is an important part of parenting, not only now but as your child grows and progresses.

Some of the babies may be beginning to stand up in their cribs. Others may not reach this stage until they are about a year old. A wide time range in this area is normal. At whatever age they accomplish this, however, the process is about the same. They stand momentarily and then fall down into the crib because they have not learned to sit down. Or else they cry to have someone help them get down.

Standing in the Crib: The Safety Precautions Required

Have any of your babies started doing this yet?

"We are just going through that now. Last night he got up during the night and could not get down. I heard him crying. All he wanted was to be put back down."

This is another stage of development: The baby can get up but can't get down. It usually is quite upsetting both for the parents and the baby. Sometimes babies fall down with quite a bump. This process may be repeated many times during the day, and unfortunately also at night. But this problem is of short duration because in the course of a week or two, babies master the procedure of getting up and sitting down. If one thinks about all of the muscle coordination needed in order to get up, release one's grasp, and then sit down, one can be more sympathetic and supportive of the baby and control one's impulse to get angry.

> "I think my baby is about to learn to sit down. He stands up, hangs onto the rail with one hand, looks behind him, and tries to size up the situation. Then he gives up and holds the rail with two hands again, bouncing just a little. I help him down before he cries. I can hardly wait for him to put it together and sit down. My husband likes to watch him and thinks it is very funny. We just couldn't imagine sitting was so hard to learn. I guess if he cries during the night because he can't sit down, I may not be so amused, but I don't think I'll get angry."

There are many activities that adults take for granted but that babies must learn. If we watch our babies carefully, however, we will see how much difficulty a baby can experience in learning how to do some things. Later on, you will see what a complicated experience it is to learn to sit down on a small chair. Parenting involves a great deal of observation and understanding that you might not have anticipated; this is one small example. It is a great satisfaction both for parent and child when the skill has been mastered.

Once the babies begin to stand in their cribs, the bumpers may become a hazard rather than an asset. Bumpers are used as a protection so that the baby will not bump against the edge of the crib or get wedged between the rails. When babies can stand in the crib, they may stand on the bumper. Then they can lose their footing and fall back into bed. Some may even be able to elevate themselves sufficiently on the bumper to lean over the rail and fall out of bed. Parents need to watch for this new development and be ready to remove the bumpers if necessary. Whether the bumpers will become a problem depends on the baby's height, the height of the rail, and the baby's competence and temperament.

> "I took the bumper out because the baby was standing on it, but you know what she did? She used the crumpled blankets and quilt to stand on and was able to lean way over the crib rail."

In that case, you have to be very careful to come in as soon as the baby wakes and take her out of the crib. Another possibility is to attach extenders to the crib rails to increase their height. But you have to be certain that they fit the crib firmly and are not made of flimsy plastic.

> "I asked about extenders in the furniture store and was told they were not safe. But I found good wooden ones in another store. I was worried because my sister's child fell out of the crib. I haven't bought them yet because the baby can't even pull himself to his knees."

Perhaps you can give us the information about those extenders so that we can share it. Some cribs have rails that are quite high and won't need extenders, and some babies are not so venturesome and don't become "climbers." Each family must assess the situation for itself.

BEGINNING SELF-FEEDING

A short time ago, we talked about teaching the baby to accept food offered from a spoon. Now, most of the babies have learned to do this and are beginning to use their hands to put bits of food in their mouths by themselves. They often reach for the spoon the mother is holding and try to advance it to their mouths. Some babies are advanced enough to get the spoon to their mouths, though they will most often invert the spoon. It is important at this stage that the food be thick and pasty so that it clings to the spoon and the baby gets some food and also develops a sense of self-feeding. Even with spoons, babies are not neat eaters, and you should not expect them to be. In time, they will all learn to hold spoons right side up and get them into their mouths without mishap. Now, however, they are at the reaching, spilling, messy stage.

Besides reaching for the spoon, babies also put their hands into the dish to pick up the food by themselves, again producing quite a mess. Some are also becoming ready for food which they can hold in their hands—for example, crackers, zwieback, teething biscuits, hard crusts, or toast. These signs of progress may cause concern because they interfere with the mother's usual feeding routines.

How are you coping with your babies' advances in the area of feeding?

> "My baby takes some of his food when I feed him. Then he likes to mess around a little in the food that's left if I don't take it away fast enough. If some spills on the tray, he loves to pick at it and feed himself. He seems to enjoy cold and messy food. Is that all right?"

Most babies of this age don't care if their food is the temperature and consistency that we think is enjoyable. Some may indeed prefer to eat it cold and messy. It is perfectly all right for him to feed himself bits of food left on the tray.

> "My baby seems to like only a few foods. It's very hard to introduce a new food. He prefers fruit to vegetables and likes his cereal cold and congealed."

That's another example of a baby's individual preferences and should be respected. It is good that you recognize his tastes and don't force him to take the food in a form he does not like. As we've said before, forcing the baby to eat something he does not like is a good way to initiate an eating problem which may be very hard to overcome.

> "My baby is so greedy for the cracker or toast that I give him that he puts too much in his mouth and almost chokes. I've almost decided not to give these things to him because I'm afraid he will choke."

Babies don't have good judgment. Moreover, their ability to swallow solids may not be fully developed, so they do have a tendency to choke or cough at times. It is best not to let a baby eat crackers or toast without supervision and to monitor how much the baby puts in his mouth until he matures enough to manage on his own. Some teething biscuits are very firm and do not break off until well-softened by saliva. This helps cut down on difficulties in swallowing.

No matter how worried you are, you do have to give the babies a chance to learn to feed themselves as soon as they show signs of readiness. Each mother has to experiment with her baby to see when to do this and which foods are most suitable for this stage. Pediatricians usually suggest a proper time to start the baby on certain foods.

> "My baby reaches for his food and makes such a mess that I have swaddled him in a towel so he can't get his hands free until I have finished feeding him. He doesn't like it, but he eats."

That seems like a rather drastic solution. If you keep it up over a long period of time, you may make the baby angry and inhibit his desire to feed himself when he is capable of it. It would seem to me that there are other alternatives. One (which I would consider third choice) is to hold him in your lap, cross your free arm over his chest to inhibit arm movements, and then feed him while talking to him and approving of his eating. Another technique is to sit the baby in his high chair and give him a spoon in one hand and a bottle cap or piece of bread in the other hand so he has something to do with his hands while you feed him. Or you could see if he was ready to hold the spoon himself after you have filled it and then help him guide it to his mouth. This is the best way for you to respond to this situation. If you find he is ready for self-feeding, progress has indeed been made.

"My baby is getting tired of his cereals, and I don't know what to substitute. I've tried them all."

Sometimes babies tire of the bland taste of cereal. If your baby likes fruit, mix some fruit with the cereal to enliven the taste. Also, toast and zweiback have the same food value as cereal and can be eaten as is or softened with milk. Oatmeal cookies are also a good substitute for cereal.

"I had that problem, and I solved it by sometimes giving the baby French toast. He likes to pick it up with his hands and eat it."

"My baby sometimes won't eat cereal. When she sees me eating toast with cream cheese and jelly, she almost jumps from her chair to get it. So I give some to her. She eats the jelly and cheese mostly. She seems happy and it agrees with her. My pediatrician says it's okay."

There seem to be several alternatives. The babies are getting older, and we have to respond appropriately to their maturing tastes and changes in habit.

"I'm introducing meat to my baby, and I give him a teaspoon from the jar. I continue with that same meat until the baby gets used to it. I finish one meat before I start another. Someone said, however, that I should vary the food more, so the baby won't get tired of just one kind."

It is safer to introduce a small amount of a new food (a teaspoon or half a teaspoon at first) until one is sure the baby likes and can digest it. Then gradually increase the amount to a tablespoon or two depending on the baby's appetite. There is too much concern about variety too early. It is better to be certain one food agrees with the baby before introducing another.

Some of you may wish to prepare your own baby food in the blender and freeze it in ice cube trays as one mother suggested earlier. One is then sure of the contents of the food. A large percentage of the commercially-prepared food is water and thickening (that is, cereal). The advantage of these prepared foods is their convenience, not their nutritional content.

Learning to Drink from a Cup

The babies are also now beginning to put their hands around their bottles to hold them themselves. This should not be a signal for mothers to stop holding the baby for the feeding. This is still a time for closeness. However, it does signal the time to introduce cup feeding. You need to offer only a little milk or juice from the cup, holding the cup for the baby, who may put his hands around it, helping the parent guide it to his mouth. This should be done regularly, so that the baby gets used to the experience of drinking from a cup. Parents should not expect that large amounts of liquid will be taken in this way at first. The introduction of the use of the cup needs to be systematic and gradual, just as spoon feeding was gradual. At first, the cup should be introduced at only one feeding a day, but its use may be increased as the baby becomes more accustomed to it.

Have you tried cup feeding yet? How are the babies doing?

> "Yes, I've started with the cup; I had to. He reached out for my cup whenever I was drinking tea or coffee, so I put a little of his milk in a cup, and he seemed to like it. Now he lets me drink from my cup. He can't really hold his cup, but I sit by him and hold his in one hand and mine in the other hand. It sounds hard, but it really isn't."

Your description shows that you have found a way to respond to this new development that suits you. This is an excellent way to "cue in" to the babies' needs and move with their readiness.

> "My baby did the same thing with me, and I tried the cup. Most of the milk spilled down his front, so I stopped."

Of course there will be much spilling at first. That's the reason for bibs. But the baby needs the experience of drinking from a cup. There are special cups with lids and spouts to facilitate drinking and prevent spilling. They are useful at first for some babies. A cup with a curved lip that fits over the baby's lip often helps in drinking. Learning to drink from the cup is achieved slowly but should be started when the baby shows readiness.

> "I don't like to cup-feed because it takes so much longer. I just want to get finished."

Feeding the babies and teaching them how to eat and drink takes time. Mealtime should not be rushed. It should be leisurely and pleasant for baby and parent. Too many adults gulp down their food in a rush, and want to set up this pattern for the babies now, and, in most cases, it is impossible to do because the babies' central nervous systems do not permit hurrying.

THE BABY'S INTRUSION ON THE PARENTS' TIME TOGETHER

We have just been talking about the time to feed babies and to help them develop on their own timetable. Perhaps what some mothers are really complaining about is not that each event in the baby's day takes so much time but that so much time is spent in dealing with the babies' needs that the mothers have no time to spend with their husbands or with other adults.

As we have mentioned a number of times, parents have little idea of how much time baby care takes. No one who has not had a baby can quite envision just how much time, effort, and physical work is entailed, especially when baby care is combined with maintaining a household. This can sometimes become a real threat to enjoying the baby and may even endanger the marriage.

When the parents feel that the baby is taking too much time and begin to get angry about it, they need to communicate this annoyance to each other and see how they both can try to arrange for more time together. They should not harbor their feelings in silence but should deal with them openly so they can decide together how to cope sensibly and positively with the situation.

Do you find that your baby is taking too much time away from your relationship with your husband? How have you been coping with the situation?

> "In the beginning I felt the baby was taking too much time, but now that he goes to bed regularly at seven o'clock and doesn't get up till about seven in the morning, I don't feel that way anymore. I'm glad when I see him awake in his crib in the morning."

> "My baby stays up too late in the evening. It's because my husband comes home late and needs to see her. By the time she is asleep, I'm too tired to even talk to my husband."

Perhaps you should reorganize your life so that you take a rest when the baby naps. That way, you will have some reserve energy and will be able to spend time with your husband after the baby is in bed.

> "We wanted our baby so much. We went to classes before he was born, and we decided we would put in the time needed to care for the baby by sharing as much of the work as we could. That way, we would be together even though we knew the baby would make many demands on our time. Our plan has succeeded beyond our wildest expectations."

Good for you! That is the ideal way to handle the situation and the way most of us would like to handle it, but some parents are not as well prepared as you were to cope with the changes in living patterns a new baby in the household entails. Most parents have to learn by trial and error after the baby is born. We think it is worthwhile to discuss problem situations because they can be resolved if the parents can communicate their feelings to each other and help each other to deal with them. If they cannot resolve a problem situation by themselves, they can always seek professional help.

Aside from being with the baby and relating to each other as caretakers, parents need time off by themselves as a couple to do the things they enjoyed before the baby came.

Have you begun to arrange time together for yourselves and your husbands? Have you been able to find the time to resume some of the activities you both enjoyed before the baby was born?

"No, we haven't gone out by ourselves yet because both of us are afraid no one else will take as good care of our baby as we do. We don't mind staying home, and when we go out, we take the baby. We visit friends with him. That was always our main way of relaxing, anyway."

That seems to suit your way of life now, but you do seem to be a bit too anxious about the baby. Perhaps you could get over your anxiety by starting to let a trusted friend or relative take some care of the baby while you are there to supervise. Then you will feel comfortable enough to leave the baby with her, for a short time at first and then for longer and longer periods. The length of time you leave the baby should increase gradually. It will be good for the baby, too, to learn to relate to another person, in addition to his parents. Of course, this should only be done when you feel ready for it.

"We have tried to go out on a regular basis—one night a week—so that we can get the same baby-sitter. We use a student nurse. Unfortunately, her schedule is so irregular that sometimes we haven't been able to use her, but we keep trying. My husband used to get a little annoyed that I was so particular about the arrangements, but now that he plays with the baby more and is getting to feel that the baby is his too, he has become just as particular as I am."

Your husband's response is very supportive. Fathers really care about their babies, and they care more as they take on more responsibility for the babies' care and have more contact with them. Some fathers like infants and are very handy with them; others are a little afraid to handle infants and do better with older babies or children.

"We have neighbors with a baby. All of us have a problem with the cost of sitters, so we exchange baby-sitting services once every week or two. When our neighbors go out, we stay with their baby in their apartment; they do the same thing for us. It's working out well."

That is a very good arrangement. It's a way of extending your social attachments and those of the babies, especially if the babies play together as well.

"We are lucky because our families live nearby, and both sets of grandparents are pleased to sit for us. It gives them a chance to spend time alone with their grandchild, and the baby gets to know them better."

You are lucky indeed to have your families so close by. It is a problem nowadays that families do not live near each other. Many children do not get to know their grandparents, and family socializing is sometimes limited. We will talk more about how babies begin to socialize in the next chapter.

Babies beginning to socialize and play
with parental assistance.

Chapter Nine

Age: 36 to 40 weeks _____

The baby is now sitting unsupported for a longer time and may be able to return to an erect sitting posture after leaning forward. Some babies may be able to maintain a standing position when holding onto the crib rail, although most cannot pull themselves to a standing position yet. This indicates further extension of the maturation of the central nervous system down to the legs.

The increasing competence of the baby's hands is evident in his attempt to pick up a marble-sized pellet with a **scissors grasp** (a grasp in which the thumb is opposed to the index and middle fingers). The baby can now grasp the third block while holding two others. He can also push one cube against another and touch a cube to the cup when it is offered. The baby is now interested in manipulating the string instead of reaching only for the red ring. These advances indicate increased fine motor coordination as well as the exploration of the relationship of objects.

Babies should be demonstrating increased vocalization and making recognizable sounds such as "da-da" and single syllables like "dah," "bah" and "mah." Babies will begin to imitate sounds made by the parent, if they are carefully and slowly enunciated. Some differentiations may begin now; for example, "da-da" may become "da-dee." Babies may respond to their own names and may even respond to "No, No" momentarily. This is early evidence of the comprehension of language.

By this time, some of the babies may be able to clasp their hands around the bottle but they still need help in holding the bottle for feeding. Emotionally, they still need to be held by the parent during feeding as well. The babies may be able to hold and eat a cracker or baby cookie but they are still not able to feed themselves alone.

THE BEGINNING OF SOCIALIZATION

Some of you have noticed that the babies are paying more attention to each other. When placed on the floor near each other, they

Rough Play with Other Babies

look and smile at each other and make reaching gestures. Sometimes one baby reaches for the toy another is holding. Sometimes one lunges toward another, and the encounter seems rough and dangerous. Babies are not intentionally rough; they simply do not have the coordination, control, and social experience to regulate their approach. Often the awkward approach of one baby will frighten another. For that reason, the babies should be carefully watched.

Have you noticed that your baby has begun to socialize? How are you coping with your baby's actions and reactions?

"I notice my baby gets very excited when she sees another baby sitting beside us in the park. She smiles and watches the older children playing for long periods of time. Does she really know that they are children?"

Yes, the babies are beginning to recognize the difference in size between a grownup and child. They seem to have the capacity for socialization earlier than we had been prepared to expect.

"My baby is just the opposite. He screams and is frightened when a child comes near him in the park. What should I do?"

When he seems frightened, he has to be held and comforted. For some reason, something connected with the children—perhaps the sounds they are making or their gestures—appears menacing to him. If you do not seem upset with the baby but comfort him and, if necessary, allow him to observe from a greater distance, he will eventually enjoy contact with other children. He should not be forced to engage in this activity, but should feel protected by you as long as he seems to need it.

"I find that when babies touch each other, they are very rough. I get angry and pull my baby away when he is rough or when another baby is rough with him."

Anger is spontaneous response on your part; it may be your way of dealing with your fear of possible negative consequences of the babies' socialization. It would be better for you to handle the situation by separating the children gently and demonstrating to children how they should play. For example, pat your baby gently with the other baby's hand and say "Nice and easy" or "Nice baby." Then pat the other baby gently with your baby's hand. Repeat the demonstration as often as necessary. Eventually both babies will begin to understand and get control of their movements.

"My baby is rough when she touches my face. She also pulls my hair and even pinches me sometimes. I get very angry and scream at her. That frightens her and she cries. Then I regret my reaction."

It's only natural for you to cry out when the baby hurts you, but there is no point in being angry at the baby. She really meant no harm; she was only attempting affectionate or exploratory contact with you. In trying to find out what you feel like, she pinched you. In exploring your hair, she pulled it—but not to hurt you, just to find out how it felt to touch your hair. It may feel like a slap when the baby pats your face, but the baby does not know she is being rough. She must be shown how to touch and explore. When she reaches for you face, intercept her hand, and guide it so she will not hurt you. Show approval of this approach, and gradually she will be able to understand what you are indicating and control her exploration. Roughness is all part of the baby's immaturity, and it's part of the parent's job to help the baby explore or express affection in a more acceptable way.

Some time ago we had discussed traveling with an infant and all that it entailed. Many families do not have the means, opportunities, or time for long trips but do go visiting with their baby. Mothers often take their babies to a friend's house for an afternoon, especially if the friend has a baby of a similar or even somewhat older age. Some babies will sleep throughout the visit, allowing mothers to have some adult social exchange. If the babies are awake, they are often left in a playpen together or on the floor with toys, and the mothers stay nearby trying to exchange a few words. Usually this does not last for long because babies of this age do not have a repertoire of play activity that is extensive enough to allow for a prolonged visit. They look at each other, touch each other, perhaps even pull hair, poke at eyes, or reach for each other's toys. This is the beginning of their socialization.

The babies' actions are entirely exploratory at this age. No matter how dangerous the contacts they make may appear, they are not malevolent, just exploratory. But babies of this age need careful monitoring and managing by the mothers. This disappoints some mothers because they have been looking forward to visiting with a friend and it seems that the babies are interfering. The truth of the matter is that the mothers' expectations of their babies' social ability are too high. If the babies can manage to amuse themselves in adjacent areas for a few minutes, or at closer range in a protected setting, such as on each mother's lap but within reach of each other, they can learn to touch and wave a toy at each other. That is all that can be expected in the way of play. The mothers may continue to hold them in their laps, feed them a bit of cookie or fruit, and try to finish their own refreshments. Then the mothers can play with the babies on the floor, rolling balls, pushing a toy to each, or playing "Peekaboo." At this age it is impossible to leave the babies to their own devices. The adults must participate in their play.

Because the adults have to participate so much, the visit may seem like a useless exercise, but it is the beginning of socializing. If

Taking the Babies on Visits; The Social Level of Babies of This Age

repeated with compatible mothers and babies, with the mothers intent on developing the babies' social responses rather than on conversing with each other, it can be a good learning experience. As the babies grow older, the mothers can take pleasure in seeing the maturation of their babies' social development.

If there are older children present, they may enjoy entertaining the babies. Babies are often content for a long time merely watching older children at play. This is a good experience for them and a boon to both mothers.

Have you begun to take your babies on visits? How have these visits worked out?

> "I go visiting only on rainy days when we can't go to the park and it would be misery to be penned up all day. At first, my baby sits in my lap and plays with the spoon while I try to have coffee. My friend has a younger baby, who usually is asleep, and an older boy. The boy tries to play with my baby and does amuse him a little. But mostly I have to play with him if he doesn't want to sit on the floor by my chair and play with the toys I bring. We roll the ball back and forth while I get in a word of two with my friend. Sometimes it works well, and I feel refreshed by the visit. Sometimes her baby is cranky or her son is cross, and the visit doesn't work, so I go home. But the length of time I can stay at her house is getting longer."

> "That's exactly my experience. I'm glad to know it's the same for someone else. I'm told by my mother-in-law that I 'give in' to the baby too much. She thinks I should let him cry while I have my coffee and not hold him and play with him. She thinks he should have 'visiting manners' at this age. She says her children behaved better."

Members of the older generation forget at what ages their babies developed "social manners." Your mother-in-law is probably recalling her children at a later stage in their development. For this age you and your baby are "doing your thing" appropriately. "Manners" are not learned until a very much later stage and should not be the concern of parents of babies of this age.

> "I find that the best way for me to socialize is to go walking with my friends when the baby is in the carriage watching the scenery or sleeping and their babies are doing the same. When we are in each other's houses, we can't talk; we just have to tend to the babies. If we sit down for coffee with the children in our laps, they may reach for and spill something. Coffee is too much of a hassle now, so we just settle for a coke. At least, that is not hot and can't hurt the babies if it spills on them. It worked out all right if you don't expect more. I know that babies grow fast and that this time will pass."

That's a good compromise and a realistic attitude.

> "I just can't see taking the baby out visiting when the visit is likely to end up in disaster. First of all, there is so much gear to get ready—the diapers, the bottle, a change of clothes, the toys, the cookies. Then undressing the baby when you get there and redressing him to go home. It just doesn't seem worth the bother. I think I'm just going to wait till my baby is older and less is needed."

It may seem like a great deal of work to go visiting with a baby. If you have enough company at home and you don't feel isolated and deprived, that is certainly a resonable attitude to have. Each parent has to suit his or her own needs and personality. However, you should also recognize that socialization is an important part of growing up and some provision needs to be made for it.

Now that the babies are older, you should try to resume your social life. You might begin doing this by inviting a couple or two over for the evening when the baby is asleep.

Entertaining Visitors at Home

Parents often think that the babies sense that something is going on and choose just that night not to go to sleep at the expected time. This may, in fact, happen. The mother may hurry the baby just a little because she is anxious to get the baby to bed. The baby senses this and reacts in the only way he can—by crying or being irritable. Or, when preparing for company, the mother may change the schedule a little; she may keep the baby waiting for something or let the baby get a bit overtired while she is preparing for her company. Then the baby makes his displeasure known by fussing and has more difficulty settling down to sleep.

These reactions by the babies do not mean parents ought not to entertain. You simply must take a more casual attitude to the company, or plan ahead, so that preparations are simplified. If the plans are not carried out as carefully as prior to the baby's arrival, no one will mind. The important thing is to be able to be together with friends—not whether the silver is polished or the table is set before your guests arrive. Good friends can always pitch in and help after they arrive if all is not ready in advance. Some such compromises may have to be made.

There are some parents who have been accustomed to entertaining a great deal by dividing the work. They can continue this after the baby comes. One parent attends to the baby's needs, and the other prepares for the company. After the baby has been taken care of, they both tackle what still remains to be done.

Sometimes one's guests have children, too, and know what to expect. They can be useful and not critical. They, too, are glad to get out again and value the adult companionship more than the decor or the kind of refreshments offered. Of course, there is always the short cut of sending out for Chinese food, fried chicken, or pizza.

Have you begun to entertain company again? How have you been handling the situation?

> "It's funny that this should be brought up now because last night for the first time since the baby came we asked my husband's boss and his wife over to see the baby and have dinner. We had been very friendly with them before the baby came, but I thought having them over would be a nice gesture. I cooked the night before and had everything ready. It only needed to be heated, and my husband brought home the dessert. So it really wasn't a big deal.
>
> They came a little earlier than expected, just as the baby was getting his bath, so I invited them to watch. They seemed to enjoy this, and the baby's schedule wasn't interrupted. They waited until I had fed him and put him to bed as usual. Everything went off well, but if I'd known they would get there before the baby was bathed and fed, I'd have been a bundle of nerves, and things would have been a mess."

It really takes guts to ask the boss and his wife as your first guests, but you managed very well. What you describe is the kind of anxious state some people can get into by anticipating the worst. Just taking things as they come, and not worrying about the impression you make on the boss or any other guest, makes everything come out more comfortably.

> "She was very lucky the baby went off to sleep as usual. That isn't what happened to me when I invited some relatives over. I purposely invited them for after the baby's bedtime, but they came early, played with the baby, and got him overexcited. Then I had to hold the baby in my arms for almost half an hour to quiet him down. I guess I should have been glad my guests were so interested in the baby, but I was really concerned about not being ready for them."

You may have been too concerned, and the baby may have sensed that. However, if visitors do come at bedtime, there is nothing wrong in telling them that the baby will be too stimulated to go to sleep if they play with him. Just ask them to look at him and leave the room, so the baby can be put to bed. One can say very pleasantly: "It's his bedtime now, so it's best just to have a 'look-see.' That way, he won't get too excited and not be able to go off to sleep." Very often, the father can say this as he leads the guests into the room in which the baby is being cared for, or the mother may say it if the father is taking care of the baby.

> "What can you do when visitors come during the day? Suppose the baby isn't napping, and they hop all over and upset him?"

Some babies, depending on their stage of development and personality, take to strangers and can be amused by the visitors while you prepare something, provided you are close by and in sight. If the babies are going through the period of stranger anxiety, they may howl. In that case, the baby's interests have to be defended. The baby has to be held close and the visitors asked to pay no attention to the baby and allow him to get used to their presence. Later, the baby will respond to their advances if they are gentle and not intrusive.

The parent can ease the way a little by having the visitor offer the baby one of his favorite toys or a cookie or dangle some object, not too vigorously, to attract the baby's attention. When parents know their baby's temperament and stage development, they can guide the visitor so that the encounter will be as pleasant as possible.

If all of this fails, just take the baby into another room, settle him down, and go on with his regular schedule. If the visit works, fine. If not, ask the friends back for another visit when the baby is asleep. There is no need to feel embarrassed or guilty if such visits aren't successful the first time.

"Well, if you are always catering to the babies like that, how will they ever get to be sociable, and how will we ever get to have friends around during the day?"

Adults who have no experience with babies have to be helped to understand their needs. The baby will learn gradually as he develops and is exposed to social situations with which he can cope. His coping repertoire increases as his successful encounters with visitors increase. It is important for the baby to have a sense of parental support and understanding rather than to feel their displeasure and disappointment at his social failures. This is not catering to the baby but moving with the baby's readiness to socialize.

"What do you do if the baby fusses when you go visiting at a house where there are no children and the grownups make a big fuss over your baby? They are practically standing on their heads to entertain the baby, and still he responds to them so negatively."

If you know from previous experience that the baby responds that way to strange people and places, warn the hosts. Tell them in advance that he is at the stage when he gets very upset if new people make advances to him, and that he needs to look the situation over and relax. Always take some of his favorite toys with you to distract him. Hold him yourself; don't let anyone take him from you. For example, the natural thing for the host to do is offer to hold the baby while your remove your coat. Don't let the host have the baby. Also, talk to the baby in a comforting, reassuring voice, and soon he will relax and be his usual self.

"That's what happened to me on my first visit to old friends of the family. I was so embarrassed, and my husband was a

little angry with the baby, which made matters worse. Finally I took the baby, held him, and walked around the living room showing him things. He gradually settled down. Then I gave our host the baby's favorite rattle to hand to him, and he was all smiles. The rest of the visit was fine. My husband thought the baby was spoiled because he cried."

That seems to be the usual interpretation adults make when the baby doesn't fulfill their expectations. The baby is not a "spoiled" baby because he is upset in a new situation which he does not understand. He expresses his anxiety in the only way he knows how—by crying. It is the parents' job to understand him and his need, and not to be so concerned with the reactions of other adults. The baby is not able to say: "I don't know you. I don't know if I can trust you. So just let me get used to you, please, and decide if I like you." That's what he is saying when he is crying. He is not spoiled; he is frightened.

The parents are a little frightened at first, too, because they think their visit is going to be disrupted. They are afraid that they won't have a good time, that their friends won't invite them again. They think: "We're doomed to having to stay home with the baby all the time. What a brat we are raising." That's not the case at all. Parents often feel that way because of their own inexperience. That's the reason for talking over such situations. The babies will gradually learn about socializing from happy visits, and visiting will get easier.

CURRENT MANIFESTATIONS OF SEPARATION ANXIETY

We have mentioned before the stage which a baby passes in learning to separate from the mother. Babies are born not realizing they are separate from the parent; they do not have a clear distinction of the boundaries of each. At about six months of age, a baby begins to get a sense of his/her physical distinctness from the other and his/her own physical extent.

At present, our babies are becoming much more active physically. They are beginning to crawl, stand, and adventure beyond mother's lap. But they still need to see the parent. They still do not know the parent exists when the parent is out of sight.

For some babies, being put to bed at night causes separation anxiety. Some cry and need to be patted to sleep or have a parent by the bed until they fall asleep. Others cry when the parent leaves the room to answer the doorbell or go to the bathroom. This is distressing and annoying for mothers and fathers unless they understand the baby's need to keep them in sight. Parents need to learn to deal appropriately with the situation. Instead of getting angry or frustrated, you should call to the baby, return as quickly as possible, and reassure the baby. Your might even take the baby with you on such errands.

What experiences with this stage of attachment and separation anxiety have you been having?

"Well, I have had the bedtime problem. It just began recently when I thought my baby was getting more grown-up."

"All my friends and relatives have said: 'Let him cry; he will get used to it.' The first night I did that. He sobbed and coughed and gagged up some food, so I knew I wasn't doing the right thing. From then on, I stood by his crib and patted him a little. Now he knows that when I turn him over and pat him it is sleep time. He goes to sleep in a minute or two that way."

You were very perceptive to catch on so quickly to what his need was. Some babies will need a little more soothing. They must have a great sense of trust to be able to relax that easily and go off to sleep quickly.

Some babies require rocking or singing. What do you suppose was the origin of lullabies which have come down to us through the centuries? Babies have always been the same, and mothers have intuitively known what was needed. It is a satisfaction for parents when they "cue in" to their baby's needs and get a good response.

"Every time I have to answer the doorbell and don't take him, my baby cries. It's quite a nuisance."

It is a nuisance to you, but it is agony to the baby because he doesn't know that you will come back. He has no sense of time or of how long you are away. He just knows his mother has disappeared, and he is not ready for that. Some babies, if they can crawl, follow their mothers to see where they are going. In that way, they can continue the attachment and feel in control of the situation.

"The worst part for me is getting to the bathroom. It is a little better now since the baby can sit and crawl. I take her with me, and she sits on the floor or crawls around. Now she is satisfied just to sit near the doorway so she can see me through the open door. Still when I pull the shower curtain, she comes right over and peeks in. It has to be a very quick shower."

"I have my baby in a walker, and he can follow me everywhere. He can even go away from me too. Sometimes he gets too far away and begins to cry, or he gets wedged into places and can't get back to me. But most of the time, he seems to like the walker, and it's easier for me."

The walker seems to work for you, but we usually do not recommend walkers for two reasons. One is that it encourages a baby to walk before his central nervous system has matured enough for him to walk on his own. The second reason is that the walker permits babies to get farther away from their mothers sooner then they would on their own. The incidents that you describe when the baby cannot see you and can't get back to you may be interfering with the natural development of your baby's ability to separate from you and may be causing him more anxiety that satisfaction.

Walkers make very nice, low seats in which babies can bob up and down. They are best used as seats, with the wheels off, so the babies can't walk. Then the babies can enjoy the walkers as a new play situation.

There is another objection to using walkers: They have a tendency to tip over easily. Babies really need to be watched when they are using them.

This stage of the process of separation is tough for both parents and children. Accommodations need to be made. Babies learn to be independent individuals by separating gradually from their parents; yet parents need to get out together and renew some of their activities. We recognize the needs of both babies and parents. How can we satisfy everyone's needs?

One of the ways of solving this problem is to leave the baby with a relative the baby is very familiar with. That used to be the commonest solution when there were large, extended families living together. It's not so easy to do now. Often we have to rely on friends the baby knows and likes.

If it is not possible to have the baby with familiar relatives or friends you should arrange for a regular baby-sitter. We have discussed this before, but it is an important topic, and you may wish to discuss it further. Adequate substitute child care is one of the most frequent problems for parents.

> "I am lucky. My baby is very happy with her grandmother. I can take the baby to her grandmother's house, and she seems happy there. My mother comes to our house if we need her help at night. I thought the baby didn't notice when I left, but she does get excited when I come back and only wants me to hold her."

She likes her grandmother, but she still needs you, as evidenced by her clinging when you come back. It's a good idea to make your departure brief and have the caretaker get the baby quickly involved in something interesting. Then, make your return enthusiastic by picking the baby up and holding her close. Emphasize your return, rather than your departure.

> "The other day I was out from 9:30 in the morning until 9:30 at night. The sitter said the baby did all right, but for the next few days he was clinging to me all the time and wanted to be held."

Twelve hours was a very long time to leave a baby. He missed you in ways the baby-sitter did not recognize or report, but he let you know by his clinging. If you must leave for such a long time, it is a good idea to prepare the baby for such extended absences by leaving for a short time, an hour or two at first, and then gradually lengthening the time so the baby gets accustomed gradually to the longer separations.

> "My baby cries so when I put on my coat to go out that I have taken to sneaking out because I can't bear the crying. But when I come back, he cries and clings. It happens more and more each time, and it's annoying. We do have to go out some of the time."

Sneaking out never pays off. It is better for the baby to see you go and then be engaged by the sitter in some pleasant activity. Sometimes the activity of going to the window and waving "Bye-bye" is engaging enough. Then make the homecoming the important event.

When a parent sneaks out and the baby suddenly finds the parent gone, he is usually very upset. He loses his sense of trust in the parent and does not let that parent out of sight again because he never knows when the parent may disappear. However if the baby gets used to saying "good-bye" to you and then begins to remember that you do return, his basic trust is not undermined, and he can begin to deal with separation. Sneaking out is a common practice because it appears easier, but it starts the parent on the deplorable road of dealing with a child deceptively. We will be discussing the importance of dealing honestly with our children again because it is so important for healthy character development.

_____ THE PARENTS' FEELINGS ABOUT THE CHANGES THEIR BABIES HAVE MADE IN THEIR LIVES

Now that the babies are older, they may be affecting parents' lives in different ways. The babies' level of development requires new attitudes on the part of the parents. What changes have you been noticing?

> "For one thing—and I think if affects me most—I can't get out as often. I think my husband feels the same, don't you?"

> "Yes, if we want to go out at night we have to get a baby-sitter. So that means I can't come home and spontaneously suggest going to a movie, or visiting friends, or taking a walk. Such things become a project. It used to gripe me a little at first, but not so much now. Of course, it's more a problem for my wife; she's the one who has to make all the arrangements."

> "When I come home at night, I'm tired. I'm glad that we are not going out the way we used to. I'm happy to play with the baby and help put him to bed. Then I watch TV. I guess that's dull for my wife. I'm more ready to go out weekends."

"I don't mind not going out during the week. I'm pooped at the end of the day. I do wish I could sleep late one morning once in a while on weekends. We go out shopping with the baby during the day or just walking or visiting. At night we get a sitter, or we exchange sitting services with a neighbor. But I do miss the morning sleep on weekends."

"Well, I like to play golf weekends. It's no fun for my wife to wait at the golf course with the baby, so she stays home. This has caused some hard feelings at times, so now I stop by noon or early afternoon. That way, we have some of the day together to do what she wants."

"It took me a while to adjust to my husband's golf, but then I figured that he's cooped up all week and needs exercise and unwinding. If I want to go out, I can go out with the baby. Sometimes I get a baby-sitter or leave the baby with my mother and go to the golf course too. I stopped feeling like a martyr, and we're all happier, but it took a little time. We both have had to give up a little for the baby. We're young. He'll grow up. We'll have time together later."

"What seemed to bother us both most was dinner time. That used to be the time that the baby cried most, and needed most attention, and was hardest to handle. Sometimes we couldn't get him to bed so easily. When I came home, dinner was never ready, my wife was a wreck, and I got mad. Now the baby is older, he goes to bed more regularly and easily, and I enjoy putting him to bed while my wife gets dinner ready. We had to learn the right way to put him to bed. We developed a regular pattern as you and our pediatrician suggested, but it took time. We were, as you say, impatient, the way most parents are."

"The difference I mind most is that I can't bring friends home from work for dinner on the spur of the moment. I have to give my wife notice, and even then, if the baby's had a bad day, it doesn't work out. So I usually have to take my friends out to dinner, and my wife has to stay home. Sometimes she can get a baby-sitter and comes too, but that's rare.

"What I mind most is the mess of toys and baby junk around. Does a baby need so much? Why can't it all be picked up before I get home?"

Each family seems to have had to make some adjustments to the baby's presence. Most of the problems were due to not understanding in advance that there would be changes. At first, parents think babies sleep all the time and only wake for feedings and changings. Some few babies are like that, but most have difficulty learning to develop a pattern of sleeping and eating. You learned to cope and helped the babies develop their physiologic rhythms. You have had to adjust your social lives a great deal. We must remember that we are dealing with a being who has to be helped from total dependence to independence, and that's a long process entailing a whole career of parenting. If parents understand this process, it can be interesting, fun, and very rewarding. It does seem that most of you have worked out your individual adjustments.

If fathers hate to see toys strewn around, they can get a toy chest or basket where all the toys could be gathered together quickly. Some fathers come from homes where their mothers waited on their fathers, and they expect the same of their wives. Some wives can manage to do that if the baby isn't too active and demanding; others cannot. There are certain things that adults have to be mature enough to accept. After all, putting a few toys away is no big deal, so whichever parent can get to the chore first should do it. Bringing up a baby is a job for both parents. Dad has to have some input, too. His share of responsibility for the baby can't always be just the fun part of playing with the baby.

"Don't you think that taking care of the baby and the house is the wife's job if the husband spends all day working?"

For most jobs outside the home, the working days lasts from 9:00 a.m. to 5:00 p.m. The job inside the home, usually lasts from 6:00 a.m. to 12:00 midnight, with occasional night duties. By any standard, this is a long work day! In our society, most children are cared for by their mothers, but this may be changing. The mother caring for an active child and a home rarely has time to rest during the day, although she should. So a mother is not being inefficient, lazy, or inconsiderate, if she needs some help from father by the end of the day. The more the father participates in the child's rearing, the better for the child—and the stronger the bond between the parents too. We know that many young couples are partners in the parenting effort, and we recommend whatever arrangement suits each family's lifestyle, desires, and needs. There are many different ways of sharing the duties and pleasures of rearing children.

CHANGES THE FATHERS HAVE NOTICED IN THE BABIES' DEVELOPMENT AND PLAY

We have been talking about the fathers' feelings about the babies and the demands a child places on parents' time and energies. We are also interested to learn what the fathers have observed about the babies' development and how these observations have affected their involvement and fun with the baby.

Acceptable
Forms of
Play

"The things I notice most is that the baby is more fun. In the first weeks, it seemed to me that the baby was mostly pesty if he wasn't asleep or being held. There was no real play. Now he plays a lot."

That certainly is a nice change. What kind of play do you do now that you weren't able to before?

> "I especially enjoy roughhousing. I get down on the floor, make funny sounds at him, and chase him as he crawls. Sometimes I let him go after me as though he were chasing me. He couldn't do that before because he couldn't crawl. We have a great time. Only, my wife says that that kind of activity is too strenuous before bedtime, and that I get the baby too excited and he won't go to sleep. Sometimes we have a hassle about it. That's bad, so I don't do it too often, but I miss it."

> "My baby likes me to throw him in the air. I enjoy that and she seems to enjoy it too, but my wife goes into a panic and puts a damper on the fun."

> "I noticed my wife was right about the baby's having difficulty getting to sleep after rough play. I think maybe the baby is too young and a little scared. So now we sit quietly on the floor. I place a toy a little distance from us and have him crawl to get it and bring it back to me. Then I put it a little further away, and he brings it back. Then maybe I'll put several around, and he'll get them all. This way we are doing something together, and it's not too exciting before bed. Sometimes now he hands me a toy and wants me to put it somewhere so he can get it. He's learning."

> "I play by handing my baby a toy—say a ball or an animal or something and right away it goes into her mouth. That bothers me."

It seems that the fathers are playing more with the babies and deriving more pleasure, but there are certain aspects of play that seem to need some discussion. One is the "roughhousing" before bed. Some of you have noticed that it interferes with the baby's ability to go to sleep quickly. That is because the baby becomes overstimulated and has difficulty settling down. This is not a reason to stop a pleasant encounter with the baby, but the father then must help the baby "simmer down." He should engage the baby in some quiet activity for a while, such as looking at a book with the baby, walking around holding the baby and pointing out objects in the house or cars passing in the street, holding the baby and singing to him or handing him a toy to place on a shelf or in a chest. If this pattern of play followed by a quiet period is carried out consistently, it can become a pleasant bedtime routine for the baby. While the father is getting the baby to bed in this way, the mother can be getting dinner ready.

We must also discuss throwing the baby in the air. Mothers do have some reason to worry because this kind of play can be dangerous. On more than one occasion a baby who has been thrown in the air has not been caught in time. Babies are not predictable; they can swing away from the parent and fall. Sometimes, while being caught, they can swing their heads back and then vigorously forward, producing a "whiplash" injury similar to the results of a car accident. This doesn't mean that the father must desist from vigorous play, but that such play should be done in a safer way. Instead of throwing the baby free into the air, hold the baby under the arms, and lift him overhead and down again. Babies may shriek as though in glee when thrown in the air, but they are usually more frightened than delighted. It is really best not to let go of them in the air.

Another thing that seems to cause concern is that some of the babies are still putting toys into their mouths. This response is appropriate for the baby as the mouth is still one of the main avenues of exploration. It may still be the way the baby derives pleasure from that toy. The toy should, therefore, not be pulled abruptly out of the baby's mouth. Instead the parent can try to induce the baby to extend the toy toward the parent; the baby may even be able to give it to the father and then take it back. A nice game can develop from this activity.

> "Well, we are doing something like that. What I do is hand my baby a small block, and he dumps it into a box. Then I give him another. His interest is sustained for about two or three minutes. Then we dump the blocks out and start all over again. I enjoy this activity very much. I guess in time the baby will be able to sustain interest for longer and longer periods of time."

That's a good game because, like the other games we have been discussing, it involves motion and stimulating the baby's motor skills.

Do any of you play games involving communication, such as talking to the babies, imitating their sounds, or naming things for them?

> "I never really considered talking to the baby. He makes a few sounds which seem to be the beginnings of speech—for example, 'ah-ah,' 'da-da,' and 'yiggy-yiggy,' which his mother thinks is the name of his toy bear—but I haven't really tried talking to him yet."

> "Is it important to talk to the babies in their own 'language,' to say back to them what they seem to be saying? Or should we speak to them in real words?"

When we speak to the babies, we should use real language. If you are pointing out an object—a doll, for instance—say the word "doll" or "dolly" in a lilting tone, so they will get the modulation and rhythm. This modulation helps them imitate what you are saying. If you are giving the baby a bottle, say "bottle" ("bah-tell") in a lilting voice, so the baby can distinguish the sounds.

However, when they vocalize, making a few syllables with their own distinctive inflection, you should make similar sounds back. In this way, the babies get the feeling that their vocalizing is important and that the parent is on their wave length. Doing this consistently sets up a sort of conversation, which is a very pleasant and productive game to play with the baby.

> "My husband does that with the baby by the hour. She talks more with him than with me. It's their thing. He couldn't come tonight, or he would have told you. It's a joy to watch."

SAYING "NO" AND SETTING LIMITATIONS

> "I don't say much to the baby, but I think he understands when I say 'No' to him in a loud voice. He stops what he is doing; sometimes he even cries. I feel badly then."

It is possible to be too emphatic and frighten the baby. However, if the baby is doing something you don't want him to do—and this happens often during this period of increased mobility—the parent should say "No." As we have said previously, these "No's" should be consistent—always for the same things. Then the baby should be immediately provided with an approved activity, and the parent should indicate his or her approval of the substitute by saying "Good," "Nice," "That's fine," or whatever is the parents' natural and usual expression of approval.

> "Sometimes I say 'No' just to see if the baby will stop. Then he will reach for something else, and I'll stop him again, until saying 'No' becomes a kind of game. Somehow it didn't seem just right to me to make a game of it; yet the baby seemed to enjoy the activity."

It is best not to make a game of saying "No" because the parent is now beginning to teach the baby limitations. There may be very real and very negative consequences if the baby doesn't learn that "No" is a serious prohibition and not a game. In limiting a baby, one doesn't have to use an angry voice but a firm tone and a serious facial expression are necessary. No matter how endearing or cute the baby may be, you should not smile when you say "No" because you confuse the signal you are giving the baby. We have to remember that what is cute now may not be cute later on.

The Conse-quences of Expecting Too Much

> "I've noticed that when I say 'No,' the baby stops for a minute but then goes right ahead. So what good does it do to say 'No'?"

That's a very accurate and perceptive observation. At this stage of the baby's development, he can only respond briefly to "No." The parent must immediately substitute an alternate approved activity. The impulse to perform an act has gone out from the baby's brain, and the act has to be completed. The check mechanism which causes a person to stop and not finish an act is not yet developed in babies of this age. This development in the central nervous system comes at a much later time. That's why the parent has to give the baby a substitute way of discharging the impulse.

"But how long will we have to wait for the babies to be able to obey a command instantly?"

Their control mechanisms may not mature sufficiently until about eight or nine years of age or sometimes even later. Parents expect this self-control now, but it's not physiologically possible. All the babies can do now is stop momentarily when parents say "No." If the baby does that, he is doing very well.

If parents expect more than a baby—or child of any age—is capable of delivering, the parent becomes angry and disappointed. Overestimating the child's ability and misunderstanding his behavior may lower his self-esteem or make him angry. A series of such unhappy encounters between parent and child may mar their relations and endanger the child's healthy personality development.

That is why we feel it is so important for parents to understand their baby's development, so that they may avoid the consequences of expecting too much too soon.

"That makes sense. I understand all that better now. My wife and I have discussed setting limits, and I felt she wasn't firm enough. That is why I yelled so loud and was a little annoyed when she tried to calm me down. But what do you do when you understand this, but others like grandparents or friends don't?"

That is hard because it's natural for us to want to show our parents and friends how well our babies behave and what competent parents we are. However, there are some things that have been learned in recent years about child development that they may not know. It is quite in order for the parent to explain to the grandparents, other relatives, or friends about the baby's level of development and that the goal of so-called "obedience" is for the future when the baby's nervous system has matured. Explain that you are taking the first steps by limiting the baby and then giving him a substitute approved activity.

We have talked about the increased mobility and exploration of our babies. We discussed the balance between housekeeping needs and the babies' need to explore and satisfy their curiosity, to learn from more interaction with their expanding environments.

Exploration: The Need for "Baby-Proofing" and Setting Limitations Consistently

Increased mobility is probably increasing the number of situations in which the parents have to restrict the baby and say "No." While this limitation of the babies is necessary for their own protection and the protection of your possessions, it is important that the babies not be confronted at every turn with parental "No's." Too much limitation can be highly frustrating to a healthy, curious baby.

Parents also have to be careful not to use too many "No's" because the admonition will lose its impact and be ignored.

A baby needs to explore and have outlets for his curiosity, a chance to learn about the world around him. Some "baby-proofing" therefore has to be done. The most valuable or dangerous objects in the house should be removed from the baby's reach; safety plugs should be put into electric outlets; poisonous cleansers, bleaches, paints, and medications should be put on high shelves and in cabinets with safety latches. Parents have to provide an environment which is reasonably safe so that the child's exploration does not have to be constantly limited.

> **"If you take everything that's interesting away, there is nothing for the baby to explore."**

Only dangerous or valuable items should be removed, so that the number of objects which the baby cannot touch is limited. Then the number of times a parent has to say "No" can be tolerated by the baby and can provide a good learning situation instead of a source of friction between parent and child.

> **"Our main problem is when we visit one of the baby's grand-mothers. She is a very old lady and has a house full of antiques. Before we come to visit, she clears away as much as she can, and she assures us not to worry if something gets broken. But we find we are constantly running after the baby and saying 'No.' When we leave, we are all pooped, and yet we want to visit her."**

Visiting with an inquisitive ten-month old baby is often a trying experience. You are probably more tense than you need to be and ought to accept the grandmother's assurance that she will be able to cope if something is damaged. If you make the visits short but frequent, the baby will begin to learn what is available for her to explore there, and she will have an enriching experience. You can hold the baby, show her some of the pretty things her grandmother has, and then give her special things to play with. Since you visit often, the grandmother can arrange a special toy corner or shelf for the baby. Things the baby is allowed to play with can be placed there.

> **"When we go visiting, our friends have things which are break-able on their coffee tables, while the things we leave on our own coffee table the baby can touch. Isn't that confusing to the baby?"**

It is confusing to the baby when she can do certain things in one house and not in another. So the parent should try to regularize the situation by saying to the hostess, "Let's put this out of the baby's reach, so we won't have any problem." Put out the toys or things the baby can touch, and replace the objects you have removed when you leave. It will make the visit easier and happier, and the hostess will appreciate it, even if she says she doesn't mind if something is broken. Then you'll be welcome again.

"We have a glass coffee table in our living room that has very sharp corners and is breakable. It's just the right height for the baby to pull himself up with, and then he bangs on it with whatever he has in his hand. The atmosphere becomes very tense when he is in the living room, and that tension is getting to us. Should we just wait it out, or move the table?"

If possible, it is best not to prolong situations that frustrate both parents and child. It seems that you are taking too much of a chance with the baby's safety and the life of the table. It probably would be easier to put the table out of the way until the baby is older and has learned to respond to your limitations.

It is also a good idea to have a place in each room with toys, cloth books, or blocks—pots and pans in the kitchen—that the baby is allowed to touch and manipulate. If the baby goes where he shouldn't, say "No" firmly, pick him up, and take him to the area where he is allowed to touch everything, giving affirmative approval by the tone of voice and words ("This is for baby," "Good," "How nice").

Parents must realize that the "No-No" items are very tempting. The babies are not at the stage where they can remember the "No" yet and control their desires. The procedure of saying "No" and providing an approved substitute will take several months before it will finally yield results and the baby gets the idea. The length of time varies with each baby.

"I know it's important to be consistent with the 'No's,' but sometimes the baby is so cute I just have to laugh. Does this set back her learning?"

Behavior you disapprove of may indeed be very cute and amusing, but what is amusing at this age may not be amusing at a later stage. The parent, therefore, has to be firm and consistent, and try to save the laugh or smile for emphasizing the achievement of approved behavior.

If parents smile when they say "No," babies get two conflicting messages. This confuses them. Parents must say "No" with their whole demeanor and facial expression. The message must be clear and immediate. A parent shouldn't test to see if a baby of this age can stop by himself without parental reinforcement.

Some parents get very angry when a baby does not respond at once to their admonitions. They lose their "cool" and slap the baby to reinforce the "No" and to relieve their feelings. Most adults do not

Slapping and Spanking to Reinforce "No"

realize how long it takes for the baby to be able to respond to "No" and how often the admonition will have to be given before the baby learns what is meant. Parents sometimes feel the process will be hastened by slapping.

"That's exactly the way my husband thinks. He thinks the baby should stop at once, and if she doesn't, she should get slapped. My husband sees no harm in it. That's the way he was brought up, and his mother agrees with him."

That is indeed the way most of us were brought up, and some of us have lasting marks of it in our character structure. We are impatient with others, get angry easily, and use our hands to reinforce what should be conveyed only by words.

Such negative personality traits are usually the results of mishandling in childhood, and usually this mishandling comes about because there has been no understanding of the responses that the babies' immature nervous systems can make. There is a long lag before the message to stop gets to the appropriate centers of control in the baby's brain and is translated into action. Babies are not being naughty or stubborn when they don't respond promptly; it simply is not possible for them to do so. Slapping the baby just jams the overloaded nervous system more. In addition, it gives the baby a negative model of behavior. At some later time, the baby will try to slap the parent or another person.

"If a baby slaps you, shouldn't you slap him back to teach him a lesson?"

No, if you do that, you will be teaching the baby to slap rather than not to slap because you are providing and reinforcing a behavior model. Also, slapping the baby back will only aggravate an already tense situation and may seriously damage the parent-child relationship.

While we are talking about slapping, we might as well talk about spanking. Spanking an older child to "teach him a lesson" does indeed teach a lesson—that when one is bigger and more powerful, one can hit another person and get away with it. We have seen in our groups here that the children who were spanked tend to hit others to settle their differences. Those who have been restrained verbally, in a way appropriate to their age, tend to settle their differences verbally.

We are not saying that an occasional slap will create a violent or overly submissive child. None of us is perfect, and there are times when babies and children can be exceedingly trying, usually just at the times when we as adults are tired or upset ourselves. If we realize, however, the bad effect physical discipline can have, we can try to control our own actions. Those adults who cannot control their own actions can become child abusers. All of us have the potential to become that kind of parent. Sometimes if your child angers you, it is best to put him in his crib, call a friend or your husband, and **tell that person** of your anger. Or else, you could put the baby in the carriage and go for a walk, or put the baby to bed and wash the kitchen floor. All of us have to learn how to handle and dispel our own anger. No one should feel guilty about having angry feelings. They are a natural part of our human makeup, but we all need to help each other learn how to release our angry feelings appropriately.

> **"That explanation helps me to understand my baby's behavior better. My mother said to slap the baby's hands. She was angry with me when I refused. She said: 'You and your new ideas. I brought up five and they are fine.' I just couldn't tell her how many of us have had or need psychiatric help."**

> **"I am so relieved to hear that other parents get angry. It makes me feel less guilty. The next time that happens, I'll try to think of this discussion."**

Being a parent is a full-time job and takes patience and ingenuity. It's not easy to keep your wits about you and act positively all the time, but it pays off in helping the child accept limitations with the minimum of stress for both parent and child. As in any other profession, parents need "time off." No one can be patient and positive twenty-four hours a day, seven days a week.

No one works efficiently if the work is continuous without any time off for rest and recreation. In industry, when people are overworked and overtired, the accident rate goes up. At home, when parents are overworked and overtired, yelling and hitting increase. Therefore, parents must have time off in order to do their job well. Then physical punishment will not become part of their interaction with their children and be perpetuated in the next generation as a model for parent-child interaction.

To summarize, then, it is best not to slap or spank the baby. It does not have a good effect. Say "No" and mean it. Then remove the baby from the undesirable activity and offer her and approved activity. Try to reinforce the good, not the bad. Make the good activity the one recognized by smiles, approving gestures, and voice.

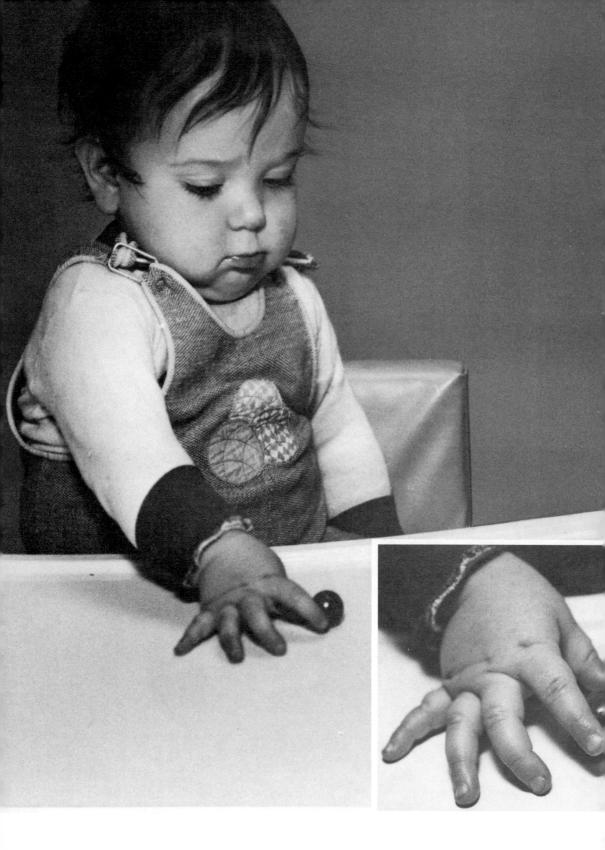

Ten-month-old baby picking up a marble-sized pallet
with pincers grasp.

Chapter Ten

Age:
40 to 44 weeks _____

The baby can now usually get to the sitting posture with a minimum of assistance or entirely on his own. Once sitting, he can maintain that posture indefinitely without falling over. He can also extend himself to the prone position and push himself back to a sitting position. The baby may now pull himself to a standing possition. (The rail of the crib should, therefore, be up all the way from now on.) He may get down from a standing to a sitting position, and begin crawling movements.

The baby can now release a block by extending and releasing her fingers. She tries to pick up a marble-sized pellet with a beginning **pincers grasp** (opposing thumb and index finger) and can manage to pluck the string holding the red ring using the same grasp.

The baby is beginning to observe more carefully objects held in each hand and may try to match them together. When he notices a block in the cup, he may touch it but not yet be able to remove it. This is evidence that the baby is learning to understand the relationship of objects. When presented with a bell, the baby grasps the handle and may spontaneously wave or bang it. However, he is just as likely to suck or bite it. The baby may get pleasure from the sound he is making, but not understand its source.

The baby should be beginning to say "Mama" and "Dada" in a more recognizable way and even have one other single-syllable word in her vocabulary, such as "Hi," "Bye," the beginning of some-one's name, or perhaps even "ba" for "bottle." (It is important for parents to repeat what they recognize of this rudimentary vocabu-lary; parents can foster the use of words by repetition and approval.)

Social play may have advanced to the point where the baby will respond to "Bye, bye" with a gesture of the arm or hand, if not yet a real wave. "Pat-a-Cake" may be responded to by patting the table and finally opposing one hand against the other. At first, parents should demonstrate this game with their own hands. Then they can hold the babies' hands and show them how to do it. In time, with maturation and approval, the babies will begin to do it on their own. This game is great fun for both parent and child, as well as a profitable learning experience for the child.

WAKING AT NIGHT

Caused by Teething, Dreaming, or Other Discomforts

During the first few weeks in caring for the baby, the pattern of sleep was of great concern to all of you. At first, the babies were waking frequently for feedings, not sleeping through the night, and getting up very early. You were not getting enough time to sleep, which made you a little edgy. Some of you were alarmed because you were afraid this was to be your way of life forever. We assured you that this period would pass in time.

By about four months most of the babies had, with the help of regular sequence of daily activities, together with their own natural development, begun to settle into longer sleeping intervals. Many have now begun to sleep through the night, though a few continue to need a late night bottle. In general, most of you have been getting more sleep and are more rested.

Now there is a new development: Some of the babies are waking during the night, again causing anxiety and loss of sleep to parents. This waking also will be temporary. Some of it is caused by teething. The gums becomes inflamed and sore. During sleep, the baby may clench down on his gums, causing pain. The pain wakes the baby momentarily and he cries. When he cries, he opens his mouth and is no longer biting down on the sore gum. But he is awake, so he has to be put back to sleep. To get to sleep, some babies may need to be changed and given some water; others may require a bottle; still others may only need to be comforted and patted back to sleep.

Have any of your babies awakened during the night because of teething problems?

> "That may be what's happening with us now. The baby's gums look very swollen. We can't see or feel any teeth yet, but she is drooling a lot and biting on everything. She wakes sometimes. It's not every night and not the same time each night. Do you think teething is what the problem could be?"

Your description of the baby's drooling and swollen gums certainly indicates teething. What do you have to do to soothe her back to sleep when she wakes up at night crying?

> "I just pat her and cover her a little, and then she drops off to sleep. But I'm wide-a-wake."

It doesn't sound like you're having too bad a time of it. Now that you know that the problem is not so serious, maybe you won't awaken with such a start or stay so wide-a-wake. You'll be able to relax and get back to sleep more easily. The crying periods come in spurts and subside until teething again becomes bothersome to the baby. Somehow parents usually get used to this periodic waking.

"My baby has begun to wake too. At first I was very worried because I thought he had colic or appendicitis or something terrible. But he goes off to sleep again after I've changed his diaper and given him some water."

"You are all very lucky. When my baby wakes he is wide-awake. He wants me to stay in the room with him and play. So I stay awhile. Then I get angry and say, 'You go to sleep,' and put him down firmly. But it doesn't help. He wants to play, and he cries."

When you go in to him do you turn on the light?

"Yes, I do. I need to see what's going on."

It's better not to put on the light in the baby's room but to do everything for him in the semi-dark of a night light or a light from the hall. Speak very softly and give no encouragement for play. Put him down in the same position you do at bedtime and repeat whatever you say when you leave the room—"Nite, Nite," "Sleep time." It will help you get the baby to sleep again if you repeat your pattern for getting him off to sleep at his normal bedtime.

The baby has no sense of time. He has been asleep for several hours; he is rested and ready for play. He has to get the message that this is not playtime but sleeptime. Sometimes the baby needs a little patting and comforting. Parents must be careful not to play or turn on the lights because then the baby thinks it's time to get up.

"I found that out. When the baby cried a few weeks ago, I got all excited too and turned on the lights. After that I used a night light. Since I've done that, things have been going better. But getting up in the middle of the night is murder, now that he is into everything all day. I need my eight hours sleep."

It is hard to lose sleep. All of us can appreciate that, but losing sleep is unfortunately part of parenting. In most cases, however, the periods when you lose sleep are intermittent. Also you and your husband can take turns getting up.

"That's what we do, but not on a regular basis. Whichever of us hears the baby first or is less tired or not fast asleep, gets up to tend the baby."

"I don't mind getting up, but my husband is the light sleeper. He is the one out of bed first, and he gets the baby settled down pretty well."

"Well, I feel it's my job to get up at night because if my husband lost sleep, he would not be able to concentrate on his job. I can always nap in the daytime when the baby naps, or if

I'm tired, I can let something go until another day. My husband can't do that."

"Our baby has been eating so poorly during the day that when he wakes at night, nothing satisfies him except a bottle. Now I have one ready. If he has a bottle at night, sometimes he doesn't get up as early in the morning. It's a comfort to learn that the problem won't last forever, though sometimes that's hard to believe."

All of you seem to be going through this phase in different ways. Each mother has to deal with her own child according to the child's needs and her understanding of those needs. Each mother learns what method works best.

"Aren't there other things that wake babies besides teething? I have heard that they dream too, and that sometimes bad dreams wake them up."

Babies do dream. Experiments show that babies have the same REM patterns found in dreaming adults. It is conceivable that babies have anxiety dreams which wake them. One of these, it has been postulated, is a dream of falling. Babies often seem to jump in their sleep as though bracing against a fall, much as adults do. Also, babies often make sucking motions during sleep which suggests they are dreaming about feeding.

"I'm very glad to hear that because I thought my baby was dreaming. When I come in, he seems frightened and needs a little cuddling. Then he goes right off to sleep. He doesn't seem in pain, and his gums are not swollen. I wondered about dreaming, but I thought he was too young to dream."

There are other things too that cause babies to wake at night. Anything that changes the environment the baby is used to may cause poor sleep and awakening in the night. Such changes as going visiting, or on a trip, or moving to a new home are disturbing to the baby's routine.

Have you noticed whether a change of routine affects your baby's sleep pattern? How?

"I go through that every weekend. We go to our country place because my husband likes to do some of his work there. Every weekend the baby wakes once or twice at night. At home he sleeps right through. I just didn't think the change could make such a difference because he is in the same kind of crib and I take his toys with him."

First, there's the trip itself. Then, the baby knows the room is not the same: The pictures may be different; the light may come in a different way. Babies are sensitive to such things, and they disturb their sleep patterns.

Taking a
Baby into
the Parents'
Bed and its
Conse-
quences

"When we went away for the weekend with our baby, she wouldn't sleep in the crib the hotel provided. We had to take her into our bed. When we got home, I tried to put her into her own crib, and she would have none of it. She just cried and cried. So now we have to sleep with her in our bed if we want to get any sleep at all."

Perhaps being in a hotel and not wanting to bother neighbors, parents feel justified in taking the baby into bed with them. However, it never proves to be a good solution. Sleeping with parents re-evokes the early feeling of oneness with the parent for which the baby always yearns. To be reunited and separated again is very hard for the baby. Of course, he will protest. Even in a hotel or at a friend's house, it is best to stay by the baby's crib, patting and comforting him until he falls asleep. You can always pull the crib close to you, but it is best for the baby to go to sleep in his own bed.

If visiting undoes an established sleep pattern, you should expect to have to go through the original routines you used to establish the pattern in the first place. Therefore, once you are home again, make the same preparations for bedtime as before going away. Keep repeating your routines until the baby resumes his normal sleep pattern.

This change of sleep pattern also happens after a baby has been ill. When the baby is well again, the old sleep pattern has to be reestablished.

Have you experienced any difficulties getting the baby to sleep after you have gone on a trip or the baby has been ill? Have they arisen because you took the baby into your bed?

"We went to my in-laws for a week, and the baby just would not sleep until we took her into our bed. Then when we got home, she still wanted to sleep with us. My husband wouldn't put up with that. So I lay down on a sofa in her room and pretended to sleep, but that didn't work. So then I put her on our bed, and she fell asleep. When she was asleep, I moved her to her crib. She didn't seem to mind being in her own crib when she woke up. Now she is going to sleep again in her crib, but I'll never take her in my bed again."

"My baby had a bad cold, and he coughed and seemed to be choking. We got scared, and my husband said we should take the baby into our bed where we could watch him. When the cold was over, the baby made a terrible fuss about going back to his own bed. I won't try that again."

When a baby is so ill that he must be watched during the night, it's better for the parents to take turns sitting up in the baby's room and really taking care of him. This is a rare situation and has to be met in a way that really deals effectively with the crisis. Just because the baby is in the parents' bed does not insure that the parents will awaken and attend to the baby's needs.

"I've heard that some houses get so cold at night that babies should be taken into the parents' bed to keep them warm."

To take a baby into bed for that reason doesn't seem to have too much justification except in very unusual situations. Then one does what seems best and deals with the consequences later.

Most babies, if warmly covered, however, usually generate a great deal of heat under the covers and often they perspire because they are too warmly wrapped. However, babies do have a way of moving about and getting uncovered. The covers need to be fastened under the mattress so that they cannot be pulled out. Also the baby should wear warm outer pajamas in cold weather. Sometimes babies sleep better when the room is cooler.

"Isn't there also the danger of rolling onto a baby and injuring her if she is sleeping in the same bed as her parents?"

That is one of the reasons that having the baby sleep in his own crib became customary. There is also another reason. We now have better forms of birth control, so that the baby does not have to be kept between the parents to separate them from each other.

"I've heard of that, too, and I guess some parents still resort to it. But isn't there any time that's all right to take the baby into bed with the parents?"

There is no reason why, for a few minutes in the morning when the parents want to stay in bed a little longer, the baby can't be taken into bed to play with them. For some parents, this is a regular morning procedure; others do it only on weekends when there is no rush to get off to work. However, it is not a good idea to allow such an activity to develop into a prolonged morning nap with the parents because then the baby wants to sleep with his parents at night too.

EMERGENCY MEASURES FOR ACCIDENTS

Cuts, Bumps, and Other Accidents; Breath Holding and Loss of Consciousness; Burns

We have talked about some safety measures that are necessary now that the babies are more mobile. We suggested that plugs be inserted into electric outlets and that safety latches be put on cabinets containing pills or cleaning substances or that such items be moved to high shelves. It also helps to put gates by staircases. In spite of all these safety precautions, we can't prevent all the bumps, falls, scratches, and scrapes which babies experience. Because of their increased activity and lack of motor coordination, babies are bound sometimes to hurt themselves. If the injury causes bleeding, it is very alarming to parents. We will, therefore, talk a little about this type of accident and what first-aid measures are appropriate.

Have your babies had any accidents so far? How have you handled them?

> "My baby somehow fell this morning before we came here. I don't know how he did it. Fortunately, he just bumped his chin."

Sometimes, if the babies have teeth, a tooth may cut through the lip or even the tongue when they fall. Usually just the application of pressure for a few minutes is sufficient to help the blood to clot and stop the bleeding. If the bleeding continues, any longer than five minutes, then the baby should be taken to the doctor or emergency room to be certain no stitches or other treatment are necessary.

A common mistake that is often made is to use a wet cloth to wash away to blood. This only encourages more bleeding because the natural clot is being continually washed away.

> "I thought you should wash the wound to be sure that it was clean, so that there will be no infection."

That is true if the injury occurs in a dirty area like a sandbox, for example. However, if the bleeding is very profuse, the blood usually washes the dirt away from the wound. This however, has to be determined by careful inspection. For outdoor accidents and those that cause jagged dirty wounds, it is best to consult a physician.

> "My daughter fell, bit her mouth, and loosened a tooth. The gum was bleeding. I rushed to the neighbor, and she said the tooth would turn black. What should I do if that happens?"

When teeth are injured, it is best to consult a dentist. Sometimes, when the tooth is loosened by a fall, it will heal by itself and become firm in the gum again. If the nerve is injured by the blow, the tooth may darken. In either case, a dentist should be consulted.

> "When a baby falls and gets a bump and that swells but does not bleed, what should one do?"

Usually a cold compress is soothing and helps the swelling go down. You must also determine whether the bump was severe. If in doubt, it is always best to consult a doctor. However, remember not to panic and scream because this only frightens the baby more. It is more important to soothe and comfort the baby first and then to pay attention to the actual wound. Sometimes a parent is so upset that, instead of comforting the child, she scolds him. This is particularly true if the child hurts himself by doing something which the parents had previously told him not to do.

> "I'm afraid that's just what I do. I get so excited I scold my baby. I remember that is what my parents did to me."

We behave a certain way spontaneously and then often regret it.

This is natural human behavior. It often takes a great deal of repatterning and learning new ways of controlling ourselves to get over this "reflex" behavior. We unconsciously imitate things our parents did. They may not have been perfect and we are not either, but we can try to improve. It's never too late to try to learn a better way of doing things.

"When my baby hurts himself, he cries and holds his breath. This scares me, and I shake him to make him breathe again. It seems like hours before he does take a breath."

The baby holds his breath because he is frightened, and shaking him will only frighten him more. It is a very scary experience for the parent. The quickest way to get the baby to stop holding his breath, however, is to soothe and comfort him. He will take another breath as the need for oxygen builds up. Natural physiological processes will take care of that, if the situation isn't intensified by the parent's alarm.

"My mother said that when a baby or, I guess, anyone loses consciousness, the thing to do is to shake him and wake him up so he won't go into a coma."

If the injury is so severe that the baby loses consciousness, you couldn't do anything worse than shake him or try to keep him awake because you can injure him further by what you are doing. Instead, you should wrap the baby gently in a robe or blanket, keep him quiet, and take him at once to the nearest doctor or hospital.

Actually, serious accidents are not common. Most of you have taken precautions so that serious falls are prevented. We have suggested that you put carpets near cribs as your babies reach the climbing stage, so any fall will be cushioned. It is also good to keep staircases carpeted, with gates at the top and bottom. We also need to try to keep cords and protruding tables out of the way to prevent tripping and bumping.

Another type of injury which becomes more prevalent now that the babies are getting more active and moving faster is burns. Babies reach out and touch hot radiators or the oven and occasionally overturn a hot beverage. Sometimes, these actions cause only small and superficial injuries with only a little redness occurring. If blisters form, however, the burn is more serious and needs medical attention. The blisters should not be broken or opened. A cold compress should be applied **at once** to **all** burns.

What precautions have you taken to prevent burns? What do you do if such an accident occurs?

"I know prevention is the best policy, so when I'm cooking, I keep the baby in a highchair or in his playpen. But our radiators have no covers, and he likes to touch them. Yesterday, they

were quite hot, and he put his hand on one before I could reach him. A big red line formed on the palm of his hand. He didn't seem to mind; he just cried a little. I didn't know what to do, so I just held it under cold water a little."

Your instincts were right to put something cool and moist on the burn. What you have described sounds like a first-degree burn, which is superficial and will heal by itself when the initial sting is taken away by the application of a cold compress.

"I always thought the thing to do was to apply butter or oil right away if you don't have a special burn salve. That's what my mother always did."

That used to be the favorite remedy, but butter and oil are good culture media and invite infection in open wounds. One often can't tell immediately whether the burn is more than superficial and will blister. The best thing is to apply a clean, cold compress and, if in doubt, go to you doctor or a hospital emergency room. Even the commercial first-aid salves may not be the right thing to use, so it is best to have medical care as soon as possible.

The best approach to burns, of course, is to keep children away from something hot. Radiators should be covered, or a barrier should be put in front of them, so that they won't cause constant parent-child conflict and unnecessary anxiety.

"I am very concerned that the baby will swallow or choke on something. What should we do if that happens?"

Swallowing Small Objects and Choking

If the baby actually swallows a small, smooth object, the most important thing to do is keep calm and not frighten the baby. Then, it is a good idea to give her something soft, like bread or thick cereal, to eat so that the object will be coated. If the object is sharp or jagged, and could cause a perforation, you should also give the child something soft to eat, and then get in touch with the baby's doctor immediately.

If the child is choking on an object or piece of food, again it is most important to keep calm and not frighten the baby. The first emergency procedure is to inspect quickly the baby's mouth to locate the object. If it can be reached, it should be pulled from the mouth immediately. If it is in the baby's throat, do not try to dislodge it with your fingers because you may just push it further down and cause more difficulty. The best procedure is to make use of gravity by inverting the baby and slapping his back firmly. A good way to do this on your lap or along your extended legs. If the object is not dislodged, place the baby face down along your forearm (or, for a larger child, use your knee) so that his abdomen rests against your arm (or knee). Then press down with your clenched fist firmly and quickly three or four times on the baby's back. This usually causes the baby to cough up the object so that you can remove it from his mouth. (This procedure is known as the "Heimlich Manuever.")

If these emergency measures fail, take the baby immediately to the nearest hospital emergency room. Even though an object is obstructing the baby's throat, enough air may be getting through to allow him to breathe. Soothing and calming the baby is important at this point, so that the spasms or crying are not intensified. Crying itself constricts the throat muscles, creating less air space.

We have talked about these emergency procedures to help you feel prepared. We want to reassure you that such serious accidents as we have been discussing are quite uncommon, and you probably will never need to use most of the information we have supplied.

"If you always protect your children that way, how will they ever learn? Shouldn't they learn not to touch hot things by experience?"

We are always in the process of teaching the babies what is forbidden. But until we are certain that the "No" has been firmly fixed in the baby's mind and that he has control enough to desist, we can't afford to take a chance. Until the babies mature and have the ability to exercise the necessary control, it is the adults who have to take the precautions. Parents have to get to know when their baby has reached that level. Each baby will reach that level of self-control at a different age. Some will learn "Hot, don't touch" quickly; others may learn not to pull down books first. It depends entirely on the individual baby's maturational level and the consistency with which the parents have pursued the training.

NEED FOR EXPLORATION: APPROPRIATE TOYS

In taking precautions and safety measures, do not forget that the babies must explore. In our zeal to keep them safe, we must not inhibit safe exploration. As we have mentioned before, if exploration is turned off now, it may be difficult to restimulate it for formal learning in school. We have to arrange for safe areas for exploration and then encourage the babies to explore them.

Babies need to be able to play with small toys which they can manipulate and explore. Blocks which are small enough for babies to grasp but not small enough to be swallowed, such as the one-inch blocks which we use in testing, make excellent toys. Another good kind of toy is a stuffed animal that has appendages which can be moved, but not pulled off. It is also good if the eyes, nose, and mouth are embroidered on. At this age babies can pull button eyes off and swallow them or put them in their ears or noses. A rattle that can be banged against a firm metal or plastic cup and a small red ball that can be grasped and rolled are other toys which are good for exploration. There are also chains of big pop-out beads. As we cautioned earlier, the most important thing is to be certain that the toys the babies play with do not have parts that can be swallowed.

Now that the babies are exploring on the floor, they pick up things they find there. After some visual inspection, and sometimes without it, the babies put the things they find into their mouths, still their primary means of exploration. By putting things in their mouths, they test texture. They find out if the object is hard, soft, or just a little pliable, and whether its taste is pleasant or unpleasant. They also put things in their mouths as a reflex action because the hand-to-mouth reflex is still prominent.

Making Oral Exploration Safe and Clean

Such behavior does not always meet with parental approval and often causes an unpleasant situation. This isn't totally unreasonable on the parents' part, of course, but it may seem so to the baby. He has just discovered this exciting object when suddenly mother or father pounces on him and removes it. Perhaps it is some small object that he could swallow or might aspirate and cause choking.

The parent is right to remove the object for the baby's safety. How the parent handles the situation, however, makes a great deal of difference. The parent can frighten the child by grabbing the object too suddenly. So it is best to offer a substitute as you remove the dangerous object from the child's grasp. It is important to try to make the situation a learning experience for the child, so that he comes to understand what he should not put in his mouth.

What experience with such situations have you had? How are you handling them?

"I am really afraid to let the baby crawl on the floor because we have a dog and it sheds all over the rug. I don't know just what the baby may pick up, so I only let him crawl in his own room. That has a linoleum floor I can keep clean. When the baby is in the living room, he has to stay in the playpen or his highchair."

Limiting the child in this way for a short time may work, but soon it will seriously limit the variety of his experiences.

"Why don't you vacuum the rug just before you put the baby on the floor? We don't have a dog or a cat, but I always vacuum the floor so it will be clean for the baby."

"Of course, it helps to vacuum, but, somehow or other, my baby always manages to find something I missed. He puts it right into his mouth, if I'm not watching. He specially likes to pick up cigarette butts and matches."

These are items that should be kept out of the baby's reach. If he should get hold of something like that, it has to be taken away. Then it is important to give the baby something more suitable to play with. Babies like to play with tops of jars, cups, and sets of measuring spoons on a chain or string. It is well to keep a supply of suitable play objects handy wherever the baby is playing on the floor.

> "My baby is crazy about paper. He can spot the smallest piece before I do, and right into his mouth it goes. I scoop it out because I'm afraid he'll choke on it."

> "My baby is wild about paper too—the newspaper, magazines, cellophane wrappers—all those things. At first he crumples them because he likes the sound and feel. Then he pulls a piece off and plops it into his mouth. I take it out. When he does it again, I just take the paper away."

Babies go through a stage of enjoying playing with paper. At first it's the sound and feel that interests them, but everything ends up in their mouths. Babies are not very discriminating about their tastes, at least from our point of view. Babies also like the feeling of mastery involved in being able to tear the paper. Some exploration of paper needs to be allowed. Chewing on paper has to be limited because occasionally babies do gag or choke on it. They should never be left alone with paper; someone needs to keep a good watch on this part of their activities. This stage will also pass as the babies become more competent and have new interests.

> "What about toys that drop on the floor? Do they all have to be washed before giving them back to the baby? I was taught that it was unsanitary to let them play with things that had fallen on the floor, and at first I used to be running back and forth washing everything that fell. It got to be too much."

> "I did that at first too, but now I just wipe off the toy a little and give it back."

We used to make a big fuss about making sure the baby's things were sterile. We know now that the baby develops some immunity to the germs around his own home. It is sufficient to wash toys off once a day or more often if they get sticky or visibly dirty. It's impossible and unnecessary to try to keep everything about the baby as sterile as an operating room. The baby could not develop natural immunity that way. If you are outside, however, and the toy drops on the street or in the bus, it should be washed. When you are outside, it's a good idea to have some kind of toy that you can attach to the baby's jacket with a ribbon or string so that when he drops it, it doesn't fall to the ground. A set of measuring spoons or the red ring is good for this purpose.

When we take an educated guess about which is better for babies—constant restriction in the cause of cleanliness or exploration in the cause of learning—it's probably better to allow exploration—in most cases, anyway. Parents have to deal with their own backgrounds and inclinations and make the compromises that suit them best. However, some avenues of exploration must be left open to the baby. Much that parents often call "naughty" is really exploration and should be recognized as such.

> "I used to feel that the baby was 'naughty' or trying to test me when he dropped a toy on the floor. Then I would take it to the sink, wash it, and bring it back. Then he'd drop it again. I used to get angry until I understood he was exploring and wasn't doing it just to annoy me. Now I stop picking up when I'm tired of picking up, and do something else with him. I don't get angry. It's a help to understand what he is trying to do."

The babies need to have small toys to play with so that they can learn to manipulate them. Putting these objects in their mouths is a natural exploratory avenue for the baby. After putting the toy in her mouth, the baby tries to use it in other ways. She may bang it against something, push it along a table, or drop it. These are all experiences the baby needs to have to help her understand the world around her. This early understanding of space is essential to the later understanding of mathematics and other types of learning.

MORE ON FEEDING

Preparation and Temperature of Food

As the babies get older, their preferences for certain foods may become more pronounced. Besides trying to offer babies a nice variety of foods, most mothers are also very careful about the temperature of the food. They put the jars in hot water or put the portions to be eaten in a special hot plate. Then, much to their surprise, the baby doesn't want the food. If left in front of him, he may play with it, mushing it up all over his tray. This is very upsetting to mothers, who want the babies to eat the food when it is nice and warm.

Have you had this experience yet?

> "This happens to me at least once every day. I get the cereal ready. It's nice warm and appetizing. When I give it to the baby, he just clamps his mouth shut and won't take it. So I take it away without a fuss. Then sometimes just before I throw it out when it's cold and congealed, I take a chance and offer it again. That's just the way he wants it."

You were doing what you thought was correct. Indeed, that is the way mothers are instructed to serve the baby's food, particularly the bottle—at body temperature. We often test the temperature to see if it is just right by squirting a little of the formula on our wrist. That's a time-honored procedure. It just so happens, however, that some babies like their food best when it is cold and we are ready to discard it.

> "Is it possible to give the baby cold things? Doesn't everything have to be heated up to room temperature?"

That's what was always taught in pediatric and nursing classes. However, some recent studies have reported that there were no ill effects from giving the baby the formula cold from the refrigerator. The food was warmed by the baby's body heat as it was consumed. So perhaps all our efforts to heat food are not entirely necessary for every baby. Perhaps heating food in only a cultural matter and not a natural need. Some babies are very slow in eating; by the time they get halfway through a meal the food is cold, but they seem to like it all the same.

> "My baby does that, and it makes me angry because I have taken such pains to get the food just right, and I try to hurry his eating so he'll get it while it is still warm. It makes me very tense."

Being tense when feeding the baby and trying to hurry the eating process, which should be leisurely and pleasant for both of you, may make the baby a poor eater. As we have said before, it is important not to make the mealtime a battleground between parent and child.

> "I guess that's a carry-over from my mother. That's the way she fed me. When she comes over, if I don't get the next spoonful into his mouth before he has quite swallowed the first one, she criticizes me. If he dawdles a little, she gets frantic."

That can't be a very pleasant experience for any of you. Perhaps you could explain to your mother that the baby is really a good eater. Nothing serious will occur if he takes a little longer and the food cools a little. Tell her you discussed this with a doctor, and you were advised not to hurry the baby.

> "You don't know my mother!"

We are not trying to prove grandparents wrong. They did what they were taught was best. In many instances, they are still correct. You must realize that child rearing wasn't so easy for them either. But some new things have been learned about child development since they brought up their children, and they probably would like to hear these ideas. Many ideas we teach here have been documented by careful observers and experimenters and should be shared with grandparents, other relatives, and neighbors.

> "My baby has a funny way of eating. I hesitate to mention it, but it has been bothering me. When I feed him, some of the food drops on the tray table on his highchair. That's just the food he is most anxious to eat. He doesn't seem to care for what's in the spoon. He'd much rather put his fingers in the food on the tray, mush it up, and then put it in his mouth. If I

wipe it away, he gets irritable because that's what he wants. So he takes one spoonful that I feed him and some from the table with his hands, then another spoonful from me and then more with his own hands."

Babies often do that. They are getting pleasure from the ability to feed themselves on their own. This is often the way self-feeding begins. Perhaps your baby is signaling that he is ready to try feeding himself. Some babies like to hold a spoon in their hands and feel that they are participating in the feeding. You can help the baby dip the spoon into thick food so it will adhere to the spoon long enough for him to get some of it into his mouth. This is a great achievement for the baby.

Readiness for Self-Feeding

"But it makes such a mess!"

There are many things about a baby that are messy by adult standards, but babies are messy and clumsy while they are developing certain skills like eating or walking. They are not ready to be neat, and adults should not expect them to be. It is not the time for table manners yet.

"What about entertaining and distracting a baby while you feed him so he won't know he is being fed?"

That is a way of getting food into the baby that many parents resort to. Your goal, however, is to teach the baby to eat food from a spoon, and the experience of eating should be pleasant for the baby. He develops a desire to eat from the spoon by the approval he gets. Mothers can show their approval by their smiles and expressions like "Good" and "That's nice." If the food is surreptitiously given to the baby or shoved in between distractions, the baby is not learning to eat from a spoon and gets no sense of achievement. In some cases, the baby may begin to clamp his mouth shut and refuse the food.

"I tried playing with the baby to get him to eat, and pretty soon I ran out of ideas to entertain him. He didn't eat so well for a few days. Now we just sit down quietly when it's mealtime, and he takes what he wants. It is probably enough because he is gaining weight. And I'm not a wreck at the end of the meal. My pediatrician approved of what I was doing, too."

"That doesn't bother my baby; she is a great eater. She can watch the company and eat too. I never force her."

As we've said before, mealtime should be pleasant for both parent and baby. Babies eat well and learn to feed themselves best when parents are patient and recognize their achievements. The quantity of food consumed is less important than the atmosphere in which the feeding takes place. With the right atmosphere, the feeding process goes much more smoothly, and more food is ultimately consumed. Parents use a variety of techniques to achieve success in feeding, but, in general, the less forcing or deception, the better the results.

GAMES AND SOCIAL ACTIVITIES

"Pat-a-Cake"   Now that the babies are older, they are awake more of the time. This means there is more time to spend in play. Parents need to develop a repertoire of games which are appropriate for the babies' ages and which utilize the babies' competence and enhance their learning. One of these early games is "Pat-a-Cake." Interestingly, this game seems to be present in some form in the early play rituals of all societies.

At first the parents should demonstrate this game by clapping their hands together and reciting "Pat-a-Cake." Some parents simply say "Clap Hands" repeating the words in a rhythmic manner to arrest the babies' interest. The baby, who can transfer objects from hand to hand, may now try to make his own hands approach each other in a clapping gesture. Sometimes the baby will watch the parents intently and rise his arms and drop them in response to the parents' activity. This response may be as far as the baby can go at this level of development, and it should be recognized by the parent with a smile and pleasant comment such as "Good," "That's nice."

Some parents take the baby's hands and put them together for the baby in a clappng position and recite "Pat-a-Cake" or "Clap Hands." Most babies chortle and enjoy this. It usually takes many weeks of watching the parent and having the parent manipulate the baby's hands before the baby begins to respond himself. For some babies, the clapping response may be to bang on something with one hand. After several weeks of this and further demonstration by the parents, they may begin to bang with two hands. Later, they learn to put their hands together, passing one hand with the other before they are actually able to clap them together. When they finally can clap their hands, they seem very pleased with themselves, particularly if the parent acknowledges their accomplishment by smiling, laughing, expressing approval verbally, or clapping in unison with them.

Have any of you begun to play "Pat-a-Cake" or "Clap Hands" with your baby?

> **"We began several months ago, but we gave up because the baby would not let us hold his hands to guide them. That dampened our enthusiasm."**

That's too bad; it only means you may have begun the game too early. Perhaps the baby needed to watch you clap hands for a longer time before he was able to respond. It may be that he wanted to move his arms on his own in what he interpreted as imitating you. You can't expect the babies to have the coordination to copy your actions exactly. Clapping one hand against the other is actually quite a skill for a baby. He may be more ready now. Try again, and keep encouraging him. He will respond in his own good time.

"I guess you are right. We expected too much too soon. Now that you mention it, he does sort of lift his arms and rock a little. I guess he is trying to use his whole body in rhythm because he isn't ready to put his hands together. We read that a baby his age should be ready for 'Pat-a-Cake,' and we just assumed he would do it as soon as we showed him. We were afraid there was something wrong with his development. Now, we'll be more patient."

"We tried 'Pat-a-Cake' too, but all our baby would do was laugh at us. She wouldn't do it herself, even though she let us take her hands and do it. She enjoyed it so that we got pleasure and didn't press her. We decided she just wasn't a genius, and we'd have to be satisfied. Now I feel better about her."

"We've been going through this too. Our baby lets us clap her hands. When we say, 'Clap Hands,' she puts her hands out for us to put together. She seems very pleased, but we can't get her to do it by herself. We wondered why."

This is another example of how parental expectations may be too far ahead of an individual baby's level of development, causing the parents unnecessary disappointment and worry. It is fine to read about development and see if your child has reached the level indicated for her age. However, we have to remember that the book is written about babies in general and that each baby has his or her own maturational timetable, even in playing games. No general developmental chart can be right for every baby. Usually babies do things in the same sequence: They sit before they crawl, crawl before they walk, and so on. But few children begin walking at exactly the same age. It is the same with learning to play games.

"Bye-Bye"

There is another activity that is appropriate for babies of this age. It is part of socialization, and can also be a game. It is "Bye-Bye." It is best to start this "game" when guests, relatives, or strangers are leaving after a visit and are waving "good-bye." The parent can then demonstrate the "game" by waving in response as she holds the baby. Later it can be done when Daddy leaves in the morning. After these preliminaries have been repeated several times, the mother, or whoever is holding the baby, should wave the baby's hand in a return gesture and say "Bye-Bye." The words should be said in a musical, rhythmic manner, so the baby can get the rhythm of the intonation and learn to imitate it. After some repetition, the baby may be able to respond by waving her own arm. Some babies do not at first wave their arms but flex their fingers. Later they learn to use their arms to wave. This activity is an especially good one because the baby is not only learning to wave "Bye-Bye" but is also learning about leaving and separation. She is adding to her vocabulary and beginning to verbalize a new concept.

When the baby has achieved a "Bye-Bye" wave, parents will often try to show off the baby's achievement by saying "Bye-Bye" when no one is departing. The baby may not respond because she has associated "Bye-Bye" with someone's departure. If the phrase is then used when no one is leaving, the baby becomes confused. Saying "Bye-Bye" should always be accompanied by the appropriate activity, even if someone only goes out of the room for a moment. As a matter of fact, leaving for only a moment is a very good activity because it gives the baby the experience of having the parent or other person return quickly. Then "Bye-Bye" is not always associated with longer separation or loss.

Have any of you begun to teach your baby "Bye-Bye"?

> "We have been saying 'Bye-Bye' every time we go out of the room. The baby smiles at times and looks serious at others. He seems to know it's something special, but he hasn't moved his arm or his hand yet."

> "Our baby just lifts his arm once and puts it down quickly. It's more of a bang than a wave, but he only does that particular gesture when we say 'Bye-Bye' and leave. I'm sure it's his way of saying 'Bye-Bye,' but my husband says I'm just imagining this because I want the baby to seem bright."

You are describing the early steps in learning "Bye-Bye." These very early gestures should be recognized as achievements and not dismissed as meaningless. As the babies get reinforcement from their parents, they go on to more accomplishments as soon as they are capable.

> "I'm afraid we were so excited because the baby does actually seem to respond to 'Bye-Bye' that we've been showing off his ability to everyone, but not just when someone is leaving. So we are really using him like a trained puppy instead of realizing that he has to learn the meaning of 'Bye-Bye' too."

That's a very good observation. Indeed, we are not training puppies. A baby is a person, a human being whom we are trying to help develop all of his potential. Sometimes when the babies are so young, it is hard to remember that.

"Peekaboo"

There is another game for this age which is closely related to "Bye-Bye" and that's "Peekaboo" or "Peek." Babies usually like this game very much. Begin to teach the baby this game by covering your eyes with your hands. Then uncover your eyes and say "Peek" or "I see you." Usually, the baby's expression becomes very serious when you cover your eyes or face, but she becomes all smiles when your eyes or face reappear. Later, the baby may begin to play the game by pulling part of her blanket or clothes over her face and then reappearing, or the parent may cover the baby's face and then expose it again saying, "I see you."

The significance of the game, in addition to its fun for both parent and child, is that the baby begins to experience appearance and disappearance. The baby begins to deal with the concept that something which disappears from sight does return. It takes a long time for the baby to develop the understanding that there is existence beyond her field of vision. At first, she does not know that the person who is out of the room or out of sight exists. This is why the departure of the parent from the room is traumatic. It is also why you should not hide completely from the baby when playing "Peekaboo." That can become too threatening. "Peekaboo" is a game which helps the baby learn that someone or something exists even though not visible to the child at the moment.

When playing "Hide-and-Seek" with four-or five-year-old children, adults are often told to hide in a specific place. The children then joyously look for the adult because they are not made anxious by the adult's disappearance. When the children hide from the adult, they often call out to announce their hiding place in order to make certain they are found. They do this because they are still not sure the adult knows of their existence. This behavior seems strange to adults. They feel the child is not playing according to the rules. Actually, the children are playing according to their needs. This is what the adult always has to keep in mind in dealing with children. Their timetables and needs are not the same as the adult's. They need time and support to achieve concept formation on an adult level.

Have any of you begun to play "Peekaboo" with you baby? How are you going about introducing the game?

> "I began the game by hiding below the baby's changing table when he was on it on his stomach and could look over the edge. Then I'd rise up and stand, and he'd have to look up to find me too. He likes it, and his father does too. We began it as you showed us when the baby was four months old. As he began to respond to words, we began to say, 'I see you' when we got up, and he laughed and flung his arms out."

Yes, that is the early form of "Peek," and it is a very good way to introduce the game—the action first and then the associated words. Have you extended the game now to covering your face with your hands or partially hiding behind something?

> "Yes, we have, and the baby likes that too."

"I began a few weeks ago just hiding my face and then saying, 'Peek, I see you' very loudly, I guess too enthusiastically. I think it scared the baby. So now we do it gently, and it is working all right."

"We've been playing 'Peekaboo, I see you' a long time with the baby just with our hands. The other day, her father came home and hid behind the open door before coming in. When the baby couldn't see him, she cried. We couldn't understand why."

Perhaps it was because the baby expected to see Daddy when he came in, and was disappointed. The baby could not understand that he was behind the door. He may have been completely hidden from view.

"Well, yes, he really was. My husband thought she was very silly to cry. He was a little bit upset too. Now that I understand, I can explain it to him."

"My husband is like that too, and so is my mother. They both think the baby should know they are there when they are completely hidden. But the baby usually cries, and they become annoyed. My husband sometimes says 'Dummy.' It makes me angry."

Your husband doesn't really mean that. It is just that he is disappointed that what he intended as fun turned out badly. Now perhaps you can practice with the baby in the appropriate way and then show Daddy and your mother how he responds. When they can evoke smiles and laughter from the baby, they will be happy too.

"Our baby enjoys it more when we cover his face with a diaper and then remove it saying 'I see you.' Now he is beginning to pull the diaper off himself, and his grin when he sees us is just so nice. It's good to know that something that is just a game and such fun can also have real learning importance."

That's the point of all these sessions: To help you enjoy bringing up the baby and to help you understand just how much what you are doing means to the baby.

"So Big"

Another game you have been playing already is "So Big." By now the babies should be getting to the point of putting up their arms to show you how big they are.

Have you continued to play "So Big"?

"Yes, and the baby can put both arms up now when we say, 'How big is baby?' She really gets a kick out of the game."

"I still have to pick the baby's arms up, but then he laughs and smiles. He likes me to do it over and over again."

"I am very glad that there are more games to play. We were getting very tired of 'So Big.'"

"Our baby gets mixed up between 'So Big,' 'Bye-Bye,' and 'Pat-a-Cake.' When we say 'How big is the baby?' or say her name, she may clap or wave 'Bye-Bye.' Why is that?"

She knows she gets a positive response from you when she responds, but she hasn't quite sorted our which response is appropriate. Perhaps you introduced these games too close together, or ask her to do one after the other—for display rather than as meaningful play.

"You know, that's it, because when she first learned a game, we'd have her do it to show off her tricks ('tricks' is good, isn't it?), and we may have mixed her up."

That's the puppy-dog routine again, and we just have to remember that these babies are not puppies. The importance of "So Big" is that it teaches the babies some idea of the extent of themselves. Like the other games we have been talking about, it is a learning game, not just a "trick." As we have said before, playing is a baby's work because he or she learns through play.

We have discussed all these games for another reason as well: They provide a way for parents and baby to spend a happy time together. The parent-child relationship gains from this pleasant interaction.

Eleven-month-old baby touching ball to mirror (top left),
examining clapper in bell (top right),
and removing block from cup (bottom left and right).

Chapter Eleven

Age: **44** to **48** weeks _____

The baby may now have the ability to stand and move along the rail of the crib. She may even be able to hold on to a couch or chair and move along it. Most babies will be quite adept at crawling, though some going better backwards than forwards.

The baby may be able to take the bell by the top of the handle and may finger the clapper. She shows more manual dexterity and curiosity. However, she does not know yet that the clapper causes the sound of the bell. The baby notices the block in the cup and may reach in and get it out. She may be able to put the block back into the cup, but she may not release it. With this activity comes the beginning of the baby's understanding of the concepts of "in" and "out."

The baby may now be saying "Dada" and "Mama" more clearly. She may also have another word or two in her vocabulary. Acquisition of language is very uneven; some children may have no words and others five or six.

The baby is beginning to comprehend "Bye-bye" better, and while still concentrating on watching the adult make the gesture, she may lift her hand a little in imitation. She may respond to "Pat-a-cake" by banging on the table with one hand, or she may begin to bring both hands together.

The baby can hold out a toy to the parent but will not yet release it. With a ball in hand, he reaches for his image in the mirror and may touch the ball to the mirror. He is beginning to accept the cup and drink better from it when the parent holds the cup for the baby.

HOLIDAYS

The Significance of Holidays for Babies

(The comments in this section are relevant for any time during the first year of life).

Adults often feel that babies are not involved in big holidays like Thanksgiving, Christmas, Chanukah, Passover, and Easter because they are too young to understand what the holidays are all about. It is true that babies do not comprehend the significance that holidays have for adults and older children, but holidays do have a significance for them. It is important for parents to realize this because most parents have some holiday traditions they would like to continue or revive for their children.

> "I was wondering about that. At Christmas we always used to have a tree and hung up stockings when I was little. For me it always was such a happy time. But I was wondering about a baby that is under a year old. What is appropriate for the baby? Is it right to expose her to all that excitement?"

Of course, the baby won't understand the meaning of the holiday, but she will sense the excitement. There will be a number of new and exciting happenings which will be fun for the baby. The baby will watch with great interest as the parents put up and decorate the tree, particularly if she can play with a harmless ornament. The baby will also enjoy seeing the tree lit up. Young babies love to look at the lighted tree and often engage in lots of cooing and babbling. Even though they will not understand the ceremony, babies will also enjoy the lighting of Chanukah candles. Babies may also enjoy playing with the colored wrappings of presents more than they enjoy the actual present. They will also like to watch presents being wrapped and later opened.

Entertaining at Home; Disruption of the Baby's Routine

At holiday time, there may be disruption of the babies' routines. For some babies, an occasional disruption is taken in stride and doesn't upset them provided the parents are there. Other babies get out-of-sorts just when the parents want to show them off to guests. The babies are irritable, won't take their feedings, have difficulty falling asleep, or don't stay asleep as long as usual. Although parents may think that they are doing things just as they usually do, they are usually under pressure to hurry a little and babies sense this. This tension usually is felt when company is expected in the baby's home, and mother and father have extra chores to do to entertain their guests.

What plans are you making for entertaining at home during the holidays? How are you preparing for them physically and emotionally?

> "I'm worried. We are having a lot of visitors from out of town. The house will be full of people."

Do you expect the baby to mind all the new faces?

> "Oh, no, he doesn't mind at all. He has a ball. I'm the one who doesn't like it. I think he gets overstimulated, and then when the company leaves, he becomes bored and wants the same attention from me just when I'm trying to clean up."

That's one of the kinds of extra pressures, the hurry to clean up afterwards. Since you have been through this experience before, why not have a quiet "winding-down" period with the baby and let some of the chores wait? If you can afford to have help, this is a good time for it. If not, just let things go until later. Perhaps some division of labor can be worked out with the rest of the family. Some of your relatives might be willing to stay and help with the cleaning up. If that arrangement is not to your taste, just do the cleaning up later. As they say, "cool it." Things work out better that way.

> "We have a different problem. As soon as company comes, the baby just clings to me and won't let me move. It takes him almost half the time the guests are there to get used to them and sit in their arms. He sometimes even won't go to his father or my mother either. That, of course, upsets them."

Does your company usually swoop down on the baby and try to hold him?

> "Yes, that's it. Besides, they are very loud and exuberant people, and he just can't take the noise they make. They tell me I must be bringing him up wrong since he is so afraid of them. They say I should make him go to them, and that's how he will get used to them."

That's the way some older adults feel babies should be treated. We do not happen to agree with that. From experience, we know that babies go through a period of stranger anxiety and, while the are in that stage, it is much better not to threaten them by placing them in a stranger's arms. Although most babies pass that stage by nine or ten months, stranger anxiety can linger on, especially if the babies are tired or have been ill. Then well-meaning but overly enthusiastic people can revive earlier response patterns. So you have to be your babies' advocates, and tell the guests gently but firmly and explicitly that the babies need time to adjust to them.

> "We've been through that, too. We used to think the baby was unfriendly, but now we can see that we just didn't understand how visitors come across to him. He isn't looking forward to the company as we are. He has no idea what it's all about. Now we just hold him or play with him ourselves and let the company settle down as best they can until the baby is ready for them."

Trying to "cue in" to the baby's level of understanding pays off. Trying to make a baby, with his immature understanding, "cue in" to adult expectations is unreasonable and leads to trouble. Even older children can be difficult when you have guests because they feel that your attention is diverted. The baby can feel excluded from the adult activities.

"I guess we all have some problems entertaining when there is a small child in the family. Getting dinner ready used to be my worst headache, but I've worked out a simple menu that I can get ready with my eyes shut. I do most of the cooking at night when the baby is asleep. I fix a casserole that is all ready beforehand. My husband helps me clean up afterwards. If we are too tired, we leave things as they are, and I get them done when I can. I've learned that I can't be overtired. So I spare myself, and that works out better for the baby too."

That is a very good attitude and one that is helpful for the baby because it reduces the tension. The parent can function better, is not overworked, and can enjoy the holiday. The baby can too. It becomes a good experience for parents and baby. You don't have to feel that the baby has intruded into your social life. You can all enjoy the holiday together.

"I suddenly realized that's just the way I've been feeling about the baby and the holidays. Instead of thinking of how to plan to enjoy it, I'm harping on the trouble the baby makes."

It's good that you can see that. Many parents feel that way, and the holidays become unpleasant for all. You must be aware of the baby's level of development and not expect more from the baby than is appropriate for his age. The parents should not expect too much from themselves either.

"I guess we are lucky because our families realize how hard it is going to be for me to get things together for dinner. Each guest is bringing something because everyone figured it would be less of a break in the baby's routine if they came to our house. We plan to have our dinner during the baby's nap. If he wakes early, it won't be too bad either. Everyone will see him when he is rested."

Visiting and Traveling During the Holidays

If you plan to visit relatives during the holidays, you will be relieved from preparing for company. But you will still have to prepare for traveling with the baby, as you have had to do on other occasions. You have to be sure to take all the things the baby will need on the trip.

The same problem with strange faces will occur, but, in addition, the baby will be in a strange place, so it is well to take some of her familiar toys.

Some babies enjoy the new surroundings and are stimulated and interested in all the new sights and sounds. Some respond by clinging and being a little apprehensive, so they need time to get adjusted. As nearly as possible, you should try to continue the baby's routine. If the baby is able to have a nap on the trip, she will arrive more rested. If the hosts have a highchair (and most grandparents and relatives do), the baby can be drawn up close to the parents while they are eating dinner.

> "We are going to my husband's family. The baby has been there before, so, aside from taking his food and diapers and a toy or two, I think we'll be okay."

> "We are going to friends who have no children and are quite fussy and formal. I warned them that the baby might be fussy if she wasn't having a good day, but they insisted. We're looking forward to it now, but at first we had some doubts."

> "I suppose our plans are preposterous. We usually go to a club my husband belongs to for holiday meals, and we decided we'd do it this time with the baby. If he doesn't sleep in his carry-all, we'll take turns minding him, but we will be with our friends; we won't feel left out just because we have a baby."

It seems you have all thought out carefully how to manage with the baby and how to enjoy yourselves without looking upon the baby as a burden. If everyone is relaxed, the visits will be pleasant.

> "We are going to Florida. It will be the baby's first plane trip, and everything will be new to him when we get there. We are a little concerned. We'll take as many of his toys as we can. My parents are going with us, so we'll have some help on the plane."

That certainly will be a big new experience. Babies usually take to plane trips very well. If the baby has a cold, however, you might run into a problem. The variations in air pressure may cause his ear canals to become blocked. If he is entirely well, there should be no problem with that. The baby can't chew gum as we do, but he can suck from a bottle during takeoff and landing. You should always have a bottle handy for this purpose, even for an older baby.

The first night in the new crib and new surroundings may change the baby's sleep pattern a little. She may not fall asleep as quickly, and you may need to stay with her until she does. She might also wake during the night.

The important ingredient in handling such changes in routine is your availability. That's what gives the baby reassurance and makes it possible for her to adapt to the change. If the parents are less available to the baby on vacation, the baby becomes upset, and no one can have a good time. It's also important to try to keep up the same sequence of daily events as at home. Sometimes the baby may sleep well in the new setting but not eat as well. All of these changes are temporary. The goal is to enjoy the trip and enjoy observing the effect of new experiences on the baby.

Whenever families go away for the holidays, they run the risk that the baby will not respond with pleasure. This happens because babies don't understand that such trips are for pleasure. They only know that something is different in their lives, and they can't quite cope with it. It may take a few days for them to settle down in the new environment and again when they return home. This does not happen in all cases, but parents should be prepared for their babies' responses and not feel that the babies are being "bad" just to spoil their holidays. Irritability, poor sleeping or eating responses, and the like are simply the baby's way of expressing her feelings about strange surroundings.

> "If babies sometimes respond so poorly to change, isn't it best to just stay home with them until they are old enough to understand what is going on? It's always such a hassle to get everything ready to go anywhere with the baby, and some-times mine behaves so badly that it just doesn't seem worthwhile."

Certainly babies are more comfortable in familiar surroundings, and it is easier not to try to take them on trips. However, parents must decide for themselves what sacrifices they want to make for their children. If parents understand, they can cope with their baby's behavior. The important thing is for the parents to be supportive of the baby and not become annoyed because the baby needs their support.

> "We've had different experiences with our baby. Sometimes everything turns out fine; other times it's just not her day and we go home early. We just play it by ear."

Yes, that is frequently the story. Babies are not always predictable. Parents must get to know their baby and learn how to cope with the child's needs. It is not easy, but being aware of the baby's immaturity and need for help often makes the burden lighter.

Visiting and taking trips are part of the process of socialization, and some babies are able to socialize sooner than others. But being able to socialize is itself a process of maturation and learning, and here parental help and patience can really enhance development.

TAKING TRIPS WITHOUT THE BABY

The Babies' Reactions

We have talked about parental plans for spending the holiday sea-son with their babies. There are some parents, however, who may be planning to spend the holidays or part of them away without their children. This may be the baby's first experience of prolonged sepa-ration from the parents, and it may be a very difficult situation for the baby to cope with. The babies are not yet old enough to understand that you are going away and will return. If the parents feel they must, need, or very much want to go away without the baby, they also need to make careful plans for the baby during the period of time they are absent.

"We've been discussing going away for a four-day vacation over the holiday. We haven't been away together since the baby was born. My husband is very tired and needs a rest, which he can't get at home because the baby wakes us up so early. I could stand a rest myself. Do you think it would be so devastating for the baby if we were away just four days?"

That depends on a number of things. Certainly your absence will have some impact on the baby. He will miss you, and when you return, he will show it in some way. If you are prepared to give the baby the extra attention he may need for a few days after you return, and if you can leave him with someone he is familiar with, then your absence won't be devastating. It's one of the decisions parents have to consider carefully. Sometimes, it is a very difficult decision to make. Occasionally, parents do need to get away for a short interval, but they must be prepared to deal with the baby's reactions after they return.

"What would the baby do when we get back, or while we are away, that we should be prepared for?"

When you come home, the baby will undoubtedly cling to one or both of you for several days. This is one of the most frequent reactions. Another thing the baby might do is wake at night. The baby will do this because he needs to be reassured that the parents are still there. Some babies get cranky and difficult to satisfy. Others change their eating habits for a few days.

Parents often think: "The baby will miss me and be so glad to see me that he will cuddle and be very loving." This is rarely the baby's response. Sometimes the baby may turn away from the parent and show his anger at being left behind. This is often the response that upsets parents the most. If parents are prepared for such behavior and understand that it is the baby's way of saying "I missed you very much," then they can respond without anger and disappointment.

The question was also asked about the baby's behavior while the parents were away. Besides the initial crying at the time of the parents' departure, the baby may show no other signs of missing them. Much depends on what arrangements are made for the baby, who takes care of the baby and where. The indications that the baby missed the parents may only be evident when they return.

In some cases, babies do give the caretaker some concern. It may be hard for the baby to get to sleep. The baby may keep looking for the parents, starting every time the outside door opens. The baby may be hard to console when he cries and may not eat as well. Some babies sleep longer than usual, as though to pass the time until the parents return. Some babies, if they have reached that level of speech, call for Mommy or Daddy when anyone comes in. These reactions may be minimal and hardly detectable, or they may be quite overt.

One more thing: We're not bringing this matter up to try to frighten you into not ever taking a vacation without your babies. Such an attitude would not be realistic. We are trying to help you understand the babies' needs so that you make the best possible arrangements for the child when you leave.

"What is the best way to arrange to go away? We were planning to have my parents, whom the baby knows well and who know the baby's routine, stay with the baby in our house."

Making Appropriate Arrangements for the Baby

That sounds fine. The best arrangement is to have someone who is close to the baby and whom the baby knows and trusts come and stay with the baby in the baby's own house. Then the baby continues to have the security of his own familiar bed, room, toys, and equipment. The grandparents, other relatives, or close friends can carry out the familiar routines. That kind of arrangement is the least traumatic; the baby is less apt to miss the parents. It also gives grandparents or other relatives a great chance to get to know and enjoy the baby, as well as enlarging the baby's circle of trusted people.

It is a good idea if the substitute caretakers can come a day or two before the parents' departure so that the takeover of responsibility for care can be effected gradually. That way, the parents' departure is not so abrupt—at least, in the baby's eyes. The parents can leave for short intervals during this time, so that the baby has the experience of their leaving and returning; he may thus develop some sense that they will return again after the vacation. In this way, you will be giving the baby a few trial runs of short separations before the longer one.

"In our case that won't work. If my parents come to us, it would mean a long trip for my father to his office. So we have to take the baby to my parents. We can go there a day or two before, settle him in, and see that all systems are 'go' before we leave. My parents' house is a place the baby is used to because we go there often for dinner and my parents have a highchair and a portacrib which the baby has used before. Besides, we'll bring his favorite toys and of course all his clothes, diapers, blankets, cups, and bottles. There will be many aunts and uncles with their children popping in, so the baby won't be lonesome."

That sounds like a good alternative solution. Each family must work these things out to suit its own circumstances.

"We've given a lot of thought to leaving this baby because we had a devastating experience with our first child. When she was a year old, we had an opportunity to go away for a month. We just took her to my parents' house and left her there without staying at all. She was upset all the time we were gone, so we know all about the clinging and crankiness you described. We didn't understand then what had happened, and we were very irritated at her when we got back. We thought my mother must have 'spoiled' her. Now we understand better about a child's reactions, and we don't expect the baby to understand. As a matter of fact, we are postponing a long vacation until the baby is old enough to understand. Our older one now needs more help to adjust to such a change than she would have needed, had we not made the first mistake."

"What do parents do if they must go away and have no one who will come to their house or in whose house the baby is comfortable?"

This often happens in small families far from their relatives. In that case, it is a good idea to hire someone who does this kind of extended care for a living—trained baby nurse, a practical nurse, or an experienced babysitter. It is not always easy to find such people at a moment's notice, but they are available. There are some agencies that specialize in this kind of assistance. Given sufficient time, appropriate arrangements can be made.

It is important to interview such a person first. Have the person come for a few hours to take care of the baby, and observe the baby's response. Then leave the baby for a short while in the person's care. If all goes well, you can feel comfortable leaving the baby for an extended time with the hired substitute.

"Can you get hired caretakers to make such trial runs? Don't such things tend to make them feel from the start that you don't trust them?"

The question here is not what the caretaker feels; the important issue is whether the particular caretaker in question is someone whom the baby can trust. Most people who care for babies professionally understand this concern on the part of the parents and will cooperate. If they do not, don't engage them. Many such caretakers are very glad to get acquainted with the baby and the baby's routine while the parents are still available because no one likes being left for several days with an unhappy, disoriented baby. Caretakers don't like to be left in such a set up any more than the baby does, so it is mutually beneficial to have the trial run.

"We have some neighbors on our block who have a baby the same age as ours. We exchange baby-sitting services often. Their baby is used to being in our apartment, and our baby is used to being in theirs. Last week, these neighbors had to go out of town suddenly because of illness in the family, and they left their baby with us. He cried a little at bedtime the first night, but he settled down when I patted him off to sleep. The next day everything was fine. He was with us two nights. When his parents came back, he cried when he saw them and clung to them for a few hours. Then he was okay. My neighbor said she would like to return the favor and would be glad to take our baby for a weekend if we wanted to get away. Do you think we should do it?"

"That's a golden opportunity. Don't pass it up. It sounds like an ideal setup."

It is a good setup if your baby can adapt as well to the neighbors as their baby adjusted to you, and if you feel your neighbors would take as good care of your baby as you did of theirs. The circumstances were a little different; you were helping out a neighbor in an emergency. The emotional framework is also a little different; your neighbors are returning what they consider a debt. You have to assess the quality and sincerity of the offer and how much you want to get away. When you have done that, then you can make a well-considered decision. It may turn out that this will be a nice arrangement that can occasionally be repeated. That's the next best thing to having one's own family close by.

"What about going away to a hotel, taking the baby, and hiring someone there to care for him? There are many resorts that offer this service."

What will happen in that situation is difficult to predict. The baby is with you part of the day and may take to the baby-sitter at once. All may go well. However, you must remember that the baby will be in a strange place and may have difficulty adjusting to new sleeping and eating arrangements with different people around. Some parents take care of the baby during the day. They put the baby to sleep and have a sitter there in case the baby wakes. The chances of the baby's waking in the new surroundings are good, and he will be confronted by a strange person. That may be traumatic. In that case, he may have difficulty getting back to sleep, and the next night the baby may not go off to sleep readily because he has fears of being left by his parents again. So even in the hotel setting—even if you are in the hotel dining room or elsewhere within reach—it is best to have the baby establish some sense of relationship with and trust for the baby-sitter before being left with her.

"We had that experience. The advertisement seemed very enticing, so we went. We put the baby to sleep. Then the baby-sitter came. She was just a kid, and I was troubled by that, but since we were just downstairs in the dining room, we left the baby with her. The baby woke, took one look at her, and screamed. The sitter didn't know what to do, but she was very gentle and nice. The next day we took her with us to the beach, and the baby got to like her. That night she came before the baby went to sleep. He did wake up, but she gave him a bottle, and he went back to sleep. So it worked out all right. We just didn't use our heads the first night. We were too anxious to be free. It would have been better to hire the sitter for the first afternoon so the baby could get used to her. Even though we were together, it took several days for him to settle back into his routine when we got home. But now we understand that we should plan for the baby first and for ourselves second. It's not too awful, and it's certainly easier and more fun in the long run."

That's a lesson well learned. It doesn't make so much difference who the caretaker is if the baby is given a chance to get used to her and the parents are confident that the caretaker can deal appropriately with the baby. Sometimes paid sitters are better at doing this than relatives are. Some grandparents and relatives get too anxious. You have to judge each situation for itself. But remember: Your vacation will be pleasanter for everyone—baby, parents, and caretakers alike—if you take the baby's needs and level of development into account when you make your arrangements.

"Well, with so much attention being paid to the baby, what about the parents' needs?"

You have hit on one of the big needs of our society: support and consideration for parents. This is one of the main purposes of our program, and that of many other parenting programs being established around the country.

Part of parenting is developing the ability to consider the baby's needs first. Yet, many parents are annoyed because the baby is inconsiderate of **their** needs, but we have also considered your needs as well. In this case, by planning well for the baby, you will ultimately profit by getting away for a rest, knowing that the minimum trauma will result. You will get a sense of achievement from having discharged your obligations with good sense.

In our discussion of leaving babies for holidays or trips, nobody asked, "Why bother to go on a trip without the baby when it really isn't good for the child?"

The Effects of Parents' Vacations on Separation Anxiety

"Yes, that did occur to me. I thought we were making an awful issue about what to do for the baby in order to do something we knew was not the best thing for the baby."

That is true. Leaving for a holiday or business trip means the baby is separated from his parents. This we know from experience is hard for babies. We have recently been discussing the manner in which to leave the baby, even for a short time, with a baby-sitter. We have said that repeated short absences teach the baby to understand that the parents will return. If left with a regular baby-sitter, the baby learns to manage, but even then the baby needs to cling to one or both of the parents when they return. How well the baby can tolerate even small separations depends on the child's level of development in this area.

We know that most children cannot separate well until they are about three years old. One of the reasons for this is that babies do not realize that their parents continue to exist when they cannot be seen. We have discussed how anxiety-provoking it can be for the baby when the parent merely disappears into the bathroom, as well as how annoying this anxiety is to the parent.

Going on vacations and leaving a baby is separation. If the baby has not learned to tolerate short separations and is very clinging when the mother returns, that baby is certainly not ready for the parents to leave for an extended period.

"When would be the worst time to leave a baby for a vacation?"

You know we believe that separation is very hard on children under three years of age. There are considerations which do make separation necessary, and it is not realistic to expect parents to give up all vacations or trips for the baby. That might be ideal in many cases, but to hope that it will happen is not realistic. Babies are probably most vulnerable from six months to a year. This is the period during which they learn that they are separate from the mother and when stranger anxiety is most acute. Babies become less vulnerable as they approach three years. In the second half of the baby's first year of life the idea that a parent who leaves will return is just beginning to make an impact and needs many repetitions until the baby develops sufficient trust that the parents will return. So a vacation away from the baby at that age is not good planning and, if possible, should be avoided. However, if a separation is necessary, then you should follow the procedures we have discussed earlier.

"If parents do go away, how long can they stay away without causing permanent or at least serious trauma?"

I would begin with an overnight separation or, at most, two nights in the six-month-to-one-year period, if you have to go at all. In general, short vacations of not more than three or four days are better until the baby is three years old, or at least until the baby is verbal and can understand that you will return. It is also important for the baby to have a good relationship with the substitute caretaker while the parents are gone.

"My! That seems like a lot of sacrifice over a very long time."

"Oh, it's not all that bad! You can get a lot of relief and pleasure out of an overnight away from home now and again. You can dine out, go to the theatre, meet friends at a party, sleep late the next morning, go to a museum or movie in the afternoon, or shop."

A mini-vacation goes a long way and does little or no harm to the development of the baby's sense of basic trust. A number of short vacations during this period are really better than one extended vacation.

> "Actually the time speeds by, and before you know it, suddenly the children are three, and you don't have a baby anymore! It's sad to think how fast the time passes and how quickly the fun you are having seeing them develop from one stage to the next is over."

> "I didn't have that feeling with my first one. I just couldn't wait for him to grow up. I guess I know the reason why now. I didn't understand the stages of development, and I was in a constant battle with him because I expected more mature behavior. Then I left him for a month and didn't understand his behavior when I came back. I'm still trying to overcome some of the effects of that mistake. He is almost four, and he is still a clinging child who needs a great deal of attention and reassurance."

It's obvious that we have a variety of opinions, feelings, and experiences. Each set of parents has to weigh the consequences of deciding upon early separation and make the choice that suits the family's needs best. However, we all have to remember that the best way to develop a whining, clinging child is to force the child into separation before the child is ready. A child who is fortunate enough to have parents who "cue in" and are sensitive to his needs and level of development repays his parents many times over by the way he develops and learns to cope independently.

> **"What would be some of the consequences of experiencing separation too early?"**

One of the earliest consequences is the child who has difficulty going to school. Most children entering nursery school need to have their mother stay at first, sometimes for the first week or two. Others require their mothers longer. Some just can't separate; they are not ready for school and have to be kept home another semester or sometimes a whole year. Of course, in that case, the parents require some counseling.

Later, these children have difficulty going to another child's house to visit. They only want children to come to their house. They can't spend a night away from home visiting with Grandma or with friends. They often don't want to play outside with other children. Of course, all of these behavior patterns may have other causes, but when one gets the whole story of the child's development, early separation is often the culprit.

> "I've often heard of children who get so homesick at camp or

college and have to come home. Is that the same problem in an older age group?"

That's probably the core of the problem. Nothing can be wholly attributable to just one factor, but it is likely that early separation caused a very large part of the problem.

The effects of forcing separation too early also carry on into later life. There are individuals who, when they marry, have to live in the same apartment house or on the same block as their mothers. This can happen to a boy or a girl. In some cultures, this is looked upon as the norm, and we say such societies prize close family ties. Well, they do, but they may not be for the best reasons. However, developing such behavior may make for a more comfortable or a more secure life because it assures the individual the support of the extended family. Thus, some advantages do sometimes accrue from that situation. The trouble comes when the family must move away from their relatives. Then the problem is fully exposed and needs careful handling. When the underlying cause is understood, it can be dealt with and, to some extent, overcome, but that is not so easy to do.

FEARS: STRANGERS, NOISES, ANIMALS, THE DARK, DOCTORS, AND NEW TOYS

The separation anxiety we have been discussing is also related to the characteristic fears of early childhood. One is the fear of the unknown and the need to experience and re-experience things until they become familiar and the baby can cope with them. In separation, the unknown is the experience that the parent will return. The baby has to experience the return over and over again until he feels confident that the parent will indeed return.

Babies also fear strange people, particularly during the period from seven to ten months of age. But even later, they are usually wary of strangers, especially if the stranger is very large or has a loud voice, or if the baby suspects the stranger will try to hold him or take him away from his mother.

"My baby has developed a fear of fire engines. We live close to a firehouse, and one day just as we were leaving the house, the fire engine came clanging down the street with the siren going, and the baby began to cry. Now I try to anticipate this reaction by picking the baby up immediately and holding her. I also try to imitate the bell and reassure her. But there is just no way to avoid the problem. Even if we move, I guess there will be fire engines around sometimes."

You are doing the very best you can with something you can't control. It is sometimes helpful to visit the firehouse when the engine is in place and not making noise, so the baby can study it a little. Sometimes a toy fire engine helps. That way, the baby gets to imitate the sound the real engine makes and gradually becomes able to deal with the fear. It is common for children to be afraid of loud noises.

> "What about dogs? Are children naturally fond or frightened of them? We don't have one, and I wondered if we should get a puppy that would grow up with the baby so she wouldn't be afraid of them. I'm especially concerned because I always had a fear of animals, dogs in particular."

Pets

Most babies enjoy watching dogs and like to pet and play with them, provided the dog isn't so large that the baby is overwhelmed by its size. Dogs resemble the stuffed animals which the babies have been playing with, but they are more active and more interesting than stuffed animals. However, if the dog barks or sniffs and snorts too close to them, babies may become upset.

The usual approach to getting the baby to overcome his fears is to get him close to the dog and try to make him pet the animal. This usually only intensifies the baby's reaction. The best thing to do is to reassure the baby that everything is all right and move away from the dog to a distance that makes the baby feel comfortable again. The parent can say, "nice doggie" and pet the animal, but they should not force the baby to do so until he feels comfortable enough with the situation to extend his hand to the dog. The baby may not reach this stage until several safe encounters have been experienced. Of course, you need to be certain beforehand that the dog is safe and will not bite or snarl at the baby. For that reason, stray dogs should be avoided. Only a dog whose owner is present and can vouch for the animal's gentleness should be allowed near the baby.

It is not necessary to get puppies for babies of this age because the babies are really too young to enjoy them. Furthermore, puppies are babies too. They demand a lot of care, and providing that care may overburden the parents. Also, puppies are so high-spirited and undisciplined at first that they can easily frighten a baby. If the family already has a pet, of course, the animal becomes part of the baby's life experience. However, you must bear in mind that sometimes a pet can become jealous of a baby. If that happens, the baby may be in some danger from the animal.

Each family must decide whether or not to get a pet. We will be talking at a later time about the most appropriate age for children to have pets.

> "What about fear of the dark? When I was a child, I remember being afraid of going to bed in a dark room. Yet when I put the baby to bed, I turn out the light. She doesn't mind and goes right off to sleep."

Usually babies do not start off being afraid of the dark. However, if they awake at night and the room is dark, they may become frightened when they can't make out any familiar landmarks. Also, if they are awakened by teething pains, they may associate the pain with the darkness and become afraid of the dark. Similarly, if they have been ill with a cold and wake in the dark with a choking sensation, they may associate this feeling with the dark. In any of these cases, the babies may not be able to fall asleep in a dark room.

> "That happened to our baby after a cold. I have tried to make her go back to sleep in the dark, but she won't. So I leave her door open and a small hall light on. Am I doing the right thing?"

That's a reasonable thing to do. Some parents have a small night light attached to the floor plug. This light gives off a very dim light, just adequate for the baby to make out familiar surroundings if he/she wakes, and also enough for the parent to be able to tend to the baby without turning on the overhead lights. There are also all sorts of table lamps with night lights in them for babies' rooms.

> "We have covered a lot of fears I didn't realize babies could have, but there is one special fear I'd like to mention, and that is fear of doctors. Ever since she had her first injection at the doctor's office, my baby cries when we go into the doctor's office. She does this even before she sees the doctor in his white coat."

It is unfortunate that inoculations have to be given as part of a regular checkup. Some doctors are very adept at it, however, and understand the baby's needs so well that they do the inoculation last. Then the mother and child leave for a room with toys, so the baby can be distracted at once. That way, the doctor can also reappear in a pleasant, unthreatening setting and develop a friendlier relationship with the baby while he is giving the mother instructions. Unfortunately, such procedures take a little extra pediatric time, and some doctors are too busy to be able to provide them, but they do pay off because the baby is easier to examine when he is not afraid. Some doctors have an assistant give the inoculation so the baby doesn't become afraid of the doctor. Some have abandoned the white coat—that helps too.

Sometimes it's a good idea to bring a favorite toy to give to the baby to comfort him right after the inoculation; sometimes giving the baby a bottle will achieve this. The important thing is for the parent to be at ease, ready to console and comfort the baby, and not intensify the baby's feeling by her own anxiety.

> "My doctor gives the baby a lollipop right away. That keeps the baby busy, and he forgets his pain."

> "My doctor does that too, but my dentist says lollipops are bad for the teeth. So I just bring a cookie or cracker, give it to the doctor ahead of time, and he hands it to the baby."

It's good that many of you have worked out techniques to ease the way for your babies.

"There is one more thing I wanted to mention and almost forgot. Are babies afraid of new toys?"

That happens if the toy is very large or strange-looking. It also happens if the toy makes an odd noise or is a very dark color that doesn't appeal to the baby.

"That's what happened to us. A friend gave the baby a large green, stuffed frog. The baby cried and wouldn't go near it. I tried to show him it was soft and nice, and he just cried more. I was so surprised and didn't know what to do."

These things happen, but the mother should explain to the person who brought the present that perhaps the baby is just too young and will appreciate the gift later. Don't try to make the baby adjust to the toy to ease the visitor's feelings. It's the baby that needs the help. It's best to put that toy away, and try taking it out again when the baby is older, or after you have shown the baby pictures of the toy so he gets to deal with the strangeness in a less threatening situation. You can also make amusing animal noises for the baby and then associate these noises with the toy. The main job for the parent is to be the child's advocate and to be concerned about the child's reactions and needs, not about what an adult may feel. Sometimes this is hard to do because you may be dealing with the boss's wife, but it's the baby that needs help or consoling first. Then you can try to explain your child's behavior to the adult while showing your real appreciation for your visitor's efforts to please the baby.

DISCIPLINE VS. PUNISHMENT

Setting Limits

Now that the babies are becoming more mobile, they can explore more distant areas and try out new activities. Adults recognize some of this exploration as dangerous, destructive, or painful to other children, and, therefore, they want to stop the baby from engaging in certain activities. Not to allow the baby to do anything that may be dangerous to the baby, destructive to property, or painful to another is part of the parents' job. How parents do this varies in different societies and households.

We have already talked about this topic several times from different points of view. Because discipline is teaching and because the baby's ability to comprehend what you are teaching develops over time, the parent-child interaction in this area changes and develops as well.

How are you dealing with situations calling for limitation? What activities do you limit? How do you go about setting these limits?

"We live in a very old-fashioned apartment where the radiators are exposed. The baby likes to play with the radiator, especially when the steam comes up and begins to sizzle. When the heat's off, I'm not worried. But when the radiator is hot and he puts his hand out toward it, I say 'No,' but he still wants to be near it. At this point, I used to slap his hands. Since we've talked about the effect of slapping, however, I just shout 'No' and get very angry."

It seems to me you are doing two things in this situation that confuse the baby. First, to let him play with the radiator when it is off and not when it is on is confusing. The baby cannot, at his age, understand why at one time it is all right to play with the radiator and at another it is not. You have to be consistent in your approach to this problem. The radiator should be off limits **all the time** until the baby is old enough to understand that something hot may be dangerous.

In the second place, to slap a baby is punishment, not discipline. He needs to be taught that he cannot touch the radiator and then be given a substitute which he can touch. He must be allowed to discharge the impulse to touch with another object. The parent can say "No" firmly and show disapproval by shaking her head and looking stern. Then the parent should be enthusiastic in her approval of the substitute activity. In this way, a parent teaches what is accepted and what is not.

> "Are you saying that we should not punish children, but we should discipline them? What is the difference?"

Punishment means teaching by inflicting pain. That should not be the parent's purpose. The parent's purpose is to set limits—that is, to teach what is acceptable and what is not, what is considered right and what is considered wrong in the household. By doing this a parent disciplines, or teaches, the child. Parents are the primary teachers, the first and most important ones the child will ever have.

> "But doesn't a child learn by being hit? Isn't that a more certain way? That's what my parents did to me, and that's what my mother thinks I ought to do to my baby. She says a little slap never hurt anyone."

That is the method of trying to teach by punishment, but a baby of this age doesn't even understand what the punishment is for because he does not know what is acceptable and not acceptable. There are many parents who only pay attention to the child when he is doing something wrong. Then he is punished physically. When the baby is doing something good, the parents just accept it as the routine. They may feel pleased by what the baby did but do not overtly convey that to the child. The child then only learns what is wrong because the parent only recognizes what is wrong. If there are many things of which the parent disapproves, then the child may get the feeling that he can't ever please the parent.

8.3 look for swift run

turn left 8.0 8.9 sharp

left turn

Yourself and family, comfortable shoes and definitely a flashlight, matches, food that I will call you about later, sleeping bags, comfortable clothes, bug spray, and whatever. Carrying will be a distance, so pack light.

WHAT IS THE CABIN LIKE?

A beautifully well-lanterned, well-pot bellied heated unpolluted spring water cabin surrounded by a virgin wood (that was cut down a couple of years ago) A maze of paths to follow during the day and you will be amazed at the bugs that will follow you at night. All cooking utensils, bunk beds, mattresses, tables, staples and lanterns and an outside OUTHOUSE are there...accomodations for 12, so bed rools are needed.

COST:

Cost will be $3.00 per person per night and food will be brought by each family. I can have a check when I get there at trip.

So until we ford the "Bridge Over Troubled Camping Grounds," "" Well need a little help from our friends. Be prepared. As Thoreau says, "A bug in the bed is worth more than a bite in the rear." So see you in the moon shadow, moon shadow--leaping and hopping in the moon shadow, spending a night with the moon shadow.

TO: POTENTIAL CAMPERS
FROM: FRAN DUMMETT
      6894 Garland Lane
      Columbia, Md. 21045
      997-2215

                                    Saturday July 23 - Sunday
                                    July 24

HERMITAGE CABIN :

Laurel   Pat   Pat   HERMITAGE CABIN
Jenny   Shelly   Bill   Cathy   Fran   Tim
Elizabeth Mellissa Cindy   Albin   Austen   Barbara
                     Cheryl   Andrea   Simone   Nicholas

HERMITAGE CABIN :

This quaint 1 room log cabin which facilitates 12 poeple lies in
Michaex-Mont Alto State Forest. From DC it is 82 miles. Gosvia
Frederick and US 15 to Thurmont and Emmitsburg. Gosvia
go through Emmitsburg, continue on Md. 97 to state line where it becomes
Penna 16. At west end of Rouzerville turn right(north) (zero point
at septic tanks works(which was hard to find) on hard surface road
which is Antietam Road but not marked. You might have to ask. Go
5.2 miles to Old Forge. At 5.5 miles turn left onto the Swift Run
Road(note signs) and ascend to Monument Rock turnout at 6.4 miles
on sharp left turn in the road. Park here. Go right on the blue-blazed
trail at the turn in the road, .2 miels through woods dand down a slope
to the cabin.   Welcome

OUR CABIN:

It is available from Fri 4PM to Sunday 4PM, but I think I will be going
down early Saturday morn.

To this the child can respond in a number of ways: He can give up trying to please; he can keep trying by becoming overly compliant and ingratiating; or he can become overtly angry and hostile. None of these behavior patterns or character traits makes for a healthy adult personality. The child who gives up may have no incentive to learn in school because he has never experienced success and approval at home. The child who tries so hard to be liked may become insincere and harbor real hostility. The child who is overtly angry and aggressive cannot deal with authority appropriately.

We all know adults who have no "get up and go." We recognize the individuals who are ready to please everyone, the "yes men" who really aren't sincere. We also recognize the angry people, the individuals with chips on their shoulders. Are these really the character traits that we want our children to develop, or do we want them to develop a healthy sense of self-worth and self-esteem, as well as a solid understanding of the difference between right and wrong?

Children learn to accept limitations because their parents' method of teaching these limitations has been patient, firm, and consistent, but not punitive. Children develop self-esteem because approved behavior on their part has been recognized and encouraged by their parents. The same recognition and encouragement will lead children to internalize a healthy concept of right and wrong, without establishing an angry relationship with the parents. These children will develop healthy, active conscience mechanisms.

Disciplining rather than punishing children is one of the basic issues of child rearing, and we will be discussing it again at different age levels. For now, it is important to recognize the need for consistency and firmness when setting limits and for enthusiastic and positive recognition of approved behavior.

The human being seems to have an inborn need for recognition and approval; this is the factor we should utilize in establishing limits or discipline. A person becomes self-disciplined when he can set his own limits and no longer needs parental or societal disapproval to discourage him from doing wrong. That is the kind of mature person we would like our children to grow up to be. We are setting a stage now for achieving that goal, and that's why we say 'discipline—yes; punishment—no!'

Permissiveness

"Aren't you saying that parents should be permissive? Aren't we getting into the controversy between authoritarianism and permissiveness?"

Both authoritarianism and permissiveness are extremes. Unfortunately, but rather commonly during our history, the changes that have taken place have tended to go from one extreme to the other. For example, we went from long, flowing skirts to the miniskirt and back again. Similarly, we went from enormous hats to no hats. In education, we moved from strictly prescribed courses to self-choice in the curriculum. Now we are moving back to requiring children and young people to take some basic courses again. In raising of children, we went from Victorian strictness to total permissiveness, and now we have begun to set limitations that are more appropriate to a child's level of development and understanding.

> "Why was permissiveness bad? What was wrong with it? We hear so much now about the aftermath of unhappiness in the generation that was brought up permissively."

> "Well, those children who had everything their way never knew what they wanted and were brats. I saw some children raised like that, and they and their parents were not happy."

Overpermissiveness seems to have led to quite a number of consequences which were not anticipated by the educators of the period. If everything is permitted and there are no limits, a child gets a sense of insecurity, a sense that no one cares what he does. It's a short step from this feeling to the feeling that no one cares for him. Children need help in identifying reality—what is harmless and harmful, good and bad, right and wrong. A parent can do that without being intrusive and taking away a child's initiative.

There is another aspect of permissiveness to be considered. If everything is permitted, there is little differentiation between right and wrong; there is also little special approval from parents when a child does do the right things. There is also probably less reinforcement of the sense of mastery and less recognition of achievement and both factors are important in development of self-esteem and a good self-image.

From experience it has been found that children do not derive pleasure from doing just what they want to all the time. When there are certain restrictions, the child feels a heightened sense of pleasure from activities reinforced by parental approval and contact. Permissiveness took away this special pleasure from the child's experience and removed parents to a greater distance from their children. There was not as much interaction between parent and child, and some children interpreted this distance as parental indifference. Some responded to it with hostility and what some people consider being a "brat."

> "I think I was brought up something like that. I remember feeling as a child that my parents did not take as good care of me or love me as much as my friend's parents loved and took care of their child because my friend's parents told her when to come home and what to wear. This seemed so important to me."

> "Well, my mother used to spank me a lot, and that was the way I thought children should be brought up. I soon realized I couldn't do that to my baby. Now I'm learning another way.

> But my problem isn't over because my mother sometimes baby-sits for me and I'm afraid she is going to treat my baby the same way she treated me."

Well, that punitive way of teaching children is still prevalent. The growing statistics on child abuse are further evidence of this because abuse often begins with what many people consider "legitimate punishment" to "teach the child a lesson." As we have said before, children are often punished as a means of getting them to behave in ways they cannot understand or perform. What we really need is an understanding of the infant's level of development and what an infant can comprehend at each level.

A great deal has been learned about the ways infants learn and the most appropriate methods for teaching them at different ages through the patient studies of many painstaking behavioral scientists. We are discussing these methods with you so that you can help your babies learn and grow in the best way possible. We also hope that the parent-child relationship will be made more enjoyable.

> "But the old methods are so ingrained and when we do anything different, someone—even a stranger in a supermarket—will come up and say: 'Don't you know how to raise a baby? He needs a good smack on the hand!' What do you do about that?"

People who know little or nothing about raising children are often the ones who are most emphatic and certain in their opinions. They do make it hard for others. It is good to be prepared for them with a kind but firm reply.

> "I've got one I use. I say: 'That is the way you used to bring up children, but times have changed and so have methods. Your generation didn't do a perfect job. Now I'm going to try it my way.' I use that on my family, and they are getting the point. No one is going to hit my baby."

If that works for you, that's fine. It is good that you have the courage to express yourself so frankly. Your family will respect you for it. However for strangers in a store or elsewhere, it might be easier to say something like: "Oh, I see you think the baby should be slapped. Thank you for you advice; I'll think about it." Then move on. This way, you take yourself out of the stranger's control and leave him or her little opportunity to pursue the matter further.

> "I can hardly wait to try that because I have been bothered so much by strangers interfering in the way I bring up my baby."

Probably the essence of all teaching is patience, kindness, firmness, and consistency. If that is what guides the relationship between parent and child, the results are bound to be effective, and no one will want or need to interfere with your child-rearing methods. Of course, babies have days when they are out-of-sorts and cranky, and outsiders often pick such time to comment or attempt to interfere. Parents must understand that such comments are made without knowledge of the whole picture of the baby's development and may be disregarded.

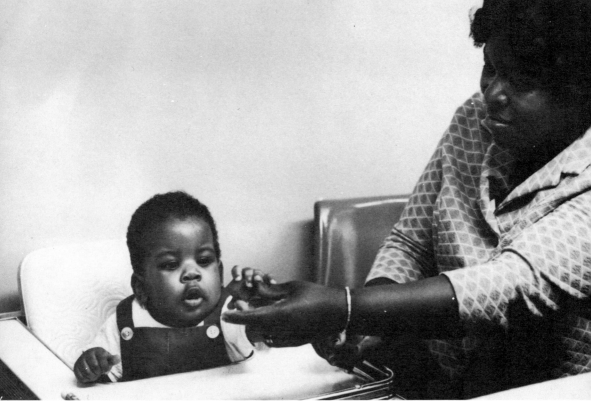

One-year-old children being assisted by their mothers during
Gesell Testing at the Early Childhood Development Center.

Chapter Twelve

Age:
48 to 52 weeks _____

While sitting, the babies can now pivot and reach for things in all directions without losing their balance; previously they could only lean forward and straighten back to the sitting posture. Many of the babies can now stand in their cribs and move around holding onto the rail. To walk outside of the crib, most babies still need support. (To provide this support, the parent may walk in front of the baby holding both of the baby's hands, or behind the child holding both of his hands over the child's head.) The babies may also be able to walk supporting themselves by pushing a chair ahead of them.

The babies are now able to pick up small objects (even small crumbs left on their highchair trays) with a neat **pincers grasp**, an important fine motor achievement. When given several little blocks, the baby can play with them in several different ways—hitting them against each other, pushing them, and rearranging them.

Babies of this age are ready to be introduced to a simple form-board puzzle with round, square and triangular pieces. When presented with such a puzzle with only the round form in place, the baby can remove it easily but will not be able to replace it. Practice with puzzles should, therefore, begin with the baby's **removal** of the pieces.

Most babies now have vocabularies including "Mama", "Dada," and one or two other words, such as "Hi" or "Bye." They should understand and be able to play "Pat-a-Cake" and "Bye-Bye" more competently.

The babies can sit in their highchairs and play with toys for a longer period of time than previously. Usually the toys end up on the floor because the babies are now at the height of the period of exploring space by throwing things down—an activity which is important to their development, although annoying to some parents.

NEW DEVELOPMENTS IN EXPLORATION

We have talked about the babies need to learn about space by pushing toys out of their cribs or off the highchair. For many babies this exploration is at its height. We hope that you are all taking advantage of this interest of your babies and teaching them the meanings of "up" and "down." This kind of teaching really assists the baby in understanding space and adds the verbal dimension to his exploratory efforts. Helping the baby achieve an understanding of these concepts can bring satisfaction to the parents as well as to the baby. There is nothing that enhances a baby's sense of achievement and mastery more than having the approving participation of the parents in his efforts to understand the world around him.

We forget how long it takes for babies to understand some concepts. They are true scientists. They have to experiment over and over again to verify their ideas. Each item that is dropped or pushed over the side of something makes a different sound or falls in a different way. The babies watch each one intently. Of course, we don't expect you to be as enchanted with this game as your babies are. For that reason, we have advised that you change the activity when you've had enough of it.

Some babies are probably already moving on to the next phase of this exploration—dropping toys and picking them up by themselves. Now that the babies are beginning to stand, they will hang on to a chair or rail with one hand and drop a toy with the other. Then they will lower themselves to pick the toy up, retrieve it, and then drop it again. They will do this over and over again because they are still not certain of cause and effect. In addition, being able to pick up a toy and throw it down by themselves without parental assistance gives babies a great sense of mastery. If your baby has not yet begun to do this, he will soon begin.

Remember: the babies will need to do the same experiment many times on their own because they were using the parent as an assistant when they could not do it by themselves.

Until now, we have been talking about throwing or dropping toys. What about food? Have any of the babies been dropping food off the table or highchair?

> **"Oh, yes! Yesterday I was so angry. The baby pushed a plate off the highchair tray. I scolded and yelled 'No' and slapped him hard. He looked very bewildered and cried and cried."**

It is very understandable that you do not find it at all amusing when the object used for exploration is a cup full of milk or the plate of delicious food you have prepared for the baby. From the baby's point of view, however, both kinds of things are fit objects for exploring space. It is hard for him to grasp the difference between a toy and a cup of milk, except that the latter falls in a more interesting way. At this age, it is better to place only a small amount of milk in a cup and sit close to the baby to intercept spills. In the coming year, we will talk about teaching the difference between toys and food because then the babies will be ready to understand.

"I'm glad to know this because I'm sure I would have been ready to punish my baby. I so much want to be a good parent and not make the mistakes my parents made."

Most mothers and fathers want to be good parents. The mistakes they make, however, do not occur because they are unkind, or unloving, but because they sometimes do not understand the meaning of their baby's actions in relation to his development. You cannot expect a one-year old, nor a three-year old to act like a five-year old.

_____ FEELINGS ABOUT PARENTHOOD: THE EFFECT OF OUR HERITAGE

In this day and age, people do not have to become parents until they are ready to, until they want to have children. Even those who do not exercise this choice for religious reasons are helped by their beliefs to accept having a child.

However, in times past, many children were not wanted by their parents. As a result, child-rearing practices which reflected the parents' anger and feelings of being trapped by the child came into use. Indeed, such practices even became the accepted ways of dealing with a child.

Many of these questionable methods of child rearing were used on us when we were being brought up, and although most of us believe that we no longer endorse such outmoded methods, we still unconsciously replicate them because they are so deeply ingrained in our behavior. Indeed, it takes a great deal of effort to overcome our heritage, especially because we are not always aware of its place in our own behavior. But don't lose heart! With time, patience, and careful consideration of what you are doing and its effects on your children, you will be able to shed unwanted behavior patterns and assimilate new techniques.

Let me clarify what I mean by pointing out one such unfortunate remnant of the past—yelling at, scolding, or slapping a baby when he touches something or engages in some activity he shouldn't.

There was a time when parents had little or no understanding of early exploration and its importance in the child's development. In particular, they did not understand that a baby could not distinguish between what the parents considered healthy exploration—for example, playing quietly with a block or a doll—and what the parents looked on as dangerous, painful, or destructive—for example, reaching for mother's hair or pulling books out of a bookcase. To the parents, the child engaged in such unapproved behavior was just being "naughty" or "willfully disobedient." Thus, the parents felt justified in "teaching" the child how to behave by punishing him for wrong behavior. Usually this punishment involved yelling, scolding, or slapping the child's hands.

From the baby's point of view, however, such reactions are thoroughly unreasonable, and we feel such "teaching" techniques are inappropriate. The baby is exploring, trying to organize his world. He does not yet know that doing certain things is "good" and that doing certain other things is "bad." Such distinctions are way above his level of development. To the baby, everything he does is part of "exploring." It's neither "good" nor "bad"; it just is.

So, reacting to unapproved behavior with a yell or slap, especially a hard one, will only confuse or frighten the child. It may even discourage him from continuing to explore because he has been prevented painfully from completing the impulse he started to carry out. That could have serious consequences on the child's development of an ability or desire to explore and learn later on in school. Moreover, such a method of setting limits does not teach the child acceptable behavior. It merely punishes him for doing something the wrongness of which he cannot yet understand. Such a technique also inevitably puts the parent in the role of an inflicter of pain and fear, rather than in the role of a trusted guide and friend. This, of course, is hardly conducive to the development of a healthy parent-child relationship.

Instead of yelling at, scolding, or slapping a child, stop him from doing what he is doing with a firm "No," and immediately substitute some approved activity. This way, the child's impulse to complete the exploratory action he has begun will be diverted into acceptable channels. Thus, the child will not be discouraged from developing a healthy instinct to explore and learn, and he will begin to perceive what acceptable behavior entails. Finally, you will enhance, rather than impede, your relationship with the child by presenting yourself as a guide and friend.

Being limited in a harsh way is something we all experienced as children, and it is so deeply ingrained in our behavior patterns that we are all likely to react to our children that way. However, if you think through the consequences of such a "teaching" technique, you will see that it inevitably does more harm than good to the child's development.

> "I see now what you mean. That's just what I find myself doing. But when I use a more constructive approach such as you suggest, and it doesn't work the first time, I'm disappointed."

Yes, of course, you are disappointed. The baby must still try his experiments until he learns, and you have to continue patiently teaching him until he does learn. The process takes time and patience, but it may make the difference between having a child with healthy intellectual curiosity and one who can't get involved in learning, or the difference between a child who learns to accept limitations and one who cannot accept them.

> "But not everything our parents did was wrong, was it?"

Of course not. There are many things which were right, and we have discussed some of them. Take, for example, picking up babies when they cry or rocking them to sleep. How do you suppose the lullaby began? We still sing babies to sleep or sing to soothe them. Similarly, we are going back to breast feeding and carrying babies on our backs or hips. Many practices from the past have value. Perhaps one of the most important of these is the establishment of regularity in the baby's day. We are returning to this time-honored practice—but with a difference—because now we recognize the baby's need for a routine that gives him a sense of security and order without the imposition of an exacting schedule unrelated to his own "biological clock."

All of the traditional practices or techniques that are appropriate and fit with the baby's level of development, we can and will hold on to. Those, however, that were not constructive, or that were harmful, we must unlearn by substituting better ways.

THE FIRST BIRTHDAY

The Party

Now that the babies are approaching their first birthdays, it may be helpful to discuss what would be appropriate for this big event. The most important thing to remember is that it is the child's birthday and should relate to his or her level of development. Grandparents naturally want to be there, and if they live nearby, that already makes a large group of guests. A very good "rule" for children's parties is to have one more child than the age of the child whose birthday it is. You will find that it is especially important to follow this "rule" when the children are two, three, and four years old. It is easy to overwhelm a child by inviting too many children and adults to the party.

> "Last week I saw that happen. I went to my nephew's party; he was two. His mother made it a great event with a beautifully decorated cake and table. There were ten children and ten mothers, plus grandparents. My nephew spent the whole afternoon crying in his room. I thought he must be getting sick. Now I understand that he was overwhelmed by the crowd invading his home."

Exactly! There were simply too many children and adults at the party. One forgets that each child comes with a parent or caretaker, and that doubles the number of guests. Following our suggested "rule," the appropriate number of children for the first birthday would be two: your child and one friend. If there is no other child available, your baby won't mind. (You must, of course, adapt all our suggestions to your own situation. If there are several siblings or other children that your baby is very used to, you may be able to have more children present at the party.) It is also important for the parent to stay close to the child to give the child a sense of security.

> "Another thing that surprised me was that none of the children ate the beautiful cake. It was a white cake with almond and bitter chocolate icing. I thought it was delicious."

All the adults probably loved the cake, but it was too fancy for the children. You must remember what they eat every day and then prepare something that is not too different. Your one-year olds may not eat any cake at all, but they will enjoy ice cream because they have had it before. Slightly older children may only eat a bite or two.

Another caution concerns the candles. Children, especially at this age, do not realize that they are hot. They are attracted by the brightness and may stick their fingers in the flame and burn themselves. It is a good idea, therefore, to keep a cake with lighted candles at some distance from the child—and then blow them out quickly after you have sung "Happy Birthday."

Remember also that one of the fears of this age is loud noise. It is a good idea to sing softly. A sudden rousing chorus of "Happy Birthday" can startle or frighten a child. The child may even burst into tears, which upsets everyone.

If you keep the party simple and at the child's level—not expecting her to understand it all—everyone will have a good time.

Appropriate Presents for the First Birthday

"We've been talking a lot about our son's birthday, especially about presents. Just what presents are right for a baby this age, and how much is enough?"

For the first birthday, there is a tendency to give a child too many presents that are too complicated. An appropriate present for a baby of this age is a small red ball that he can hold in his hand. It should be soft and chewable with nontoxic coloring because the baby will naturally try out its taste and texture with his mouth. Babies enjoy rolling balls along their highchair trays or on the floor. They also like having the balls rolled back to them.

Other good toys include small rag dolls with the eyes, nose, and mouth embroidered on so they cannot be chewed off and brightly colored, nontoxic stuffed animals of a size the baby can hold—not enormous ones.

At this age, babies are also ready for small blocks about one inch square. They can hold them in their hands, put them in and out of cups, jars, or boxes, and perhaps begin to stack one on top of another.

The babies are also ready for the peg toy which holds a number of colored rings of graded sizes. At this time, the baby will be able to remove the rings from the peg and perhaps can learn to place one on the peg in the next few months. It is a good toy because it enhances development and, with maturation and practice, the baby will be able to place the rings on the peg in the appropriate order. This ability may not come until the child is two years old, so this is a useful toy for a long time.

Cloth books with one picture per page are also good presents and can be used for a long time. Musical rattles and music boxes are nice but not essential. The baby does not need too many new presents at once.

Clothes, small chairs and tables, electric trains, elaborate dolls with real hair and fine clothes, large stuffed animals, and the like are always things that doting friends and relatives feel moved to give babies on the first birthday (or first Christmas). At this age, such items are really presents for the parents. The complicated and elaborate toys can be put away until they are appropriate, or they can be used as room ornaments until the baby shows interest in them.

What feelings and ideas do you have about presents?

> "I have been wondering what to say if anyone asked what to get the baby. I can see to it that the baby's father and I get the few appropriate toys that have been suggested. We can decide afterward to do what seems right about whatever else the baby gets—use what is right for now and put the rest away."

> "I know my husband is going to be very upset about the trains not being appropriate. He's been looking forward to giving the baby that for a present."

Actually you don't have to spoil the father's fun. We all know that getting the train set will give the father pleasure, and when he gets it set up and running, the baby will enjoy watching it for a few minutes at a time. However, you can hardly call the trains the baby's toy. A baby's toy is something the baby can manipulate by himself. Trains will not be appropriate for a few years yet.

> "If trains are really for fathers, how about the doll with change of clothes being for mothers?"

If that gives mother pleasure, why not? Mother may have been looking forward to playing with dolls with her baby. There is nothing wrong in admitting that.

> "Well, I guess I don't need to play with dolls anymore. My baby is my big, live doll, and dressing her is the real thing. I guess I've worked out my needs in real life and don't need to do it symbolically anymore."

Many women who like to sew get pleasure from making clothes for their children's dolls. Adults get pleasure in giving lovely toys. That's fine! The most important thing, however, is not to overwhelm the babies with too many presents and not to expect them to appreciate toys that are not yet developmentally appropriate.

The baby's first shoes are often given as a gift, especially by grandparents. There are differing opinions on when the baby needs shoes

The Baby's First Shoes

and what kind they should be. It is very important that shoes fit properly, and how to tell this is often a problem.

"My pediatrician says babies don't need shoes until they are walking, and my mother is having a fit. She says the baby needs high shoes to support his ankles; otherwise he'll damage his ankles, and that is why he is not walking yet. We keep arguing about this."

It's always a good idea to get your pediatrician's advice because he is the one who can best tell whether the baby is ready for shoes, and what kind of shoes to get, particularly if a special type is required.

There are some facts about foot and muscle development that ought to be better known. For example, the belief that a baby needs high shoes for ankle support is a common misconception. A baby does not learn to walk because her feet are supported by brace-like high shoes but because her neuromusculature has matured to the point that she can support herself. Her ability to stand and move is helped by the freedom to flex and contract her muscles. The more freedom to exercise the muscles, the quicker the development of motor activity. A high, firm shoe can act as a deterrent to this free exercise of the muscles and actually make movement more difficult and clumsy. We have often seen babies who clump along in heavy shoes and scamper freely when the shoes are removed.

"Well, why put any shoes on the baby's feet in that case?"

Actually, many doctors advise against shoes until the baby is walking well. However, in the winter when floors are cold and drafty, soft leather-soled moccasin-socks or slippers made out of corduroy, flexible leather, or felt are appropriate. Socks are also good if the baby doesn't slip or skid in them. These soft foot coverings serve two purposes: They keep the feet warm, and they protect them from pins or other sharp objects on the floor.

"When babies are finally ready for shoes, what kind should they be? Should they be high or low shoes?"

For normal feet, the high shoes are not necessary. Support for the child's weight comes from the bone and muscle, not the leather shoes. A low shoe is adequate. It is necessary only to protect the feet from the roughness of the pavement and such things as broken glass or sharp pebbles when the baby is walking outdoors. If the floor is carpeted, the baby certainly does not need shoes. If the floors are uncarpeted and cold, then some protective foot covering is in order. Parents have to use their judgment and find a shoe or slipper which allows freedom of movement but also provides protection for the feet.

"What are some of the things to look for when getting shoes

fitted? Stores make such a fuss about their brands, and some use x-rays, although I hear that is dangerous."

X-rays are dangerous, and their use is now prohibited because there was too much x-ray emanation.

First of all, the thing to look for is a flexible sole on the shoes; you should be able to bend the toe toward the heel easily. Then you should be certain that the inner edge of the last—that is, the line from the big toe to the heel—is straight. When the baby's foot is placed in the shoes, the heel should not ride up. The back rim of the shoes should not curve and cut into the heel. Put your finger in and feel whether it does. When the shoe is buckled or laced and the baby stands up, there should be about half an inch from the end of his toe to the tip of the shoe. There should be ample toe room, and the top of the shoe should not overlap the sole. If a shoe does that, it is not wide enough to accommodate the foot when it is bearing the baby's weight. If the shoe has to be buckled or laced very tightly to keep the foot from riding up, then the shoes does not fit properly. A different size, width, or brand of shoe must be tried. Proper shoe fitting is difficult and very important.

"Shoes are so expensive. The salespeople always try to sell you the most expensive ones. Can one tell by the price which to buy?"

Certainly not. Look for the features just mentioned. They can sometimes be found in some of the least expensive shoes. The baby's foot grows very rapidly. When the shoes are very expensive, you try to get as much wear out of them as possible, and children often end up wearing shoes that are too small. It is not necessary to get the strongest, longest lasting, and most expensive leather. The important factor is the fit, which should be checked every three months. Many babies need new shoes several times a year.

"What about boots and overshoes?"

Just now the babies are not spending enough time walking outdoors to need such footwear. In bad weather and in high snow, most babies are not outdoors very much at all. When they are older and do spend more time walking outdoors, these items will be needed. If some babies are out a lot in the rain and snow, they will, of course, need boots earlier. Parents have to decide depending on their own situations.

WEANING

Breast Feeding

Many mothers are breast feeding and both baby and mother are thriving. Some of you have asked how long breast feeding should last. That is a very individual matter. If the milk supply is good and the mother is comfortable, it can be kept up until the baby is about a year old. Many babies have a natural inclination to stop when they are about eight or nine months old, and many mothers wish to encourage this.

Whenever the mother feels that she would like to offer a supplementary bottle instead of the breast, she can introduce it. It is best to offer this bottle at the same feeding each day so the baby gets used to it. Then, if an emergency arises when the mother has to be away, the baby will be more accustomed to drinking from a bottle. Your pediatrician will advise you about this and prescribe what formula is the best to use.

When weaning is decided on, it can be accomplished gradually as the baby becomes used to taking more from the bottle than from the breast. Nature has a way of taking care of the mother's milk supply. As the baby demands less and sucks less from the breast, the production of milk diminishes. Finally, the baby becomes entirely dependent on bottle feedings, and the breast supply of milk has ceased naturally, without trauma to either mother or baby.

Have you thought about weaning? What are your thoughts on the subject?

> "I'm perfectly content nursing, and I haven't used any supplementary bottles yet. Do you think it's a good idea to use supplementary bottles anyway?"

Yes, it's a kind of an insurance, so that if an emergency arises, the baby won't be forced abruptly to use the unfamiliar bottle. But bear this consideration in mind: When using a bottle, you must be certain the milk flow is not too fast, so that the feeding isn't too quick. Breast-fed babies are accustomed to a lot of sucking.

> "If you keep up breast feeding as long as a year, isn't it harder on the baby to stop? Doesn't the baby become too attached to that method of feeding?"

> "I had to stop suddenly when I was sick, and I hadn't started the baby on a bottle. The baby cried and cried and would not take the formula for two days. We were very concerned. Finally we sweetened the formula, and he took it. I wish I had given at least one bottle a day before that. Even now, he pulls at me as though he still wants the breast, but he is getting used to the bottle."

Of course, the babies become attached to the method of feeding you've established. That is why the weaning should be very gradual. Perhaps one bottle a day for a week or two, then weaning to two and then three. The first morning and the last night feedings are usually the hardest to give up.

> "I heard that weaning should start when the baby begins to get teeth. Is that the usual guideline?"

That used to be the guideline when breast feeding was the norm. When the baby bit the mother, she would then wean the baby. Often this was done quite abruptly, and the abruptness of the change caused the mother discomfort because she still had a large milk supply and had to have her breasts bound and use some form of dehydration. The baby was also miserable. Now we know better, and try to wean the baby more gradually on a time schedule that suits both infant and mother.

"Do babies have to be weaned to a bottle? Can they be weaned to a cup?"

This is often done, particularly when a baby has also been taught to take juice from a cup. When babies are used to taking juice, you can try giving them their milk or formula from a cup. This is a very nice way to wean a baby and eliminates the need for going through the bottle stage. Success, however, depends on the baby's level of development and ability to manage drinking from a cup. Cup feeding is an especially good way to begin weaning when breast feeding has continued for nearly a year. By this time, the baby has probably had sufficient sucking activity, and if the cup is accepted well, you needn't introduce the bottle.

"What if the baby doesn't take as much milk from the cup as he would from a bottle?"

The quantity that a baby needs has to be decided individually for each baby by the doctor. Usually if cup feeding is begun later, the baby is taking sufficient other food so that his nourishment isn't entirely dependent on milk. However, this is all very individual, and the timing has to be decided by the mother's assessment of her baby, her own needs, and her doctor's advice.

"What about weaning from the bottle? Now that my baby is nearly a year old, I'm getting a lot of advice about weaning her to a cup."

Bottle Feeding

Bottle-fed babies need the same gradual weaning as breast-fed babies. Often such weaning is too abrupt because the mother does not have any personal physical need for gradualism.

Bottle-fed babies usually do not get as much sucking time as breast-fed babies because bottle nipples allow a more rapid milk flow. Bottle-fed babies therefore usually have a greater sucking need, and it is important to wean them slowly on their own timetables, not the adult's. Babies often find the last bottle of the day a comforting one to continue. If they still need to suck and are too abruptly weaned, they will find their own substitutes, usually their thumbs. Weaning from the bottle too early can lead to a habit of thumb-sucking.

"Now that the babies have teeth, isn't it bad for them to go to sleep with a bottle in their mouths?"

Doctors and dentists generally feel that allowing the baby to go to sleep with formula or milk in the mouth may result in damage to the baby's teeth. We, therefore, recommend that you do not leave the bottle in the crib with the baby. Instead, let the baby take her bottle; then give her a drink of water and put her to bed. If the baby will not relax and go off to sleep unless she is sucking on her bottle, use water in the bottle instead of milk.

Other babies who have stopped taking bottles may like to suck on a pacifier for a few minutes before they go to sleep. Such a child clearly needs the pacifier for additional sucking as well as for comfort.

"What about the two-year old who walks around with a bottle?"

This child must still need some opportunity to suck. She may also need some extra comforting. It is a good idea to look at the child's life pattern and see whether there isn't something that is causing her anxiety. In any case, you often do more harm than good by trying to take away the bottle before the child is ready. No child goes to high school with a bottle, yet some at that age still surreptitiously suck their thumbs. Most children naturally give up the bottle when they are ready. Parents must "tune in" to the signs of readiness and be prepared to help the child take this step toward more mature behavior.

"What is the latest that a child may need a bottle at bedtime or first thing in the morning?"

About three years old is usually accepted as the average limit. The time factor varies, of course, with each child. Some manage cup feeding very well before they are three and are proud of their accomplishment. A few need one bottle a while longer. At no time should a child be shamed into giving up the bottle.

"But you often see kids who are older than that walking around holding bottles. Why is that?"

Such behavior is not usual or normal. The child in question is probably not using the bottle for nourishment but as a security measure or as a tie to the mother, from whom the child may have difficulty separating. The cause of such behavior varies in each case. You must look at each child's particular situation to determine the reasons for the behavior and the ways of correcting it.

TOILET TRAINING: SOME GENERAL IDEAS

"What about toilet training? My mother keeps urging me to start training the baby. In fact, when he was four months old, she gave me a little potty!"

That is the way older generations began toilet training: The mother put a small potty on her lap and held the baby on it. She, of course, did that about the time that the baby naturally had a bowel movement. For a baby with regular habits this training could be quite successful. We maintain, however, that it was the mother who was well-trained, **not** the baby!

Other theorists held that one should start toilet training when the baby was about one year old. Once again the mother observed the natural time of bowel movements and trained herself to be ready for them.

More recently, we have come to understand that the child's ability to control the sphincter muscles of the bowels and bladder does not usually develop until the child is between two and three years old. In other words, children are physically incapable of controlling these body muscles until that time. As in every other aspect of child development, each child has his own maturational timetable. Some children may gain this control at a year and a half; others not until three years of age or later. Nonetheless, the ability develops, unless there is some physical problem, or unless the parents have tried to develop the ability too early or too punitively and the child has built up an emotional resistance to it. Such resistance comes from a battle for control between parent and child.

All of us must realize that this is the second major area over which the child has total control. The first, you will recall, is eating. No parent can force a child either to withhold or release his urine or bowel movement. The child must be physically capable of doing it, and—equally important—must want to. It is, therefore, a very complicated neurological, physiological, and psychological process. Inappropriate parental demands in this area can have deleterious effects on the parent-child relationship and turn it into an "angry alliance" which may affect the child's later development in the form of speech difficulties (speech delay and stuttering) and problems with self-control. How the child handles the demands of toilet training prepares him, more or less well, for the pressures of later life.

The appropriate timing for toilet training, the signs of a child's readiness, and ways in which parents can help the child learn this control with a minimum of stress to both parent and child will be topics for discussion in the coming year. We provide you with these general ideas on the topic now, however, to help you resist suggestions to begin premature toilet training and to enable you to relax and enjoy the developments that are appropriate to this age. They are greater motor activity, self-feeding, speech development, and concept formation; they do **not** include the ability to control the sphincter muscles of the bowels and the bladder.

It is also important that weaning and toilet training be kept quite separate. To place these two frustrations and limitations on the child's "baby ways" simultaneously is not a good idea. In the coming months, it is appropriate to begin gradual weaning. Toilet training should wait for the child's physical readiness and his greater under-standing of the meaning of the physical feelings he has and how to act on them appropriately. It also helps tremendously if the child is more verbal and can understand and discuss the process with you.

> "I am very relieved to hear all this. My pediatrician has said very much the same thing. I'm glad you agree."

Our suggestions to you on all these child-rearing topics are based not only on the thinking of child psychiatrists and psychologists but also on that of pediatricians. We always urge you to consult your pediatri-cians and certainly hope our ideas are not in conflict with theirs. All of us have the best interests of you and your children in mind.

> "My gosh, I thought we'd be getting rid of the diapers in a few months. But if the child's muscles aren't ready, I guess there's not much point in attempting to press toilet training."

Pressing a child before he or she is ready only leads to frustration for both parent and child.

> "I am disappointed that it will take so long, but I am relieved that I don't have to start in yet because my friends are having such a struggle with the procedure."

Your friends would not have a struggle if they were going about the training when the child was ready. You do not have to look ahead to toilet training as a struggle. It is a natural development which takes place without conflict or resistance if it is done on the child's timetable and not for the parents' convenience. We will be discuss-ing this matter often in the coming year and will prepare you for action when the children are around two years old.

HIGHLIGHTS OF DEVELOPMENT—FIFTY-TWO WEEKS

The child's first birthday has special significance for most parents. Development can still be quite varied, however, among children at this age. Some babies may be able to take a halting step or two alone, but most still need to hold onto a parent's hand for support. Some are more advanced and are walking quite well. It is fun for parents to recall the time when the baby's greatest accomplish-ments were lifting his head and waving his arms and legs about.

If the parent makes a tower of two blocks, the baby will try to build such a structure but often will not succeed. Even the attempt shows an advance over the last month when the baby could only bang blocks against each other. Practice helps the child to become more skillful at placing blocks on top of each other and such play is a good game for parent and child.

The babies may be able to release a block into a cup after this activity has been demonstrated to them. They can now pick up a pellet more easily but have difficulty inserting it into the small jar, often missing the jar opening as they release the pellet. These activities can also be added to the child's playtime with the parents.

By now, the baby is able to dangle the red ring by the string, whereas several months ago she would only reach for the red ring, indicating an advance in manual dexterity.

When a simple puzzle board (for circles, squares and triangles) is presented to the baby without the pieces in place and the round piece is handed to the baby, she will look selectively at the round hole, sometimes poking her finger into it. Most children do not put the piece in the correct place unless they have had some practice with the puzzle. This, too, is a good learning activity for parents to play with the child.

By now, most babies have a vocabulary of two or three words, perhaps "Bye" and "Hi" or "Ba" (for bottle), in addition to "Mama" and "Dada." The additional words in a child's vocabulary depend on what the child hears, what has been repeated most dramatically to him, and what interests him. For some it is "ca" (for cookie or car); for others, it is a syllable standing for the name of a favorite toy. In addition to expressive language, the children also show comprehension and may be able to hand toys to the parent on request, although they may not be able to release them yet.

The baby likes to gaze at herself in the mirror. If given a ball, she will place the ball against the mirror and look at it as well. While being dressed, the babies are beginning to cooperate by holding up their arms to be put through sleeves or holding up their feet for socks or shoes.

REVIEW OF THE ACCOMPLISHMENTS OF THE FIRST YEAR

The first birthday is really quite a milestone. It is a good time to review the accomplishments of this first year. What are the biggest changes you have noticed in your babies?

Communication

"For me the baby's first year went very fast. There were some bad days, and at times I wondered why I was so eager to be a mother, but on the whole it was a good experience. What we notice most is the increase in our ability to communicate and the increase in our ability to catch on to what the baby means. In the last week or two, she is really beginning to communicate with us."

What do you mean by that?

"Well, if she wants something, for instance, she gestures and grunts, and I can tell what she wants. When I get it right, she smiles and is very happy."

"As a father, I think communication is the most important thing, too. Now our baby can say 'Dada,' and I know what he means. He is calling to me; he wants me to come to him."

"Our baby only says, 'Mama,' 'Dada,' 'Bye,' waves, and calls out 'ca' (for 'car'), but we understand and that's a thrill. When we repeat words, we feel reassured that sooner or later the baby will catch on, and that language is on the way. I really have to admit that until he said a word that we could make out, we were really concerned about whether or not he would learn to talk."

Often parents feel that the baby is slow in speech, but three or four words at one year is normal. Sometimes parents do not "count" single syllables as words, even though they have meaning for the baby. Also, clear enunciation should not be expected at this age. The parents' sense of satisfaction will enhance the baby's sense of achievement if these words, no matter how rudimentary, are appropriately recognized as part of the baby's early vocabulary.

"Even though our baby has only a small speaking vocabulary, I know she understands much more. If we want her to get something like a ball or a shoe or even go to the closet for Daddy's slipper, she can do it. Her ability to understand us is very satisfying."

"Even though we can't understand much of our baby's babbling, we can tell by her intonation that she thinks she is talking. We can only guess at the meaning of some of the clearer sounds, but there is much more of a sense of communication. We feel we are reaching a goal that we looked forward to very much."

"In our house we speak Spanish, so our baby is saying words in Spanish—'Papy' for 'Daddy,' for instance. My husband is so happy. He says the baby is a real person now!"

All of you seem to agree that communication is an important accomplishment. It is very interesting that this is the first accomplishment to be mentioned tonight. Naturally, communication is the most important accomplishment for a human baby. Language distinguishes us from the rest of the animal world, and good language development correlates highly with good achievement in school. All of you must have been doing a very good job in stimulating speech. That is clearly shown by your understanding of the importance of language and your interest in helping the baby develop the ability to communicate. Some parents place greater value on walking and often try to force a baby to walk before the baby is quite ready. As you all know by now, walking is a development which occurs spontaneously if the child is given sufficient freedom to move. However, language cannot be learned without stimulation and imitation. You are certainly doing a good job of providing this stimulation.

Is there anything else that you feel has been an important development during the baby's first year of life?

> "Even though babies learn to walk naturally, it really is fun to see them take their first steps. They take a step or two ever so carefully at first. Then they sit down. Then they get up and try again or reach for the nearest table or chair. We are delighted because our baby is so pleased with herself."

Walking

> "I'm pleased the baby can walk, but I'm also a little worried. Now I have to watch him more closely so that he will not get hurt or get at something which he can break."

> "I can't wait for the baby to walk by himself. To me that's very important—maybe because I enjoy sports and I want my son to be athletic too."

Certainly, the increased ability to move around is an important advance for the babies. You'll remember the babies were unable to lift their heads from the mattress when they were first born. We understand your pleasure and the babies' pleasure in learning to walk. All parents look forward to this achievement.

> "The babies' greater mobility makes them more interesting as well, even if it makes us all work harder. We can see them explore things and try to reach out for, hold, and examine things. Sometimes they tear or break something, but I guess that's to be expected because they haven't learned yet just how to handle different objects."

Exploration

To permit exploration and provide the right playthings, such as small toys, plastic cups, measuring spoons, and small blocks, are all part of the parents' job. The baby's interest in exploration is one of the signs of progress and sets the groundwork for the desire to find out about things later in school.

> "There is one thing we haven't mentioned. I wouldn't call it an achievement, but it certainly is a condition or situation that you can't get away from, and that's the everlasting mess the baby creates in a house. My wife just can't seem to keep the place neat. I really love the baby, but the mess sometimes gets to me."

Yes, there is apt to be disorder in the house where the baby is playing. At this age, babies are "messy" from the adult point of view. They are only exploring. They haven't yet learned what each object is. Soon you will be able to teach them where each thing belongs. They learn that by observation. So, a house should not be left in a mess all the time just because it's going to get messy again. There should be certain clean-up times—for example, before lunch or before bedtime—so the baby sees the house in order and begins to absorb that image of his home. When he is able to, the baby will begin to participate in the putting-away activities.

Good Daily Routine

"Another of our baby's accomplishments that means a great deal to me is that she is now on a good schedule and can sleep through the night. Also, she takes a nap that I can count on during the day, and life is better organized for all of us."

"That accomplishment also means a lot to me. My baby isn't sleeping all through the night yet, but he wakes only once, at about eleven. Then he sleeps till six or seven in the morning. The day goes along pretty regularly. I'm not in a tizzy anymore trying to get him taken care of and do the housework too. Yes, I'd say it's quite a change for the better."

"I must confess that the first few times our baby slept through the night, I awakened, and so did my husband. We were used to getting up, and we had to go in and look at her to be sure she was all right."

All of us like order in our lives; we also like to know more or less what's coming next. Babies like these things too, as you have found out. They give the baby a sense of security.

Basic Trust and Attachment; Personality Development

"Yes, I'd have to say my baby is getting less restless and more confident. He seems to be simmering down, as though he was getting the idea that I'd be there to fix things for him. Could you say he seems to trust me more?"

That's exactly the idea. Not only are the babies' nervous systems maturing and functioning better, but they themselves are developing a sense of security in their environment due to the consistency of your care. They are less anxious and more secure. This sense of security or basic trust is certainly one of the major achievements of this year. As you know, it is a very important element in personality development and helps the baby cope throughout life.

"Of course, all the things we've talked about are accomplishments, but for me the most satisfying is the way the baby responds to us and acts like we are important to her. We see that she responds differently to her grandparents. She knows them and likes them, but her response is different from her response to her mother and me. You could say that the baby has a special attachment to each of us and that all these special attachments are different from one another."

You are saying that the attachment you feel the baby has for you and the recognition you have of the baby's emerging personality are achievements to be recorded for this first year. That is a vey good observation. It is very important to recognize the fact that you feel that each of you is becoming aware of the other as a person who counts, and, perhaps, is accountable to the other. Not so long ago, this feeling was not generally recognized as important, and babies were not thought to have such feelings and personalities until they were much older. Their wishes and preferences were never considered. But now we recognize that such is the case, and that constitutes a great advance in our understanding of young children.

_____ CHANGES AND DEVELOPMENTS TO EXPECT IN THE SECOND YEAR

We seem to have covered all of the babies' major achievements during their first year of life. Now I wonder what you are looking forward to for the next year? What are some of the things that you are anticipating?

> "I think one of the big advances will be in walking. The babies will be much more able to walk alone with less falling. It won't be such a tottering kind of walk."

Greater Mobility

That's true. They will be able to walk faster and farther and even begin to run and climb stairs with help. Also, they will finally give up crawling.

> "That sounds great to me because our baby is getting too heavy to carry around, but he isn't making much effort to walk. He only stands. When should I expect him to walk?"

Many babies walk by ten or eleven months. The average age for walking well alone is about fourteen months.

> "When should you begin to worry if they don't walk? Our baby seems so slow learning."

If the babies are able to pull themselves to a standing position and shuffle from chair to chair, or along the crib edge, you know they will learn to walk. If you have any doubts, you should see your doctor about the matter. Some babies are very cautious; some are putting all their efforts into speech or the manipulation of toys, rather than walking. Parents must also remember that each child has a different maturational timetable.

> "What about speech? I know the babies will speak more this year, but how much more? What should we expect?"

Increased Speech Development

> "Maybe the babies will be able to name more things."

> "I expect my baby to say sentences this year."

> "I can't wait to have a real conversation with my baby. When will that come?"

There seems to be a variety of expectations. Some parents are quite modest in their expectations; others want a great deal. If a baby can say ten to twenty words by eighteen months, that is an appropriate vocabulary. By two years, the baby should be able to make a three-word sentence like "Daddy go bye" or "Baby want car," and their vocabularies will have increased to about 250 words. Of course, some babies will speak more fluently than others. Some will have a larger vocabulary but enunciate this vocabulary relatively poorly; others will enunciate clearly but possess a small vocabulary. There will be a great deal of gesturing and tugging to get parents to understand, and there may be tears and frustration when the parents don't. Parents who are patient and don't lose their "cool," however, will begin to understand their own child quite well, and that makes the second year more fun for both parents and child.

Increased Socialization

"What about play? Will the babies begin playing together?"

The babies will become increasingly social and will enjoy being with other people and children. As we will see, babies of this age play **alongside** each other, rather than **with** each other, and will continue to need parental supervision.

Self-Feeding

"When can we expect the babies to feed themselves with a spoon?"

Most babies begin trying to feed themselves between ten and fourteen months of age. Many of your babies are already doing well with finger foods. Gradually over this coming year, they will become more adept at using the spoon. It is important to let them begin doing this during this coming year, even though it is messy.

The babies will also become more adept at drinking from a cup in the coming year. Here again, you must expect some spilling and messiness.

Increasing Autonomy

The desire to feed themselves is one of the examples of the babies' increasing desire for autonomy. Other signs of this desire include greater selectiveness about what they eat and the greater distance they run from the parent or caretaker. They will be able to play by themselves for longer periods as well and will be less willing to accept changes in activity. This will put greater demands on the parents' versatility, consistency, and firmness. The child's growing desire for autonomy can lead, therefore, to conflict with the parents. These conflicts can culminate towards the end of this year in the "Terrible Two's" if the child's need for autonomy is not properly understood by the parents. We will be talking more about this in the coming year to help make your relationship with your child happy and constructive.

Most of the babies are now beginning to understand that people or objects they do not see still exist. When they drop their toys, they now look for them. They are also enjoying the game of "Peekaboo," and are no longer frightened or made uncomfortable when the parent's face disappears. Some of the babies are beginning to look up expectantly when they hear Daddy's key turn in the lock. The babies' understanding of the permanence of objects will be greatly strengthened during the second year.

In addition, children's concepts about the world will be related to their exploration and manipulation of objects. They will need to examine and physically handle a wide variety of objects. Needless to say, parents will often take a dim view of this activity, but it is essential to the child's development of concepts and language. Manipulating objects is the necessary precursor to naming them. Language, in turn, will strengthen conceptual thinking, so this will be another important area of discussion in the coming year.

Now that we have had a "sneak preview" of the "coming attractions" for next year, let us say a few words about your part in your child's development this year.

You are learning the "ropes" of being parents. You have all acquired a greater understanding of your babies' developmental needs. You have helped the babies develop warm, trusting relationships with you, and you have come to enjoy them. You are learning to become your children's advocates, instead of their critics, while at the same time helping them to accept your guidance in beginning to assimilate the socially accepted patterns of our society. You have helped them to learn about their world in a way that they could understand and to begin to recognize their own achievements and develop their own self-esteem. In all, you have contributed immeasurably to the great progress the babies have made. A mutually affectionate relationship has been established, and that is the best note on which to end the first year.

Increased Concept Formation

Closing Remarks

Bibliography

Note: Titles preceded by a bullet (•) are especially recommended for parents.

Abrahamson, David. 1969. **Emotional Care of Your Child**. New York: Trident Press.

Ainsworth, Mary D. Salter. 1965. Further research into the adverse effects of maternal deprivation. In **Child Care and Growth of Love**, ed. John Bowlby, 2d ed., pp. 191–241. Harmondsworth, England: Penguin Books, Ltd.

_____. 1967. **Infancy in Uganda: Infant Care and the Growth of Attachment**. Baltimore, Maryland: The Johns Hopkins Press.

_____. 1969. Object relations, dependency, and attachment: a theoretical review of the infant-mother relationship. **Child Development** 40: 969–1025.

_____, and Bell, Sylvia M. 1972. Attachment, exploration, and separation: illustrated by behavior of one-year-olds in a strange situation. In **Readings in Child Development**, eds. Irving B. Weiner and David Elkind. New York: John Wiley & Sons.

Anglund, Sandra. 1968. Here, even infants go to school. **Today's Health** March 1968: 52–57.

Auerbach, Alice S. 1968. **Parents Learn Through Discussion**. New York: John Wiley & Sons.

Badger, Earladeen D. 1972. A mother's training program. **Children Today** (U.S. Department of Health, Education, and Welfare) 1/3: 7–11, 35.

Bayley, Nancy. 1940. Mental growth in young children. **Yearbook of the National Society for the Study of Education** 39/2: 11–47.

_____. 1969. **Bayley Scales of Infant Development**. New York: Psychological Corporation.

Beadle, Muriel. 1970. **A Child's Mind**. New York: Doubleday & Co.

Bell, Richard Q. 1971. Stimulus control of parent or caretaker behavior by infant. **Developmental Psychology** 4: 63–72.

Bernstein, B. 1964. Aspects of language and learning in the genesis of the social process. In **Language in Culture and Society: A Reader in Linguistics and Anthropology**, ed. D. Hymes, pp. 251–263. New York: Harper & Row.

Bettelheim, Bruno. 1962. **Dialogues with Mothers**. New York: Free Press.

Bijou, S. W. 1970. **Experiences and the Processes of Socialization.** New York: Academic Press.

Birch, Herbert G. 1970. **Disadvantaged Children: Health, Nutrition, and School Failure.** New York: Harcourt, Brace & World.

Blank, M. 1964. Some maternal influences on infants' rate of sensorimotor development. **Journal of the American Academy of Child Psychiatry** 3: 668–687.

Bloom, Benjamin S. 1964. **Stability and Change in Human Characteristics.** New York: John Wiley & Sons.

Bowlby, John. 1951. **Maternal Care and Mental Health.** Report to World Health Organization. New York: Columbia University Press.

_____. 1958. Nature of a child's tie to his mother. **International Journal of Psychoanalysis** 39: 350–373.

_____. 1960. Grief and mourning in infancy and early childhood. In **The Psychoanalytic Study of the Child.** New York: International Universities Press.

• Brazelton, Berry. 1969. **Infants and Mothers.** New York: Delacourt.

Bresnahan, Jean L., and Blum, William. 1971. Chaotic reinforcement: a socio-economic leveler. **Developmental Psychology** 4: 89–92.

Brim, Orville G., Jr. 1961. Methods of educating parents and their evaluation. In **Prevention of Mental Disorders in Children,** ed. G. Caplan, pp. 122–141. New York: Basic Books.

_____. 1965. **Education for Child Rearing.** Paperback edition. New York: Free Press.

Brody, Grace F. 1969. Maternal child-rearing attitudes and child behavior. **Developmental Psychology** 1:66.

Brody, Sylvia. 1956. **Patterns of Mothering.** New York: International Universities Press.

Bronfenbrenner, Urie. 1970. **Two Worlds of Childhood.** New York: Russell Sage Foundation.

Bruner, Jerome S. 1968. **Processes of Cognitive Growth: Infancy.** Worcester, Massachusetts: Clark University Press.

Caldwell, Bettye M. 1972. What does research teach us about day care: for children under three? **Children Today** (U.S. Department of Health, Education, and Welfare) 1/1:6–11.

_____, and Ricciuti, N. N., eds. 1973. **Review of Child Development Research.** Vol. 3, **Child Development and Social Policy.** Chicago: University of Chicago Press.

• Caplan, Frank, ed. 1971. **The First Twelve Months of Life.** Princeton, New Jersey: Edcom Systems, Inc.

Caplan, Gerald, ed. 1961. **Prevention of Mental Disorders in Children**. New York: Basic Books.

Clausen, John A., ed. 1968. **Socialization and Society**. Boston: Little, Brown & Co.

• Comer, James, and Poussaint, Alvin. 1975. **Black Child Care**. New York: Stratford Press.

Crandall, Virginia. 1972. Achievement behavior in young children. In **Readings in Child Development**, eds. Irving B. Weiner and David Elkind. New York: John Wiley & Sons.

Danziger, Kurt. 1971. **Socialization**. Paperback edition. Middlesex, England: Penguin Books, Ltd.

Deutsch, Martin. 1960. **Minority Groups and Class Status as Related to Social and Personality Factors in Scholastic Achievement**. Ithaca, New York: Society for Applied Anthropology.

_____. 1964. Facilitating development in the preschool child: social and psychological perspectives. **Merrill-Palmer Quarterly** 10:249–263.

_____. 1965. The role of social class in language development and cognition. **American Journal of Orthopsychiatry** 35/1: 78–88.

Dittman, Laura, ed. 1968. **Early Child Care**. New York: Atherton Press.

Escalona, Sibylle. 1968. **Roots of Individuality**. Chicago: Aldine Publishing Co.

Erikson, Erik H. 1963. **Childhood and Society**. 2d ed., paperback. New York: W. W. Norton & Co.

Fantz, R. 1963. Pattern vision in newborn infants. **Science** 140: 296–297.

Foss, B. N. ed. 1968. **Determinants of Infant Behavior IV**. New York: John Wiley & Sons.

• Fraiberg, Selma H. 1959. **The Magic Years**. New York: Charles Scribner & Sons.

_____. 1977. **Every Child's Birthright: In Defense of Mothering**. New York: Basic Books.

• Gesell, Arnold L. 1940. **The First Five Years of Life**. New York: Harper & Row.

_____. 1943. **Infant and Child Care in the Culture of Today**. New York: Harper & Row.

_____, and Amatruda, Catherine. 1947. **Developmental Diagnosis**. 2d ed. New York: Paul B. Hoeber, Inc.

Goslin, D. A., ed. 1969. **Handbook of Socialization Theory and Research**. New York: Rand McNally.

Goldstein, Joseph; Freud, Anna; and Solnit, Albert J. 1973. **Beyond the Best Interests of the Child**. Paperback edition. New York: Free Press.

Harlow, H. 1949. The formation of learning sets. **Psychological Review** 56:51–65.

Hellmuth, Jerome, ed. 1970. **Cognitive Studies**. Vol. 1. New York: Brunner/Mazel.

Hess, R., and Shipman, V. 1965. Early experience and cognitive modes. **Child Development** 36:869.

Hunt, J. McV. 1961. **Intelligence and Experience**. New York: Ronald Press.

———. 1971. Parent and child centers: their basis in the behavioral and educational sciences. **American Journal of Orthopsychiatry** 41/1:13–38.

Johnson, Dale L., et al. 1974. The Houston parent-child development center: a parent education program for Mexican-American families. **American Journal of Orthopsychiatry** 44/1:121–128.

Kagan, Jerome. 1971. **Change and Continuity in Infancy**. New York: John Wiley & Sons.

Katz, I. 1967. The socialization of academic motivation in minority group children. In **Nebraska Symposium in Motivation**, ed. D. Levine, pp. 133–191. Lincoln, Nebraska: University of Nebraska Press.

Kessler, Jane W. 1970. Contributions of the mentally retarded toward a theory of cognitive development. In **Cognitive Studies**, ed. J. Hellmuth, Vol. 1, pp. 111–209. New York: Brunner/Mazel.

———. 1966. **Psychopathology of Childhood**. Englewood Cliffs, New Jersey: Prentice-Hall.

Knobloch, Hilda, and Pasamanic, Benjamin, eds. 1974. **Gesell and Amatruda's Developmental Diagnosis**. 3d ed., revised and enlarged. Hagerstown, Maryland: Harper & Row Medical Department.

Levy, David M. 1956. **Maternal Overprotection**. Paperback edition. New York: W. W. Norton & Co.

Lewis, M. M. 1963. **Language, Thought, and Personality in Infancy and Childhood**. New York: Basic Books.

———. 1976. **Origins of Intelligence: Infancy and Early Childhood**. New York: Plenum Press.

• Lidz, Theodore. 1968. **The Person: His Development Through the Life Cycle**. New York: Basic Books.

Lief, Nina R., and Zarin-Ackerman, Judith. 1976. The effectiveness of a curriculum of parent education on a group of risk and non-risk mothers and infants. Paper presented at the meeting of the American Association of Psychiatric Services for Children, 11 November 1976, at San Francisco, California.

Lipsitt, L. 1966. Learning processes of human newborns. **Merrill-Palmer Quarterly** 12: 45–71.

Litman, Frances. 1969. Environmental influences on the development of abilities. Excerpted from a Harvard Graduate School of Education Pre-School Project paper presented at the Biennial Meeting of the Society for Research in Child Development, Santa Monica, California.

Madden, John; Levenstein, Phyllis; and Levenstein, Sidney. 1976. Longitudinal I.Q. outcomes of the mother-child home program—Verbal Interaction Project. **Child Development** 47/4: 1015–1025.

Mahler, Margaret S., and La Perriere, K. 1965. Mother-child interaction during separation. **Psychoanalytical Quarterly** 34:483–498.

_____; Pine, Fred; and Bergman, Anni. 1975. **The Psychological Birth of the Human Infant—Symbiosis and Individuation.** New York: Basic Books.

Malone, Charles A. 1967. Psychosocial characteristics of the children from a development viewpoint. In **The Drifters**, ed. E. Pavenstedt, pp. 105–124. Boston: Little, Brown & Co.

McClelland, D., et al. 1953. **The Achievement Motive.** New York: Appleton-Century-Croft, Inc.

McGurk, Harry. 1974. Visual Perception in Young Infants. In Foss, Brian (ed.), **New Perspectives in Child Development.** Baltimore, Maryland: Penguin Books, Inc.

Morris, Ann G. 1974. Conducting a parent education program in a pediatric clinic playroom. **Children Today** 3/6: 11–14.

Murphy, Lois B. 1962. **The Widening World of Childhood.** New York: Basic Books.

_____. 1963. Problems in recognizing emotional disturbances in children. **Child Welfare** December 1963: 473–487.

Neubauer, Peter B. 1968. The third year: the two-year old. In **Early Child Care.** ed. L. Dittman, pp. 57–67. New York: Atherton Press.

Newson, Elizabeth and John. 1968. **Four-Year Olds in an Urban Community.** Chicago: Aldine Publishing Co.

Pavenstedt, Eleanor. 1965. A comparison of child-rearing environments of upper lower and very-low lower class families. **American Journal of Orthopsychiatry** 35, 89.

———. 1967. **The Drifters**. Boston: Little, Brown & Co.

Piaget, Jean. 1950. **The Psychology of Intelligence**. New York: Harcourt, Brace.

———. 1970. The stages of the intellectual development of the child. In **Readings in Child Development and Personality**, eds. Paul H. Mussen, John J. Conger, and Jerome Kagan, 2d., pp. 291–298. New York: Harper & Row.

Pine, Fred. 1971. On the separation process: universal trends and individual differences. In **Separation-Individuation: Essays in Honor of Margaret S. Mahler**, eds. John B. McDivitt and Calvin F. Settlage, pp. 113–130. New York: International Universities Press.

Pringle, M. L. Kellmer, et al. 1967. **11,000 Seven-Year Olds**. New York: Humanities Press.

Provence, S., and Litman, R. C. 1962. **Infants in Institutions**. New York: International Universities Press.

• Rice, F. Philip. 1979. **The Working Mother's Guide to Child Development**. Englewood Cliffs, New Jersey: Prentice-Hall.

• Pulaski, Mary Ann Spencer. 1978. **Your Baby's Mind and How It Grows: Piaget's Theory for Parents**. New York: Harper & Row.

Rowland, L. W. 1948. A first evaluation of Pierre the Pelican. **Health Pamphlets**, Louisiana Mental Health Studies, no. 1. New Orleans: Louisiana Society for Mental Health.

• Salk, Lee. 1971. **What Every Child Would Like His Parents to Know**. New York: David McKay Co.

Sarbin, Theodore R., and Allen, Vernon L. 1968. Role theory. In **Handbook of Social Psychology**, eds. Gardner Lindzey and Elliot Aronson, 2d ed., vol. 1, pp. 488–567. Reading, Massachusetts: Addison-Wesley Publishing Co.

Schaefer, Earl S. 1970. Need for Early and Continuing Education. In **Education of the Infant and Young Child**, ed. V. H. Denenberg. New York: Academic Press.

Sears, Robert R.; Maccoby, E. E.; and Levin, H. 1957. **Patterns of Childrearing**. New York and Evanston, Illinois: Row, Peterson & Co.

Skinner, B. F. 1953. **Science and Human Behavior**. New York: Macmillan & Co.

• Smith, M. Brewster. 1968. Competence and socialization. In **Socialization and Society**, ed. J. A. Clausen, pp. 270–320. Boston: Little, Brown & Co.

Spitz, René A. 1945. Hospitalism and inquiry into the genesis of psychiatric conditions of early childhood. **Psychoanalytic Study of the Child** 1: 53–74.

_____. 1965. **The First Year of Life**. New York: International Universities Press.

• Spock, Benjamin. 1968. **Baby and Child Care**. New York: Pocket Books Division of Simon & Schuster, Inc.

• Stone, Joseph, and Church, Joseph. 1968. **Childhood and Adolescence**. Chapters 1 through 8. New York: Random House.

Talbot, Nathan B.; Kagan, Jerome; and Eisenberg, Leon. 1971. **Behavioral Science in Pediatric Medicine**. Philadelphia: Saunders.

Terman, Lewis M., and Merrill, M. 1972. **Stanford-Binet Intelligence Scale**. Form L–M. 3d revision. Boston: Houghton Mifflin.

• Thomas, Alexander; Chess, Stella; and Birch, Herbert G. 1968. **Temperament and Behavior Disorders in Children**. New York: New York University Press.

_____. 1977. **Temperament and Development**. New York: Brunner/Mazel.

White, Burton L. 1970. Child development research: an edifice without foundation. In **Readings in Child Development and Personality**, eds. P. H. Mussen, et al., 2nd ed., pp. 97–117. New York: Harper & Row.

•_____. 1975. **The First Three Years of Life**. Englewood Cliffs, New Jersey: Prentice-Hall.

_____, and Watts, Jean Carew. 1973. **Experience and Environment**. Vol. 1. Englewood Cliffs, New Jersey: Prentice-Hall.

Wilson, Ronald S. 1972. Twins: early mental development. **Science** 175/4024, 914–917.

Work, Henry H. 1972. Parent-child centers: a working reappraisal. **American Journal of Orthopsychiatry** 42/4:582–595.

Yarrow, Leon J. 1968. Conceptualizing the early environment. In **Early Child Care**, ed. L. L. Dittman. New York: Atherton Press.

Zambrana, Ruth E., Hurst, Marsha, and Hite, Rodney. 1979. The Working Mother in Contemporary Perspective: A Review of the Literature. **Pediatrics** 64/6, 862–870.

Ziegler, Edward, and Child, Irvin L. 1969. Socialization. In **Handbook of Social Psychology**, eds. Gardner Lindzey and Elliott Aronson, 2nd ed., vol. 3, pp. 450–589. Reading, Massachusetts: Addison-Wesley Publishing Co.

INDEX

Attachment
    to other caretakers, 77–78, 97–100, 128–130
    to parents, 20–22, 57–63, 77–78, 82–83, 94–101, 124,
    126–128, 270–271
    to places and toys (the implications of moving,
    visiting), 78–79
    See also Basic trust

Autonomy, 272

Baby-sitters, 20–22, 61–62, 77–78, 99–101, 125–126, 128,
    149–150, 181–182, 194–195
    instructions in case of emergency, 149–150
    instructions on daily routine, 149–150
    preparations prior to parental vacations, 234–241

Basic trust
    disruptions to, **see** Conflict, Separation anxiety
    effects of caretaking, 20–22, 57–63, 124, 126–130,
    270–271
    in relation to patterning and sequencing, 12–13, 34–35,
    44–45, 270–271
    response to crying, 13–14, 53–54, 72–76, 119
    results of lack of trust, 70–72, 121–122, 129–130
    See also Cuing in to baby's needs

Bathing, 42, 45

Birthday Party
    first, 257–258
    appropriate presents, 258–259

Bowel movements, 7–9

Caretaking
    father's role, 28–30, 59–61, 98–99, 122–127, 130–134,
    166–168, 172–176
    substitute caretakers, **see** Baby-sitters
    working mothers, 20–22, 77–78, 82–83, 97–101
    See also Attachment, Cuing in to baby's needs, Patterning
    and sequencing

Child abuse, 204–205, 248–249

Colic, 45–46, 85

Comforting, see Cuing in to baby's needs

Concept formation
in relation to object permanence, 92–94, 127, 223–225, 272–273

Conflict, between parent and child
"angry alliance," 108–114, 118, 265
eating, 56–57, 83–87, 142–145
personality differences, 148
See also Discipline, Exploration, Sleep, Toilet training

Conscience
setting limits as beginning of, 104–108, 165–168, 245–250
See also Discipline

Crying
as language, 13–14, 19, 53, 72–76, 113–114, 118–119
loudness, 19, 113–114
spoiling, 13–15, 35–38, 63, 71–77, 93–94

Cuing in to baby's needs, 70–76, 113–114, 118–119, 121–122
differentiating cries, 72–76
results of feeding as comfort, 118
to developmental changes, 118–119, 155–157

Discipline
appropriate to maturational level, 105–106, 168–170, 200–201, 245–246
as teaching, 104–108, 165–168, 170–171, 245–150
development of baby's understanding of "**No**," 170–172, 200–201, 245–250
difference between discipline and punishment, 245–250, 255–257
need for substitute activities, 109, 135–136, 165–166, 168–169
recognition of approved behavior, 102–104, 106–108, 165–168, 246–247
setting limits, 104–108, 165–172, 200–203, 245–250
spanking 203–205, 246

Emergencies
first aid for, 212–216

Entertaining
with a baby, 189–192, 230–232

Exploration
balance between baby's need and housekeeping, 168–171, 269
manual, 89, 142–143

necessary limitations of, **see** Discipline
oral, 39–41, 51–52, 79–80, 117, 163, 199, 217–219
reaching, 120–121, 135–136, 142, 163, 168–171
relation to healthy cognitive development, 137–138, 218–219, 269
spatial, 80–82, 218–219, 253–254
visual, 54–55, 79–81
with increasing mobility, 155–157, 163–166, 168, 171, 201–204, 269

Father's involvement, 3, 28–30, 45, 122–127, 166–168, 172–175

Fears of early childhood, 242–245
See also Separation anxiety, Stranger anxiety

Feeding
appropriate weight in relation to, 122–123
allergies, 46, 56, 85
burping, 6–7
demand, 5, 12–13
food additives, 85
home preparation of baby food, 85, 179
messiness, 142–143, 178
obesity, 57, 144
patterns of, 4–7, 28–29, 83–87, 142–145, 177–180, 218–221
pleasant atmosphere during, 10, 54–56, 219–221
problems, 83–85, 142–143, 146–147, 177–178
self-feeding, 83–84, 142–143, 177–181, 219–221, 272–273
solid foods, 9–10, 56–57, 83–86, 142–144, 177–180, 218–221
spitting up, 6–7, 29, 85
straw for bottle, 85–86

Feelings of parents
about having a child, 1–3, 25–27, 82–83, 122–123, 195–197, 255–257
child care as burden, 25–27, 73, 79, 94–101, 180–182, 195–197
conflicts from differing child-rearing attitudes, 131–135, 255–257
enjoyment of child, 4, 73–74, 79, 146–148, 267–273,
father's feelings, 28–30, 33–34, 43–44, 76–77, 82–83, 122–127, 130–135, 195–197, 267
frustration, 26–27, 36–38, 108–114, 118–119
mother's feelings, 1–3, 82–83, 92–97, 133–135
parents' need for time together, 126, 150, 180–182
parents' feelings of accomplishment 121–122, 180–182

Games
"Bye-Bye," 207, 223–224, 229,253

"Hide-and-Seek," 225
"I See," 50
"Pat-a-Cake," ("Clap Hands"), 81, 207, 221–223, 229, 253
"Peekaboo," 49, 125, 224–226
"So Big," 125, 226
"Up and Down," 81, 136–137, 253

Gratification
early need for, 70–72
immediate gratification seen as "spoiling," 109–114
inability to delay due to lack of neurological development, 70–71, 108–109
need for substitute gratifications, 109
relation of basic trust, 70–72
results of lack of appropriate gratification, 111
teaching delay of gratification, 110–114

Hearing, 1, 4, 25, 117

Holidays
disruption of routines, 230–232
parents going away without babies, 234–242
significance for babies, 229–230
See also Entertaining, Traveling, Visiting

Language, see Speech

Mastery
sense of, 50–51, 65–67, 120–122, 135–136, 164–165, 176
importance of parental approval, 102–104, 121–122, 135–136, 147–148, 164–168, 222, 253–255
relation to later initiative, 102–104

Maturational timetable
individual differences, 4, 17–18, 41–42, 58, 122–123, 221–224

Motor development
crawling, 155–157, 163–165, 207–208
eye-hand coordination, 49, 64, 69, 119–121, 135–137
hand-to-mouth coordination, 39–40, 50–51
handedness, 22, 55–56
head control, 1, 25, 49, 69, 89
manual coordination, 1, 32–33, 65–66, 69, 89–90, 117, 119–121, 135–136, 141, 147–148, 163, 185, 207–208, 229, 253, 266–267
sitting up, 69, 79, 117, 123, 141, 163, 185, 207
standing up, 141, 148, 157, 163, 185, 207, 229
turning over, 63; 117
walking, 229, 253, 266, 268–269, 271
See also Neurological development

Neurological development
achievement of quick responses and reflexes, 123–124
early lack of response from immaturity of central nervous system, 123–124
maturation of central nervous system as prerequisite to self-discipline, 105–106
need for substitute activity for impulses, 109, 135–136, 165–166
sequence of development, 4, 50–51

Pacifiers, 40–41

Parenting as a profession, 37–38, 83

Patterning and sequencing of daily routine
baby biological clock, 4–9, 12–13
disruptions due to illness or developmental changes, 145–146
father's role, 28–30, 59–62, 122–126
importance of sequence, 12–13, 43–47, 58–60, 270
in relation to housework, 3
See also Attachment, Basic trust

Pediatrician, when to consult for
accidents, 212–216
feeding problems, 84–86
general care, 14–15, 146, 212–216, 260, 262–263, 266

Pets, 243

Play, 10–11, 16–19, 38–39, 45, 50–52, 65–66, 79–82, 118–121, 125, 136–137, 159–160
achieving a balance between encouraging play and setting limits, 172
recognition of achievement, 166–167, 172–175, 197–200,
roughhousing and overstimulation, 172–175, 197–199
See also Games, Mastery, Socialization

Playpens, 119–120, 165

Safety precautions
accidents (cuts, bumps, burns) 212–216
backpacks, 155–156
breath holding, 214
choking, 215–216
cribs (bumpers and extenders), 175–176
first aid, 212–216
latches on cabinets, 171, 202
oral exploration (hygiene), 217–219
plugs in electric outlets, 202
sunburn, 87

Separation anxiety, 77–78, 92–96, 126–130, 192–195, 234–242
  during parents' vacations, 234–242
  how parents get time off, 94–96, 148–150, 194–195, 234–242
  if mothers work, 20–22, 77–78, 96–101
  in relation to object permanence, 92–94, 127, 223–224
  role of language in overcoming, 93, 223

Shoes, 260–261

Sleep
  consequences of taking child into parents' bed, 211–212
  disturbances, 45–47, 100, 145–146, 173–175, 192–193, 208–211
  dreams, 47, 210–211
  patterns, 43–45, 145–146, 208–211

Socialization, 1, 25, 49, 69, 73, 89, 117, 141, 163, 185–192, 195, 207, 223, 229–234, 272
  need for parental monitoring, 185–189

Spacing of children, 150–155

Speech
  baby talk, 27–28, 30–31, 158–159
  babbling as "conversation," 137–138, 141
  development of, 1, 4, 25, 49, 69, 89, 117, 137–139, 141, 157–158, 163, 185, 207, 229, 253–254, 267–268, 271–272
  stimulation, 15–17, 25, 27, 30–33, 49, 80–82, 137–139, 148, 157–159, 199

Spoiling, 13–15, 25, 27, 30–33, 49, 80–82, 137–139, 148, 157–159, 199

Stimulation
  from going outdoors, 18–19
  manual coordination, **see** Motor development
  motor (exercises), 1, 17–19
  overstimulation, 10–11, 45, 172–175
  play, 10–11, 16–18, 27–28, 65–66, 119–121
  sitting propped up, 64
  visual, 1, 4, 16–18, 25, 31–32, 49, 54–55
  See also Speech, Toys

Stranger anxiety, 90–92, 128–130, 190–192, 230–232, 241–242

Teething, 52–54, 208–209
  as cause of sleep disruptions, 145–146, 208–209
  care of teeth, 263–264

Television
    as baby-sitter, 101
    as stimulus, 11, 101

Toilet training, 264–266

Toys, 54, 65–66, 119–121, 136–137, 149, 159–160, 257–260

Traveling
    with baby, 47, 187–189, 191–192, 232–234, 238–239
    without baby, 234–242

Vision, 4, 54–55

Visiting with the baby, 47, 187–189, 191–192, 232–234, 238–239
    See also Socialization

Walkers, 173–174

Weaning
    general advice regarding, 261–264
    sucking needs, 40–41, 86, 261–266

Working mothers, see Caretaking, Separation Anxiety